ALWAYS MORE TO LEARN

*Joy, Faith, and Resilience
as a Career Educator*

JAN HOCHSTETLER

Always More to Learn
Joy, Faith, and Resilience as a Career Educator

ISBN: 979-8-9897247-0-3 (Paperback)
ISBN: 979-8-9897247-1-0 (Hardcover)
ISBN: 979-8-9897247-2-7 (eBook)

Library of Congress Control Number: 2019908984

Cover design by Cherie Fox at www.cheriefox.com
Cover photo by Maryam Thompson Photography

Printed in the United States of America

Jan Hochstetler
JansInkCo@gmail.com

For more information on this book, the author, programs, and events, please visit www.JansInk.org

To my parents, Cal and Betty,
who always believed in me.

TABLE OF CONTENTS

ACKNOWLEDGMENTS

To Dave:

I want to thank my husband, Dave, for your support on this project. I know it has stretched you beyond your comfort zone to allow me to open up our lives for all to read about. It really is *our* story, as you have lived every day of it with me. It wasn't always easy to see me hunker down in my office in my loungewear writing as you continued to go to work every day. Thank you for believing I could do it and encouraging me along the way. I'm forever grateful that I chose you as my life's partner.

To my editor Bruce Hurd:

This book would not have become a reality without you. The day you told me you were thinking through my book on your morning jog was when it cemented how much of a partner you have been with me in this process. You pushed me to express my emotions and it was therapeutic in bringing up feelings I didn't even realize I had. Your endless encouragement and honest feedback and wisdom are the reasons a seemingly unrealistic dream was able to come to fruition.

To my friend Cynthia Ukah:

Ever since I shared my desire to write a book you have been a constant supporter. When I found myself discouraged, you were the one I knew to call. Your ongoing optimism and confidence in my project kept me moving in the right direction.

To my son Dylan and daughter Jenna:

Thank you both for allowing me to display a "look behind the curtain" and for your constant love and support. Jenna, when you said the words "Look Mom – this is going to be you!" to me in the book store in Ponce City Market in Atlanta as we approached a new author who was doing a book signing, it made my heart soar. It was clear there was not a doubt in your mind that this project was going to become a reality.

To my inner circle of strong women:

My idea to keep this project to myself until it was done didn't last long. I appreciate each of you asking me how it was going and being willing to fill in details for me that had become a bit fuzzy. You each carry a unique attribute and blessing that I love and need in my life.

INTRODUCTION

Always More to Learn is a book about my life as an educator and the unlikely path that led me to becoming the principal of a startup Christian elementary school serving mostly minority and low-income youth in Iowa City, Iowa. It is a book about trusting God amid disappointments and using my experiences to help me better understand others. Because all of us are affected by both tragedy and joy throughout life, I also share hard things that happened to me in hopes that others can benefit from my life lessons.

While I do give details about my childhood and growing up in a homogenous Christian community in southeast Iowa, *Always More to Learn* mainly focuses on my life during my eight years at Faith Academy.

There were many interesting things that happened along the way that seemed to just be events in my life at the time they occurred. Looking back, however, I can clearly see how certain experiences readied me for my involvement in creating Faith Academy, the remarkable school I was able to help succeed as it got off the ground.

Throughout this book, I acknowledge things that I learned through a variety of ways. Many times, my growth was gained through getting to know other people and seeing what life looks like through their eyes. I learned it is necessary to recognize other people's suffering and understand it from their perspective. I want to share these experiences, as they are how I developed my compassion for others. We are a better world when we think beyond our own household and familiar community.

When I was younger, I believed I would have it all together at a certain point and there would be a time when I felt like I had taken in everything I needed to learn to be successful and happy. Presently, I know that is far from the truth. I am at the point now where I almost feel like I cannot complete this book because I find myself learning something more every single day.

In *Always More to Learn*, I touch on pivotal moments in my life. This was not easy, as I had to reach deep to access painful feelings I had been taught to keep within because they were too personal to share. For example, I talk briefly about the deaths of each of Dave's and my parents and how that affected us. While I could write an entire book on my mom's struggle with cancer alone, just touching on the loss we felt each time we lost a mother or father is an important part of my story.

I also faced a personal crisis in my professional career as I was turning 50. I had lost my enthusiasm for teaching, and I was exhausted by the experience. After a year, I rediscovered the joy of being an educator when I became directly involved with the unique mission at Faith Academy.

Like everyone in this world, I am a flawed human. I haven't always made perfect choices, and I hope to describe those imperfect decisions as part of my story. If I only wrote about the parts of my life that were honorable or without conflict, it would be a very incomplete representation.

In this book, I described the challenges we faced as a school when the Covid-19 pandemic invaded our world in 2020. As a school principal with responsibility for the well-being of all our students, teachers, and staff, this may have been the greatest educational challenge I ever faced. While our main concern was to keep everyone safe, keeping everyone content was a constant challenge during a time of great divisiveness.

Because I was an educational leader in an underprivileged neighborhood, I also look at first-hand accounts of racial injustice my students and staff encountered. These were brought to the forefront of our society and our school following the George Floyd murder.

I am hopeful that the miraculous creation of Faith Academy can speak to our hearts and show there are many wonderful people in this world who are concerned enough about others' children that they will sacrifice their time, money, and skills to help with such an endeavor. It is clear to me that teachers, as well as people in other helping professions such as social work and healthcare, do it every day.

As I describe the experiences I had as an elementary teacher and principal, I hope it is crystal clear that the good has far outweighed the bad. Along with being a parent, being a career educator has been one of the great joys of my life.

I also hope I have demonstrated how God has served as my source of peace and comfort during trying times.

Blessings to all of you, regardless of your beliefs and circumstances. We are all more alike than we are different.

CHAPTER 1

THE CREATION OF FAITH

Faith Academy was not my idea. Our group in Belize was just getting to know each other when I heard DeDe Parker make an off-handed comment to someone else on the mission trip. "Some of us at The Spot" – an organization sponsored by our church that holds after-school and evening programs for youth groups in southeast Iowa City – "are seriously thinking of starting a school." That was the first I heard of this grand undertaking.

I remember being both startled and incredulous as I thought, *A school? Good luck! It's not easy to work in a school, let alone create one from scratch!*

I also remember thinking it was a good thing neither DeDe nor our pastor Doug Fern had worked in a school before, or they probably never would have thought it was possible to open one. Pastor Doug had built a solid reputation on the southeast side of Iowa City as a Christian youth worker. This part of Iowa City was where the largest Black population lived, with many of the people having moved there from the south side of Chicago. Doug had coached boys in basketball teams at Iowa City's North Dodge Athletic Club and done other fun things with groups of kids as the leader for The Spot. A devoted Christian, he also led Bible Studies.

Most importantly, he walked the walk by engaging in life with not only the kids, but their families as well. Years later, when I was teaching second grade at Faith Academy, one of my student's sisters stopped by to see her. Andrea didn't live in town anymore and was just on her way through. This was her first time seeing our new school. She made a comment about how she couldn't believe the school had really opened. I asked her if she knew Doug. Her response was so telling.

"Oh yeah, Doug has been in our family for years!" She used to be a regular at The Spot.

The Spot opened in 2005. The outreach started because there was a need for a safe place for kids to hang out on the southeast side of Iowa City. Parkview Church began leasing a building on Cross Park Avenue to provide such a space. Importantly, it included a gym and a kitchen. Doug and another young guy had already been interacting with members of the community prior to having a building and they had already established a presence. Pastor Doug eventually had his office in the building so he would be easily accessible to the kids he was working with in the neighborhood as well as their families.

The idea of creating a new, faith-based school came when a junior-high boy, who was part of the regular crew at The Spot, was having trouble in school. It appeared to Doug and the others that the boy's school had just kind of given up on him and was satisfied to transfer him to the alternative junior high school in the district. The behavior that precipitated that final step sounded nothing like the boy they had come to know through The Spot. He struggled with academics as well. As a teacher I didn't want to believe that he would have been placed somewhere that he didn't belong, but also knew how difficult it is to serve the range of students that make up the classes. While I didn't know this boy personally, I understand that's where the idea of creating Faith Academy began. After witnessing this boy's struggles, Doug and DeDe said to each other, "We need to have these kids more than just one or two nights a week."

I wasn't aware of the backstory at the time I heard DeDe's comment about starting a school, but I knew how extraordinarily difficult that would be. I was doubtful that their desire, as strongly as they felt about it, was ever going to get this massive project off the ground. At that point in my life, I was feeling burned out and bitter toward education because of the insensitive actions of the most recent administration at Mid-Prairie Schools, where I had worked as a teacher for the last 11 years. Because of my disenchantment toward education, it is ironic that I eventually became the first Principal of Faith Academy.

Before Faith Academy, I wasn't a big fan of private schools. I now see that private schools are sometimes able to meet a need for some students, in ways that bigger public schools find difficult. As a public-school teacher, it irritated me to see a group of kids separate themselves by attending a private high school, thus leaving the remaining classes in the public school smaller. In addition to leaving us with smaller numbers, the private school took many of the students who were higher achievers academically and were most likely to participate in extracurricular activities, leaving a disproportionate number of the more challenging students in the public school.

By choosing to enroll their children in private schools, it also gave the appearance that families elected to send their children off to an exclusive school to be surrounded by people who had mostly the same beliefs, heritage, and social class as they did. When this happened, it left less opportunity for understanding other people who are not like them. It also appeared to me that at least some of those parents didn't care what happened to the rest of the kids in our community.

As their teacher, once I got to know "those kids" in public schools, I loved them and saw their unique value. I appreciated the things they had to offer and who they were. A public school population is a more realistic cross section of society and more representative of what the world is really like. I think back on the children that I taught over the years, and I feel fortunate to have had the opportunity to do just that; to get to know all of them. A powerful example of a parent not realizing the value of getting to know a kid who is different from their family takes place in one of my favorite movies, *Remember the Titans*. In the movie, one of the team's white football players, Gary Bertier, is asking his mom to give his new Black friend, Julius, a chance and to get to know him. Her reply was, "I don't *want* to get to know him!"

I desired to teach the underserved by letting them experience high expectations while providing a caring connection. Doing this at a private Christian school where I could share openly about Jesus never appeared to be an option to me for a couple of big reasons. The cost of private school tuition and the necessary marketing to bring in students of color or low income made this combination seem highly unlikely. Faith Academy was designed to be different by providing a high quality, values-oriented, faith-based curriculum to an underserved community at an affordable price.

Of course, none of this would have been possible without the vision, dedication, and enthusiasm of Doug and DeDe. Doug was one of our pastors and DeDe sang in the worship team. They both were prominent members of Parkview Church, the church Dave and I had been attending for about 10 years at that point, so I had seen them frequently. I got to know them much better on a church mission to Belize in the summer of 2012. My husband Dave and I as well as our two kids went on the trip. Even though all of us going to Belize together was my idea, Dave was 100% in favor of it. That trip changed the trajectory of my life.

Dave and I met during college in 1984. As a Mennonite, I went to our church school, Hesston College in Kansas. For those who may not be familiar with it, being a Mennonite is not synonymous with being Amish. Mennonites are considered a mainstream religion with pacifism and believer's baptism as two of our core beliefs. Hesston College is a small liberal-arts school in the town of Hesston, Kansas. Because of the small number of students and emphasis on core general education as well as Christian classes, it was a good choice for me. It was a way to transition from a tiny public high-school class of 43 students to taking on college life.

I was also only committing to a two-year college, as Hesston just taught students at the freshman and sophomore level. I was a first-generation college student, and my parents were completely comfortable sending me to a college that many in my extended family had previously attended. I was also able to participate in choir and play basketball for the women's team, something that wouldn't have happened at a larger school.

I hadn't even considered going out for basketball until two members of the women's team came to my dorm and asked me to think about playing my freshman year. Somehow, they had learned that I played in high school. I was in our lounge with a group of girls and saw two silhouettes coming down the hall. It was still early in the first semester and I didn't know very many people yet. Having these two players seek me out left a big impression. I set up a meeting with my advisor to get his feedback on whether or not it was something I could handle along with my coursework. His encouragement was the tipping factor I needed. I decided to give it a try.

It was a big adjustment for me because Iowa was one of only two states remaining that played six-player girls' basketball in high school. The rules for that type of basketball were that we couldn't cross the half-court line and were only allowed two dribbles before passing or shooting the ball. As a result, if I wanted to play basketball in college I had to learn how to play five-player, full court women's basketball and the nuances that went with it.

Learning the plays was the trickiest part for me. Despite the major adjustments to this new type of game, I earned a starting position and enjoyed the opportunity to continue playing a sport I loved. I got along easily with my teammates and coach, which was a good thing, as we spent a huge amount of time together during the season. For example, we all went directly to the dining hall after practice each day. There was just enough time to get in and eat before it closed for the night. For away games, we would do our homework while riding in the van our coach drove to various junior colleges around the state of Kansas.

I had a similar experience getting to know people in the Hesston College Concert Choir, even spending both of my Spring Breaks traveling on a chartered bus during our annual choir tour. Each year the trips were different; one went as far as Pennsylvania to the east and the next year took us as far west as Portland, Oregon. Through these choir experiences I got to be close friends with Ruth Brenneman, and we enjoy living in the same community today. In addition to our experiences together during the two school years, we both had the privilege of traveling across Europe for a month one summer.

Between our freshman and sophomore years, our choir took an optional trip to The Netherlands, West Germany, Czechoslovakia, Austria, and Switzerland. Not fully realizing what an amazing opportunity it was at the time, Ruth and I now look back at the places we were able to see and the variety of settings where we performed and are genuinely appreciative of the enriching experience.

We flew into Amsterdam, and we gave our first concert at the Singelkerk Mennonite Church. From the outside, it looked like living quarters typical for the area. Once inside, we discovered it was a large church built among three houses, with each of them being three stories tall, complete with balconies. The church was constructed in this way during the 1600s so it would blend in as part of the surroundings. Mennonites were not openly accepted during the Protestant Reformation.

One event in particular stands out from our European trip decades after it happened. Crossing from West Germany into communist-controlled Czechoslovakia we were stopped at the border checkpoint. A large mirror fastened to the end of a long pole was run under all sides of our bus by the border guards as they checked to see if we were smuggling anything. The guards actually boarded our bus and carefully looked through the items we had placed on the shelves above our seats.

This was all very intimidating. Since 9-11 many of us have experienced this type of scrutiny when crossing borders, but this was years before that. At that point in our lives, none of us had ever been through these types of security checks, except our director, who had previously traveled to communist countries. Our chartered bus, with more than 50 college students and chaperones, had never been that quiet.

A government chaperone got on the bus with us at the border and accompanied us during our entire stay. Because Czechoslovakia was ruled by a repressive communist regime in 1984, we weren't allowed to have an official concert when we were in their country. As a result, we had no contacts inside the country to arrange home stays. Hotel International in Prague, a five-star hotel, was where we called home for several days.

Our conductor, Dave Rhodes, got last-minute permission for us to sing in a seminary classroom in Prague. The tense feeling of being unsure whether we would be found out hampered our usual 40 voice a cappella choir from being at our best. The opposite was true in West Germany when our voices reverberated off the 150-foot-high vault of the Cologne Cathedral (Kolner Dom). We were thrilled to sing two songs after the official mass had ended in the largest cathedral in Europe. Completion of the cathedral took more than 600 years. The United States hadn't even been a country for *half* that long.

Learning first-hand about the history and culture of these fascinating European countries enriched the way I was able to teach elementary students. The Oliver Wendell Holmes quote, "A mind that is stretched by a new experience will never go back to its old dimensions," rings true here. Remembering the anxious feeling we experienced as we crossed the border and throughout our time in Czechoslovakia were experiences I could share with my students. This made our "Current Events" lessons that much richer as I taught social-studies classes to fourth and fifth graders at Garton Elementary in Des Moines when the Berlin Wall came down in 1989. My knowledge was much deeper than it would have been had I learned solely through a textbook in my teacher-prep program. Entering the hidden church in Amsterdam gave a new meaning to freedom of religion and provided me with a point of reference when teaching about that as well.

Participating in choir at the collegiate level gave me the necessary experience to be able to take on directing school musicals at Faith Academy as well as lead our daily worship in Chapel. Having played on the varsity basketball team at Hesston gave me the insight to coach my daughter's club basketball team for four years. It also inspired me to be the coach for a two-month program consisting of a weekly basketball clinic with our girls at Faith Academy. I wanted our girls to be able to have athletic opportunities like the boys had. The clinic culminated with going to a University of Iowa Women's basketball game at Carver Hawkeye Arena. This was pre Caitlin Clark, so tickets were readily available.

I also went to Hesston College with Maria, my best friend growing up. At the time I started, my brother Joe had already been attending there for a semester. So even though Hesston was out of state, there was a lot of familiarity for me. One weekend during the spring of our freshman year, Maria invited me to go with her on a trip to visit her boyfriend, Mike – now her husband – at Iowa State in Ames. I was game to go along and planned to visit Shari, our good friend from high school.

In addition to being a fun road trip for Maria and me, I was interested to see what life was like at a big public university compared to our Christian campus of only 600 students in the middle of Kansas. It was there, at a Jones House Party — a party in Mike's dorm – where I met Dave. "Stretch," as they called him, knew my high-school friends through other older WACO guys. WACO is the consolidated school district where I grew up – it is shorthand for the three communities in the district: Wayland, Crawfordsville and Olds. Dave and the others had taken some of the same Agricultural (Ag) Business classes, played intramural sports together, and things like that.

Dave was already a senior and lived off campus. In addition to being good-looking, athletic, and having beautiful blue eyes, he was tall. This was a major bonus for me as I am 5'10". While, admittedly, this sounds pretty shallow, his height was simply a positive aspect that I appreciated. Of course, there's far more to Dave than his athleticism, height, and good looks.

As I got to know him better and fell in love, I saw that we were a fabulous match in so many important ways. He was fun to be around and was a calming presence for me. He grew up Mennonite, as did I. I knew he was from a Christian home and would likely be a stronger Christian as time went on, as that was important to me. Looking at that word "likely" causes me to acknowledge that I am fortunate. Dave and I did a lot of growing up together and fortunately we grew toward God in the same way.

I told Shari that weekend, "I'm going to marry that guy." As romantic as that sounds looking back, there were some details that stood in the way. One big one was that we both were going out with other people at the time, so it took a while for us to even start dating. In fact, I thought he had forgotten about me until he called unexpectedly when I was home from college over the next Christmas break. Cell phones weren't a thing yet, so he had to make some effort to reach me. He called my house and my mom answered. I was babysitting my twin niece and nephew at the time and wasn't home. My mom gave him the number to reach me at my brother's house. Two and a half years later, we were married.

Dave and I were married at Sugar Creek Mennonite Church -
Wayland, Iowa in June 1987

I chose to attend Iowa State University (ISU) after graduating from Hesston with an Associate of Arts degree in Liberal Arts in 1985. I finished my bachelor's degree in Elementary Education from ISU two years later. I am thankful that my mom graciously gave out the phone number where I could be reached that day when Dave called. She later became one of his biggest fans. There were times I jokingly said she liked him more than she liked me. He was her only son-in-law as I am the only girl in our family and grew up the youngest behind four brothers. My brothers all liked Dave and he was easily accepted.

Dave is a high achiever and has always been a stable husband and father to our two kids. He is quiet and competitive, and his interests are varied. He's intrigued by cars, music, travel, and sports – both playing and watching. Dave grew up on a farm and has always been a hard worker. Appreciation for Dave's hard work was something our son Dylan verbalized at the end of our mission trip. As I would discover, our life-changing trip to Belize would impact all of us in so many ways.

CHAPTER 2

THE MAGIC OF BELIZE

Our kids each had finished their freshman years when we went to Belize with a church group on a mission in 2012. Jenna was about to become a sophomore at Mid-Prairie High School and Dylan was studying accounting and finance at the University of Iowa. I was at a difficult point in my career as an elementary school teacher. I felt our staff at Mid-Prairie Schools was no longer cohesive. I had challenging students, and the relationships between some teachers and the school administration were strained, causing additional problems. But it was summer break and what had been a very problematic school year was behind me.

On top of everything else, my dad had just passed away from Parkinson's Disease in March. I always had a close connection with Dad and it was difficult to see him in the debilitating condition caused by that ugly disease. He had been the one to teach me to play basketball and golf; and there he was – trapped in this body that would not cooperate with him. He had been living in a nursing home in Wayland for a couple of years and it was indeed a blessing for him when he passed.

Whether it was ever said out loud or not, I had been concerned that his failing health might cause our church's mission trip to happen without us. In other words, if he died right before the trip was scheduled to take place, we wouldn't be able to go. Or, if he was still lingering in his debilitating state, we would not have wanted to leave him and travel out of the country. So, as the trip began, relaxing and recharging were my main objectives for that time of year, as they often are for those of us who work in an intense school setting.

The first night of our mission trip was a Sunday and we were all attending worship in the host church in Dangriga, Belize. I was unsettled. It seemed like 95% humidity, and we were with people who we didn't yet know very well. My face was greasy, and I was tired from traveling. I hadn't even seen our accommodations yet, and I was nervous about where we were going to be staying for the upcoming weeks. Because I realized we were here for almost three weeks, my anxiety was beginning to build.

It was then they started singing the second song in the service: "What a Mighty God we Serve" – this was a song we sing at home! The accent of the Belizeans made some words sound a bit different, but it was a song we all knew. I felt a calm come over me and found warm tears running down my cheeks as I sang along. I had a complete awareness that there is **one** God over all of us, no matter where we live in the world. And there we were, worshiping that same God together. This spiritual awareness was a key moment in my life.

There were three different missions within the trip. Dave was doing construction work, and our son, Dylan, was going to be part of a sports camp with kids in the community. Our daughter, Jenna, and I were scheduled to help with Bible School. Jenna and I soon discovered kids in Belize can be just as naughty as kids in the U.S., especially as they were getting to know us. While my patience with kids wasn't what it once was, I wanted to be a good example to my daughter and to Madeline, a student who was a few years older than

Jenna and a leader in our classroom. She was planning on majoring in elementary education, as she was going to attend college soon. I tried hard not to let my jaded view of the education system seep out and taint her positive outlook.

As I served the beautiful children of Stan Creek Valley, I was drawing closer to Jesus and this group of friends I was getting to know. As the adults gradually came together, we opened ourselves up and began to trust one another. The facades fell off and we allowed our imperfections to be seen. When we left Belize that summer and traveled back home to Iowa, I fully appreciated that the trip was a bonding time for our family as well as the whole group.

On our last evening in Belize, Pastor Doug led us in a time of reflection about our time there. It included things God had revealed to us about ourselves, each other, and the people we were serving. It was one of those moments when people allowed themselves to be vulnerable and were sharing freely.

Julie Dancer and DeDe Parker on our Belize trip

14

It meant a lot when our new friend, Julie Dancer, shared her observations about Dave as a husband. She had noticed that he would come and wait outside my hotel door for us to go to supper together and be genuinely happy to see me after a day apart. The facilities were very limited, and Dave and I were not only working on separate jobs during the day, we were not even staying in the same hotel room. Jenna and I were in a room with seven females, including my new friend Jill Mabry and her two daughters, as well as two other high-school girls from our church.

Dave was in a room of six people, along with Dylan, Doug, his son Tony, and their family friends Lonnie and JJ who they knew from The Spot. I use the word "hotel" loosely here. In both rooms there were double beds pushed together so five or six people could share them and then a single bed on the side. The sheets were a variety of colorful floral patterns rather than the standard white we were all used to. Towels were not plentiful – Jenna and I shared ours. And the shower was a slow stream, at times just a drip. The stream was barely strong enough to get the shampoo rinsed out when we had an opportunity to take a shower.

Despite these inconveniences, we managed to do perfectly well with our accommodations, and had fun getting to know the Mabry girls. It still cracks me up to think of the guys in another room all sleeping side-by-side in those pushed-together beds. Being the extrovert that I am, I made it a point to get to know the new roommates that Dylan and Dave were bunking with. About the third day as we were all gathering for the evening meal, Lonnie said to me rather dryly, "Dylan… he's warming up to us."

Dave and Dylan are both men of few words, so I was surprised when Dylan spoke up on that last night under the shelter at the beach during our sharing time. He said how he had always known his dad was a hard worker, but that he had seen it first-hand this week. Dave's crew worked construction on meager houses for people in the community. They were digging crude wells and making repairs with the few tools they had. Dylan pointed out that Dave had missed supper one night because he wasn't feeling well but had worked all that day and got up and went back to it the next day. They were so dedicated that their whole construction crew missed the day that the rest of us walked to the waterfall and swam because they were so close to getting their project finished. They wanted to work instead of hiking and swimming so they could complete what they started. Dylan thanked Dave, in front of everyone, for being a great example as a dad. As a mom, that was an unexpected moment I'll always cherish.

*Taking a lunch break from their
work project on our Belize Mission trip.
From left: Jens Dancer, Doug Fern, and Dave.
Photo Credit – Julie Dancer*

That was the summer of 2012. Looking back now, it is easy to connect the dots of the path God was paving to lead me to Faith

Academy. I could see this, all the way back to my changing my major in college to education. If I could have had a glimpse at what He had in store for me, the tough times may not have been so painful. But while that is not the way life works, it is the way that God works. And I experienced just that, firsthand.

CHAPTER 3

GROWING UP

I have so very much to be thankful for as I recall my experiences growing up. My husband likes to tell me I had the perfect childhood. While we both knew that is never completely true for anyone, this was something he started saying as we were deciding where to settle and raise our own children. I spent the first 15 years of my life on an acreage outside of the small town of Wayland in southeast Iowa. At the time, Wayland had a total of three gas stations, a small grocery store, a hardware store, a bank, and a couple of restaurants.

Dad was a hog buyer. He wasn't a farmer, but he owned an agriculture-related business. He bought hogs from area farmers when they were ready to go to slaughter. He would sell the hogs to a packing plant, such as Oscar Mayer, and transport them using his own semi-truck, trailer, and driver. At that time, farms were smaller, and farmers typically didn't have the means to take the hogs to packing plants themselves.

My dad and mom - Cal and Betty - at a county fair in 1948.

Dad had other jobs before I was born, such as farmer, dairy tester, and manager of the Wayland Livestock Sale Barn. He liked to joke with us about his "college days" which consisted entirely of attending a three-week Dairy Testing Course on Iowa State University's campus and a six-week session of general studies at Goshen College, a Mennonite college in Indiana. Dad's claim to fame was that when he was at Goshen during that interim session, they pulled together a group of guys from the six-week course to form a basketball team. They played the Goshen College men's basketball team and actually beat them.

Unlike many of my friends whose dads were farmers, my dad's job didn't require the long hours away from home during the planting season in the spring or during harvesting in the fall. He was always able to attend all my school events – even the 4:00 basketball games when I was in junior high. Dad and I shared a connection over basketball, as he was a star player in his high school days. I loved it when he would shoot baskets with me in the driveway, and I always wanted him to be proud of me after games. He never put pressure on me or got upset when I had a poor performance, for which I was grateful.

All four of my brothers helped Dad at the hog station, as we called it, with Don and Bruce later making careers out of it for a number of years. Our house was nice for a family, with five kids sharing three bedrooms upstairs. One advantage to being the only girl in our family was that I always had a bedroom to myself. We had a big yard with trees to play in and a pasture with plenty of room for our horses to roam. We lived on a gravel road just a quarter of a mile off a highway where a beautiful white wooden fence bordered our pasture. At least, it was beautiful until it came time to paint it in the summer!

Our family: Dave, Bruce, Mom, Dad, and Donnie in back with me and Joe in front.

We lived just a mile away from our church, Sugar Creek Mennonite Church. Even though there were plenty of churches in the area, ours was the largest, with an average attendance of 250 people on Sundays. This is the same church where Dave and I got married when I was 22. We were married in a new, big, brick building that was completed one year prior to our wedding. It was beautiful and had a center aisle that our old church building lacked; although there were some unique features of the old church building that stand out in my memory such as the parallel open balconies with seating areas on both sides of the sanctuary. My dad served as chairperson of the building committee for the new church. He had the type of personality that was good at keeping the peace with all parties involved and bringing a big project like that to fruition.

My childhood was idyllic in that I had two close playmates right in my rural neighborhood. We remained friends as we grew up, to the point we all stood up at each other's weddings. My best friend, Maria, lived in the closest house to me, just on the other side of the highway. And another good friend, Beth, a year younger than us, lived in the next house just 200 yards away from Maria. The only other home in the vicinity was Beth's grandma. So even though I lived out in the country, I still had friends my age to play with without having to ask my mom to take me anywhere.

Beth Garrett, me, and Maria Freyenberger; our neighborhood clan playing dress-up at Beth's house in 1970 with her mom's square dancing dresses. (Such dresses wouldn't be found in our Mennonite households because square dancing would not have been something they participated in at that time.)

My brother Joe is two years older than I am, so we were close enough in age that sometimes he hung out with us, but other times we were doing things that he wasn't interested in. Joe and I always had each other as companions. We got along well at that point and had fun together. Of course, we had our moments like when he would find my hidden diary, read it, and recite quotes from me at the dinner table. I would come unglued, fly out of my chair, and try to hit him until my parents intervened.

Beth's family went to a local Methodist church, and Maria and I both went to Sugar Creek. We did everything together and had several sets of common friends, including Heather, who lived only a mile away, and went to church with us.

In addition to Joe, I had three other older brothers: Dave, Don, and Bruce. All of the boys were tall and thin like my parents. We all lived under the same roof for around six years, as Dave, the oldest -- yes, I have a brother with the same name as the guy I married – graduated from high school the year I finished kindergarten.

Don, who we called Donnie until he was an adult, was two years behind Dave and the two were a pair. They rode horses and motorcycles together, and they shared the same outdoor interests. Schoolwork wasn't necessarily a priority for either of them, and I do remember Mom and Dad being stressed more than a time or two when the two boys – okay, mostly, Donnie – would misbehave at school. This would result in a call from the high school principal or even require my parents to make trips to the school. That seemed to be when our parents would argue the most, with Mom saying "You're too easy on them, Cal!" It was the 1960s after all.

But no matter what any of us did, our parents were always there to support us and were our biggest cheerleaders. They were loving and kept positive relationships with all of us throughout their entire lives. Mom also stressed that we should maintain our relationships with each other. "There's enough people in this old world that want to run you down – you've got to stick up for each other!"

Don lived in Sarasota, Florida for a number of years. I thought it was cool that he was living somewhere else. I have a vivid memory of him returning and having gifts for Joe and me that he hid behind the couch. We each got a stuffed dog and a bag of orange gum. The gum was made to resemble oranges in a green net bag, just the way you would buy real oranges. I savored the gum, rationing it out to make it last as long as possible.

Bruce was the middle child, being about five years older than Joe and five years younger than Don. Even though he was the middle child he got plenty of love and attention and he was pretty easy going. There was a period when he had serious health issues, though. He spent two weeks in the hospital when he was in junior high after having open-heart surgery.

Bruce's health issues were, of course, a huge deal and everyone was concerned about him. Mom spent all her time at the hospital, rightly so, while he was there. I remember being sick during that time and my grandma camouflaging an aspirin in a spoonful of jelly for me to take as I was lying on the living room couch. We used the couch as a sickbed as that was customary when we were not feeling well. I knew Bruce needed Mom more, but I was sad and lonely and very much wished she could've been the one to take care of me when I was sick, instead of Grandma.

My sister-in-law, Nancy, married my brother Dave when I was just six. She has been a stable force in our family ever since. There's not much of my family history that doesn't have her in it. Two years after they married, my first nephew was born and two years after that their family was completed, with another baby boy. Being an aunt at the age of eight had its advantages. I loved playing with Brad and Andy, my oldest nephews. Nancy worked in an office of a sale barn one day a week and Mom watched the boys for her. The time she got off varied, depending on how lengthy the auction was for that particular day. I was always so hopeful that the boys would still be there when I got off the bus from school.

When I got a little older, I could actually babysit for the boys when Dave and Nancy would go out. We would arrange it so that I would stay overnight at their house on Saturday night, take my church clothes along, and then go to church with them the next day and return home with Mom and Dad afterward. I wanted to be with them as much as I could. During the summer I would get to hang out at their house sometimes and just play with the boys. My brother, Dave, would come in for lunch, as his work as a farmer allowed him to be right there. I was impressed that he would always get down on the floor and play with Brad and Andy for a while before going back out to work. Seeing them operate as a family gave me a loving example to emulate in my future family.

Joe and I were close as little kids but that changed once we were in junior high and high school. I am grateful that even though we are very different from each other, we still get together frequently as adults for lunch, coffee, and to help each other out. We were involved in the same youth group, but each had our own group of friends there. It was a tradition for our church to have an Easter sunrise service and for our youth group to be part of the service.

When I was in junior high, Mom, Dad, Joe, and I were trying to get out the door to be at the service as it started at 6:30 a.m. One of the reasons we wanted to be there so early was to take in the beautiful sunrise over the hill to the east. Mom always took a big pan of her homemade cinnamon rolls to share as part of the breakfast afterwards. Joe was ready and waiting for the rest of us in the living room. He was sitting in the Lazy Boy recliner minding his own business. I walked into the room and saw that he was wearing his leisure suit. Thinking he was too dressed up, I took the opportunity to make fun of him by saying, "You're wearing *that* to the sunrise service?"

Not liking my comment, he grabbed a shoe that was lying on the floor near him and angrily threw it at me. I dodged it and it went sailing right into our glass fish aquarium with the heel breaking the glass. Water and fish and tiny decorative pebbles flowed all over our living room carpet. Mom came running into the room and, boy, was she mad! I remember her salvaging the fish by putting them in Tupperware bowls and using towel after towel to try to soak up the water. She was hosting Easter dinner at noon that day, and she didn't need this disaster. Dad, of course, was disgusted with Joe and me – even more so when he saw how stressed-out this made Mom.

In addition to a lot of yelling, which we deserved, we had to do the dishes for two weeks as punishment. We did not own a dishwasher, and I remember standing in the kitchen with Joe for way longer than it should have taken us each evening. We either had our hands in the grungy water that had grown cold or were the person drying and putting away the dishes. Mom and Dad actually liked that situation to some degree because they were able to walk away from the dinner table and enjoy uninterrupted adult conversation and some TV in the living room while Joe and I remained captive in the kitchen.

One of the highlights of growing up were those Sunday lunches, like Easter that day, where all our family would gather after church. These gatherings continued even after my family moved. That move was a mere three miles away to a newer house in town when I was 15. Dad would sit at the head of the table while Mom served up a fabulous lunch of homemade food such as roast beef, mashed potatoes and gravy, or ham balls. Lots of laughter always went with it. Dad and his gift of storytelling never got old, at least not for me. Sometimes it was his favorite jokes, other times he retold stories about people in his past.

One of his favorites was an eating contest where a bunch of guys in the small town wanted to see who could eat the most steak. One man, who must have been somewhat gullible, was made to believe that the more water he drank, the more he would be able to eat. So the call for "More Water!" was a catch phrase that went along with that story. Needless to say, the more water he drank, the more his stomach filled up, and he failed to win the eating contest.

Our church was the center of my parent's world. We went without hesitation every Sunday morning and most Sunday evenings. My parents belonged to an adult Sunday School class consisting of about 12 couples. Except for one family that moved away, it remained constant throughout their married life. This was who they studied the Bible with, as well as who they socialized with. The downside to this comfortable familiarity was the lack of diversity and new ideas. Along with that, as is the case in most small towns, this situation lent itself to occasional gossip.

The positive side to this arrangement was the lifelong friendships we made, and the stability associated with belonging to a supportive community. The kids of our parents' friends became good friends to Joe and me as a result of their social outings. We would spend the weekend at hotels and go on camping trips. Our parents always let us do our own thing, as they were happy they didn't have to entertain us. I remember them bringing McDonald's food back to the hotel in Coralville for the kids and then going out for nice dinners. We were happy as clams and couldn't believe our luck to be left alone as a group of kids at a hotel.

Our church was supportive of its youth, involving us without reservation. I took my turn in the rotation of people who played piano for pre-service music when I was as young as 12. Two of my friends and I – their parents were in Mom and Dad's Sunday School class – started singing special music during church around that same age. Special music was when a soloist or small group sang up front for the congregation. At that time, it was sometimes accompanied by a piano, but was sometimes just instrumental.

I was the youngest of the three of us. Our trio sang together for years until the oldest left for college. There was only one time I remember it not sounding very good and that was when we tried branching out into some solo verses. I felt much more confident singing in a small group, even with my own alto notes, than when I was singing anything by myself. We didn't try that again.

The older boys still think I was spoiled because I was the only girl in our family. I am not saying I didn't have some advantages growing up that maybe they didn't have. I just think the different treatment I might have received had more to do with the stage of life our parents were in rather than me being the only girl. They were making a little more money when I was in school. We got to take a couple of vacations out of state that were more than just camping. They also had less expenses as they no longer had five kids at home.

My entire Eichelberger family as we celebrated Mom and Dad's 50th Anniversary in 1999.

Joe and I both went to college. The two older boys were not interested. Bruce, who was labeled as the smart one among the siblings, gave college a try, but missed his girlfriend and was home after just six weeks. It worked out for him though, as his girlfriend later became his wife. All three of us started out at Hesston College, a two-year college affiliated with the Mennonite Church. Because Joe took time off after high school, he and I attended Hesston at the same time. He had already been there for a semester when I started as a freshman. I was nervous, vulnerable and maybe a little homesick in my new setting. I remember he was kind and helpful to me that fall. That experience was a turning point in our relationship.

Having so many positive memories from growing up, I wanted the same for my family after Dave and I got married. After trying for many years to find a group of friends in our new town to create the close social circle my parents had, we realized it wasn't going to happen. We had plenty of friends from a variety of settings such as his work, my school, our church, his softball league, but not a group who all knew each other. Whether consciously or unconsciously, we accepted that our life was going to be different from what he and I grew up with. We knew our childhoods were unique experiences, not to be replicated.

I had the privilege of delivering a Sunday sermon at Sugar Creek in 2021. This was a significant experience for me; I felt I was coming full circle. I shared stories about my involvement at Faith Academy, and I described all the amazing things that were being done to change lives. Having them hear what a pivotal role Sugar Creek – their church – had played in my Christian walk enabled them to see themselves as an extension of the positive work happening there.

Whenever I return to Wayland and particularly to Sugar Creek Church, I feel warm and secure. People at church are always happy to see me and they know my husband now as well. When I attend church service at Sugar Creek, I find it is much quieter than where we worship now. Not only are we used to a worship band in our church, but I am now used to people responding to the service with an "Amen!" or other affirmations here and there.

God is present in both settings. Love is present in both settings. Wonderful people are present in both settings. But there is nothing like the feeling of acceptance and love I experience when I return to where I was raised. It envelops me like a warm hug when I am in the presence of people I've known from my years growing up at Sugar Creek Mennonite Church.

Yet, despite the outward appearances, my childhood wasn't perfect. There have been other experiences in my life that have caused stress and pain, and I have learned from them, too. I know it is very important to appreciate the wonderful people we love, as we honor them and the amazing experiences we've had. It is also critical to look at what has caused us pain and, more importantly, to see what we have learned from those situations and how they have helped us to grow. My next chapter is focused on that.

CHAPTER 4

JUDGE NOT

My life growing up seemed idyllic – but not everything was perfect. Living in such a tight community with people from church who were my parents' best friends created a sometimes difficult situation. I learned early on that things were easiest when we were all behaving as perfectly as possible. Our parents, like most parents, didn't want to find out their children were doing anything that would cast a negative light on our family. I can't count the number of times my mother told me how important it was to maintain a good reputation.

I discovered very early that our small community was very judgmental about who our friends were, and who we hung out with. In the Mennonite community of the 1970s this meant never drinking alcohol. Never drinking applied to everyone, even our parents. I do realize the occasional card games between Dad and his buddies were an occasion for them to partake, though. That was in the privacy of someone's home or garage. Dances were permissible for schools, but not all families even accepted that. Think of that old Kevin Bacon movie from 1984, *Footloose*. In fact, we held the first-ever dance at my Mennonite college when I was attending there. We watched the movie together and then all went to the town middle school so that it would be off campus in case the college's donors complained.

My mom wasn't hung up on that, like some others in the community, as she grew up in a different denomination where dancing was allowed. But this prohibition was strictly adhered to within most of my friends' families, as none of my friends from church had dances at their weddings. It wasn't worth even asking my parents about having a dance at our wedding as I knew that was a losing battle. After our wedding, Dave and I and some of our friends stopped at a restaurant bar called The Cove in Washington, Iowa, for our own little dance after having rice tossed on us and waving goodbye to everyone at the church. I love the celebratory feeling of a wedding dance. This was obviously not quite the same.

Something I did sense was that Mom always felt she wasn't viewed as much of a Christian by the rest of her in-laws because she didn't grow up as a Mennonite. I know the feeling of not being "good enough" was hurtful to her over the years as she told me a variety of stories that reinforced this. Strict adherence to these norms she and my father were supposed to live by encroached into their lives in personal ways. For example, she was the only one from my dad's family to have a diamond wedding ring set. His other sisters got watches for their engagement. Even though they were attractive gold watches, they were intentionally given a gift that was practical and had a use other than just adornment.

Her appearance was judged even when she was supporting the church. She was admonished for cutting her hair rather than rolling it up, as was the tradition. For her to be able to serve as a Sunday School teacher for children she was asked to take her wedding rings off because they were seen as being too worldly.

I know her goal was for us to live a life that was pleasing to God, and as a parent, I too have that goal. In the back of her Bible she wrote, "My one main hope in this life is that my children and grandchildren will all get to know and love our wonderful Lord and will live for him."

It is so simple.

It is unfortunate that people sometimes complicate it with legalism, meaning the conviction that law-keeping is the basis of God's acceptance of us.

In contrast, the Bible tells us "The Lord does not look at the things people look at. People look at the outward appearance, but the Lord looks at the heart." 1 Samuel 16:7

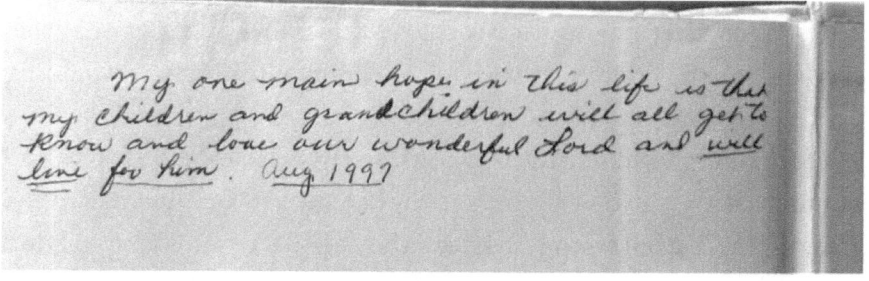

A snapshot of the back page in my mom's Bible

Of course, I realize that it is desirable to be looked upon favorably by others in our community. Unfortunately, I have seen that when this is too heavily emphasized to young people, there is a risk of turning them into over-conformists and people pleasers. Some people find it easier to simply conform to expectations than others do. Those of us with a bit of rebelliousness in our personality tend to push those conformity boundaries, especially when our brains are not yet fully developed, which doesn't happen until the age of 25.

Growing up with a strict "no drinking" rule, I know Mom and Dad were just trying to enforce what they thought was best for all of us. In addition to the church's stance on alcohol, Mom had grown up with a couple of alcoholics in her extended family. Her belief was that if you never allow yourself to drink, there is no danger of becoming an alcoholic. While this is certainly a true statement, not everyone in her family agreed with living a life of abstinence. We kids found it amusing to see beer in our refrigerator on one occasion. When Mom's brother, my Uncle Ken, and his family visited from Wisconsin, they knew they would never be offered a beer in my mother's home, so they brought their own.

This is the side of the family that was not Mennonite. Looking back, it would have been a great chance for a conversation about safe drinking. We were all at home, so no one was going to be driving. People drank it in moderation and enjoyed it. But after they left, this incident was never mentioned. That puzzled me as a kid, but I knew enough not to bring it up. Drinking continued to be a great mystery of immoral behavior to me.

Like a lot of college students, I didn't find it necessary to follow the rules. Our college had a no-drinking policy even though the legal drinking age in Kansas was 18 for beer. I didn't love the taste, but it was a means to an end. It meant that we had to leave town to drink, though, as there was no place in the small town of Hesston to purchase alcohol – it was a dry town. There were some of us who would periodically drive to Wichita 30 miles away to go out as a group on Friday or Saturday nights. I loved to dance at Pogo's to songs like "Old Time Rock and Roll" or Van Halen's "Jump." To this day, when I infrequently take a sip of beer, I say, "Reminds me of Hesston College."

At that time, I felt I had to act one way or the other depending on who I was with. I felt I was living in two different worlds. Again, this was not uncommon for college students trying out some different things for the first time. I have tried to raise my kids in a different way, where the act of drinking once you are of age, in and of itself, is not a *sin*. And I have no ill feelings on this subject, as I know my parents were doing the best they could with what they knew at the time.

Instead, I talked to our kids about the dangers of drinking and driving, and I let them know they could call us, and we would pick them up without question. They knew I did not want them getting behind the wheel if they had had too much to drink. I have, however, seen where drinking can cause serious physical and emotional problems, and I've seen drinking destroy relationships. I've witnessed marriages fall apart due to excessive drinking.

I also lost three friends in drinking-related accidents during the same year. These two separate accidents happened within four months of each other when I was in college. They were devastating and I know the experiences impacted me long term.

On a Friday night in late fall, we were leaving Pogo's, a dance club in Wichita, and our group of girls met up with a carload of guys at Burger King after a night of being out together. We enjoyed a time of energetic talking and looking to the future. I remember John Aramburu told all of us we needed to spend Spring Break in Brownsville, Texas, where he was from. He told us the weather was amazing that time of year.

We were just enjoying living in the moment as we all hopped in our cars to return to Hesston. My friend Maria had ridden to Wichita with the guys but was tired and for some reason got back in our car for the ride back to campus. I remember thinking it was so fun to have a big group of friends from a variety of different states who had connected at college. The guys needed to stop and get gas for Clair Stauffer's red Chevy retro car. He loved his car. I whipped through the gas station and didn't stop because I had over half a tank in my '78 silver Thunderbird, so we all just waved at them. I noticed John was driving.

That's good, I think Clair had too much to drink.

We took off to drive back to Hesston, 30 miles away. I parked my car, and we made our way back to our dorm, Erb Hall, without being noticed. The next morning, we found out that the other car

34

never made it back. I don't remember who it was that told me, but we were all in disbelief. They had gone past the Hesston exit, drifted off the interstate and struck a tree or rolled the car, I don't remember which. They must have fallen asleep.

We learned John was dead and Clair was in a coma in the hospital in Wichita. Another friend suffered two broken legs and our fourth friend sustained no injuries. We were shocked and overwhelmingly sad, probably more than we had ever been in our lives. We had a hard time accepting what happened, much less knowing how to react to this horrible news.

When we went to the cafeteria that Saturday morning, there was a solemn feeling among all the students. Everyone was just quiet, and the feeling was surreal. Our campus was small enough to the point that we all knew who everyone was by this time in the school year. So many thoughts raced through my head as I struggled to cope with the immensity of what I just found out. I remember one thought that stood out particularly. It was a result of the dual life I was leading, where I tried to hide my behavior from others.

Did anyone know that I was part of the group that was with John and Clair the night before?

I didn't reach out to my parents and share all of this with them. I thought they would be upset if they found out we had been partying with these guys. Just days later, the funeral for John was held at Hesston College Church, the big church on campus where we went to Chapel every day. I walked in together with a group of friends and sat behind the family. As terrible as we all felt, it was reassuring to say good-bye to John together. It was especially sad as we realized we would never have a chance to visit Brownsville with him, as we had talked about the night he died.

I also remember I felt like everyone was watching me. I could sense their eyes on my back. A couple of girls from our group became bitter about the way the accident was being talked about around campus and were vocal about their feelings of being harshly judged. My method of coping was to mostly keep quiet. I was forced to go through something that I didn't really have the maturity to handle. Sometimes in life that is the way it is. I just prayed and put one foot in front of the other.

It felt comforting to be sad with our group of friends – we had each other. When we saw John's parents who had traveled up from Texas, there was a much higher level of seriousness that set in. The hearse was not a typical hearse I had seen before, either. It was like an ambulance. I was standing outside when one of our friends, who was asked to be a pallbearer, shut the door behind the casket as it was going to drive to the cemetery. *Slam.* So final. John's parents had sent their son to college at Hesston to better himself and instead they were leaving him here, burying him in the town cemetery.

When Clair was in the hospital, a few of us drove to Wichita to see him. What we could see of his face was pale, as his head was wrapped in white gauze. His mom was in his room when we got there. Clair was unresponsive, as she was reading to him from her Bible. Again, the reality hit me that he was just a kid. We were *all* just kids. Even at the time, we knew we were living in our own little bubble, unaware of the happenings of the world as it went on around us.

We were independent for the first time, and we now knew that this tragedy is what can happen if we don't make wise decisions.

My friend Lisa couldn't stay in the room. She walked out into the hall and slid down against the wall. She just crumbled and cried. Her boyfriend Jim had been in the car, too, and he was the one who "walked away from the accident." Though his body was intact, his spirit certainly was not. He was broken.

A week later we buried another friend. Clair didn't ever come out of the coma and died within several days. His funeral was held at the same church. This time, it was a more familiar funeral for me. His family looked like mine. They were white middle class from the

Midwest and John's family was Hispanic from South Texas. Clair's body had arrived in a long, silver hearse. It was the kind of vehicle I remembered from when my grandpa died when I was 10. All the while, I wasn't sure how to process the feelings I was having. In addition to being deeply saddened, I felt guilty being associated with this terrible event. And I still had the same nagging thoughts.

How do we go on? We can't allow ourselves to enjoy anything about the rest of this school year when John and Clair lost their lives.

I don't recall ever talking to my parents about the accident, other than telling them that it happened and that we knew the boys who died.

A letter from the college president was sent out to the student body, faculty and staff. Part of it read, "I seek your assistance and cooperation as we at Hesston College address the issue of alcohol openly and honestly. The death of two friends prompt us to take immediate and responsible action in this regard. We hope that many of you will have suggestions or will wish to express your interest in being part of this important time of learning and value clarification...."

I do recall being called into the Director of Student Life's office with a small group of students. We were asked what activities could be planned to keep students on campus on the weekends. That was admirable, yet uncomfortable.

The only way I could deal with this terrible situation was to compartmentalize this experience and keep moving forward.

The second tragic accident that year happened back in Iowa. Again, a friend came to my dorm room on a Saturday morning, woke me up and told me the news. I had dated Kent for most of my freshman year, on and off. He was from Iowa as well and we met a month into my first year. The details of the early morning accident that just involved one car were unclear, but he was dead at the age of 21. He had been the passenger and the driver had died as well.

37

How could this be happening again? And to someone I cared about and knew so well? Why is all this happening, God?

I was a mess. It was February, we were full swing into the second semester, and I was in the midst of my basketball season. I felt more isolated this time as most of the friends Kent made in his two years at Hesston were no longer on campus. Some of my friends at Hesston knew him and were as supportive as they knew how to be. I had a basketball game that night and my coach put me in for a bit, but it was clear my focus was not on the game. Everyone was used to me being upbeat and encouraging at games, so my silence had the reverse effect – it put everyone on edge.

My parents were on their drive home from a few weeks in sunny Florida as empty nesters. They took two days to drive to Iowa and hadn't checked in with any of us, so I had no way to contact them. With the instant access we have to each other today, it may be hard to remember when immediate availability wasn't the case. Feeling the strong need to go to the funeral, I decided to take the train back home to Iowa.

My brother Dave and Nancy picked me up at the train station to drive me home. I remember the mixed emotions of being excited to see my nephews Brad and Andy standing there waiting with them, but not being able to muster any enthusiasm because I was so very sad.

Mom and Dad walked into the house shortly after we had arrived home from the train station. When Mom came in the door, at first, she lit up seeing me. She then sensed the somber feeling in the room, completely changing her demeanor as she knew something was very wrong.

"What is going on? What happened?"

Mom later told me that she had a frightening thought as her mind started racing. She immediately worried that something had happened to my brother, Joe. Dave and Nancy explained what happened because I couldn't speak. The situation was awkward because it was always clear to me how my parents felt – they never liked that I was dating Kent. They had friends who knew of him and didn't think he was the kind of guy I should be with. Much of their dislike centered around his smoking and drinking. That was all it took.

There were others in my life who didn't approve, either. My freshman roommate would make me leave my clothes in the hall after I had been out with Kent. It was only after I washed the clothes that I could bring them back into our room. She was annoyed by the smoke smell and didn't want it permeating our small room.

Looking back as an adult, I know my parents wanted what was best for me. At the time, I simply thought they were being judgmental and trying to control me. I felt they didn't know him like I knew him. Ultimately, I knew in my heart he wasn't what was best for me, and I had broken up with him before my freshman year ended. We had, though, connected as friends as recently as two months prior to his death.

My parents went to his funeral with me that next day. Again, it felt weird to have all these adults around in a situation where I just wanted to privately say good-bye to my good friend. Mom and Dad took the time to drive me back to Hesston later that week and stayed to see one of my basketball games. This gave me time to go on that first date with Dave, my future husband. It was two months after he had made his initial phone call to me, showing that he was interested after meeting me when I was visiting Iowa State with Maria.

When I returned to campus, I needed to jump back into life, as it continued to roll on. It was different from the tragic car accident two months prior – everyone on campus knew about that as it involved current students. Everyone was dealing with this shock. This time, it was just me and a few other people who had known Kent the year before. I did reach out to the campus pastor after a few weeks and met with him. He, of course, knew of the whole situation already. It was a relief to finally talk to a professional about it, but I didn't go a second time. It wasn't comfortable, as I felt I had to be too cautious about saying the wrong thing and causing him to judge me.

Being judged by others felt terrible when I knew the good intentions in my heart, or the good in the hearts of my friends. I was angry. I was disappointed. I was confused. I loved Jesus, and I knew He died for my sins and accepted me for who I am. I knew I could lean on Him to get me through the tough times in life. I was hurt that the adults at the college didn't reach out to me and my friends at the moment when we really could have used their support and compassion. In my "other life" as a Hesston student who was an athlete and choir member, I was having a fabulous experience. But as a hurting 19-year-old who had close friends tragically die, I felt I was on my own to try to make sense of these terrible, life-changing losses. As I reflect on my experience, I realize that Hesston wasn't unusual. I believe most Christian colleges would likely have dealt with it in a similar way in 1985.

One result of going through these painful experiences in college was that I learned a great deal about how I wanted to treat others with kindness and respect. Many years later, as Faith Academy presented a wonderful opportunity to me, I had a strong desire to be part of a school like Faith. I saw it was a school where we exemplify the Christ who enables us to live in peace, and where we know we are loved by Him.

Other schools who only value students who live a squeaky-clean life aren't where I am interested in investing my time. I know life is messy and I prefer to be with the souls who embrace the messiness and grow from the experience as they love those wonderful people around them.

Thomas Merton, an influential Catholic author, has a wonderful saying that I firmly embrace. "As Christians, our job is to love others, without stopping to inquire whether or not they are worthy."

I also learned it doesn't serve people to pretend like everything is perfect when it is not. Each of us needs to express our feelings – especially when we're hurting. That's how we heal. Along with that, I learned not to expect anyone or anything to be perfect. Perfection is an impossible standard, and we all make mistakes. We are only able to do our best, and that's all we can expect from ourselves and from others.

CHAPTER 5

ENTERING FROM A SAFE DISTANCE

"I was wondering if you would be willing to serve on the school board for Faith Academy?"

In the fall of 2013, a year after our Belize trip, I got a phone call from Doug Fern asking me if I would be interested in being one of the members on the board of Faith Academy. I took the invitation as a compliment from someone I respected. My husband was asked to serve on boards all the time as a community banker, so I was flattered to be considered. While I initially was skeptical about them opening a school, I soon realized they had actually done their homework and formed a committed group of people who fully intended to make this idea a reality.

The Visionary Team did their research and found Hope Academy in Minneapolis, a K-12 school that had a similar mission to what Doug had envisioned for Faith Academy. The tuition model and type of student that Hope Academy served – the same type of student Faith Academy was aiming for – was the drawing card to look into that particular school. Families who typically couldn't afford to pay tuition are able to attend Hope Academy because they are only asked to pay ten percent of what it costs to educate a student and the rest is paid for by churches and private donors. For most families, that meant tuition costs were as little as $50 a month.

Doug pulled together a small group of people with a variety of educational experiences from the church to investigate what was needed to get Faith Academy off the ground. They took a trip to meet with the Hope Academy administration and were generously allowed to tour the school and ask any questions they had. They were given Hope Academy's operating handbooks so that they had a starting point and wouldn't have to reinvent the wheel. If I were to serve on the new school board, I quickly realized I would be supporting an innovative school that served children who were not typical private school attendees. I happily accepted. As things progressed, I saw I would become more aware of how things were going, and I was hoping to be of some help. I didn't see that I had to be involved first-hand on a daily basis. I still wanted to kind of keep a safe distance.

I worked one more year as a fifth-grade teacher at Kalona Elementary, as I continued to put one foot in front of the other each day. After arriving home from a typical day at school, my dog Mick greeted me just inside the door from the garage. He would be wagging his tail and showing a smile that I could detect through his doggy eyes. More often than not, I responded by saying "Thank you for **not talking**!" I was so wiped out. My bag, stuffed with writing assignments to read and grade, fell off my shoulder onto the floor. My good intentions were to grade at least four of them each night. I felt that maybe I could light a cinnamon scented soy candle and work from our dining room table. But the bag was most often still there, untouched, when I walked out to go to work again in the morning.

If the kids and the paperwork were the only things that were weighing on me, I would have been able to recharge and sign my contract for teaching fifth grade for another year. But the bigger energy-sucker was the administration and even some of my fellow teachers. These underlying conflicts caused big divisions among us.

My husband certainly knew the stress I was under and that I had tried several times to get other positions within the district. He agreed that my quitting was for the best, but we both knew that I would look for another job within a year or so. I had been praying about my discontent for several years – what did it mean and what could I do about it? I could feel God saying that He had something for me. There were many times I woke up during the night with my mind spinning negatively. Sometimes, it got so bad I would go out to our living room while Dave slept. I would kneel at our brown leather ottoman and just open myself up to God.

I don't like the way this feels – why is this so hard? Why have none of these opportunities worked out for me? I'm in a low valley – please help ... I need your guidance.

To get a change from the classroom I applied for other positions within the district prior to making the decision to leave. I felt this would enable me to keep working for the Mid-Prairie School District and retain all the benefits I had earned. I had interviewed for the Educational Technology Specialist position, thinking the interview went well. In that position, I would work with teachers all over the district, as I helped them to integrate technology in their lessons.

I was excited about the possibility of not being tied down to a classroom and having something new to dive into. It would be much less risky than leaving all together. As it turned out, I didn't get the position. I was friends with the man who got the position and was happy for him, as technology was his strong suit. Of course, I was disappointed, because I knew that would have been a great solution for me.

Earlier in the year, I applied for the Reading Consultant position that was being created in the district. I had taken the time to return to school at the University of Iowa a few years earlier to complete my

Reading Endorsement certification that was a requirement of this new position. I applied and was interviewed but pulled my application before they made the final decision. There was an outside applicant that I figured was more qualified, so I withdrew. Who knows which way it would have gone, but I allowed my lack of self-confidence to not even permit myself to compete for a position I wanted. I was at a low point in my teaching career and the solutions I tried to come up with were not materializing.

This was not the first time I've been held back due to lack of confidence, either. It has taken me many years to be in a room full of people and not think that everyone else is somehow smarter and has more to offer than I do. Even as I took Dale Carnegie training in 2005, that feeling of not measuring up was firmly embedded in my mindset. Dave had taken the training through his bank, and I could see the impact it had on him, so I wanted to take it. I've always loved new learning opportunities.

I didn't want to pay the $1,800 for the 14-week class, so I reached out to the Dale Carnegie leader and asked if there would be any discount for taking their course since my employer wouldn't be paying for it, as is customary with private businesses. She agreed. I was able to attend on a scholarship in exchange for being a Teacher's Assistant for two consecutive classes. I was proud of myself for being able to experience this course and learn this material under conditions that worked out for me.

In addition to the weekly speeches, there was required reading. While I found all three books valuable, Carnegie's book *How to Stop Worrying and Start Living* was life-changing for me. After reading that book, I had new skills to access when I found myself worrying about a situation. I have recommended it to many friends when I hear them talking frequently about their worries. Both of our kids have also read it along with the other classic Carnegie book *How to Win Friends and Influence People.*

Still, when I walked into that group of about 15 men and women in the small conference room at the AmericInn in Coralville, Iowa, I was sure that others were going to be better at this than I was. When we got to know each other through the speeches we gave, it became evident to me that everyone definitely had their own strengths and weaknesses. By the end of the course, though, I was presented with the "Highest Award for Achievement," an honor which was voted on by the class. I was stunned and very pleased at the same time.

It was traditional for everyone's supervisors to be invited to the last evening of class. My principal at that time was Bill Marks and he told me he was honored to attend. I have great respect for Bill and he shared in my excitement when I was surprised with the award that evening. Since it was typically a class for businessmen and women, it wasn't something Bill knew much about. He was impressed with my achievement and reported it to the other teachers at our next staff meeting. That is the way Bill operated; he was quick to praise others on his staff and reluctant to take credit for the accomplishments that he had orchestrated. He was an intelligent and encouraging leader. He did not seek recognition and things ran smoothly under his watch.

In my fifth year of teaching at Kalona Elementary, Bill was diagnosed with cancer. He lived less than a year after the diagnosis and passed away in the summer of 2007. He had been the principal for ten years and our school had to find our new normal. The teachers who I worked with at that time – and who I continue to be in a Book Club with — still call those days when Bill was principal "the Good Old Days." Whether they were or not, the morale at school declined sharply with the next principal. It was during that time that I applied for those two other positions I didn't get. I was getting used to the idea of another year in the same role.

Despite the change in leadership and a worse atmosphere, the teachers at our end of the building got along well with each other. In most other parts of the building and district, the tension was ever-present and growing. It didn't take long for the downward spiral to come to a head.

My teaching partner Emily and I worked together to serve all our fifth graders, using each of our strengths. I was teaching Reading and Social Studies to both classes, and her role was instructing them in Math and Science. We both taught writing and language arts. This division of duties was something the previous teacher and I had worked out between us with Bill's approval. Emily and I wanted to continue teaching that way as it served the students well, and we were able to specialize.

I designed a way to integrate Social Studies and Reading by having all of our novels cover different time periods. I found that reading historical fiction such as *Sign of the Beaver* or *Bud, Not Buddy* was the most meaningful way to present American History to kids. When they had characters and stories to connect with the events they studied, it made sense to them. They learned.

We also had a "county fair" where every student reported, using their tri-fold board or a later a digital presentation, on their county of choice in Iowa. A field trip to the state capitol in Des Moines had become a yearly tradition, even though it was a two-hour drive. We had hit our stride, and our students enjoyed it. Most importantly, they learned the concepts and broadened their understanding of our world and the people in it. Students came to school eager for each new day.

Our fifth grade class from Kalona Elementary with teaching partner Karen Fisher (top right) on our 2007 field trip to the state capitol in Des Moines

When we were told that we could no longer departmentalize our teaching, it seemed to be the tipping point in my wanting to leave. We were told that a district reading committee had taken the stance that reading needed to be taught a different way and our principal, who had never taught elementary reading, was happy to enforce their idea. There's even a name for this controversial debate: "The Reading Wars." The name refers to an old disagreement about the best way to teach children how to read.

I had a conversation with our superintendent asking why it was necessary for each of our classes to be self-contained and teach all the subjects to our own homeroom. He even came to my classroom so we could talk about it in person. We were sitting at my kidney shaped table after the students had gone home. I remember he specifically told me he didn't think that specializing in subject areas was an issue at all. He said of course we could continue to specialize in the different subject areas.

Whew - that means a lot.

I felt relieved and supported for the first time in a long while.

However, the next day I got an email from him saying that he had misspoken. What a letdown. I later found out there was more to the story. At the time, though, the problem seemed insurmountable. Worse than that, I wasn't sure who I could trust.

I must have been complaining about my situation at school more than I thought. One day, I happened to see something my daughter had written. It was all about her feeling powerless because she didn't have the ability to make her own choices. It was from a journal of hers and it was lying out in her room. When I asked her to talk about it, she very wisely added her perspective.

"... at least you can change if you want to — you can quit ... I sometimes hate things that much and kids can't do anything about it."

I respect my daughter's privacy, but it was almost as if God just laid this one out there for me to see. I realized I *did* have a choice. I turned in my resignation.

In hindsight, I see verses from the Bible playing out. "...Don't you see, you planned evil against me but God used those same plans for my good, as you see all around you right now" Genesis 50: 19-21.

I felt I had been treated in a disrespectful and needlessly confrontational way and it ultimately caused me to leave my teaching job. Despite everything that went on, I was comforted by the fact that parents and students had only favorable things to say about me as a teacher. As I look back, I am surprisingly thankful for the negative events that played out. Had that not been the case, I likely would never have left the school right down the street from our home when I did. I needed to make that difficult move so God could bring the next step in His plan into place.

CHAPTER 6

WHAT NOW?

When others asked questions about me leaving my steady job in a respected profession as a teacher, most of them rolled off my back. But one question that stung was "How are you going to replace that income?" This was posed by a friend at church who was very analytical — not a word ever used to describe me.

And thanks for pointing this out to my husband, buddy!

I felt I was forced to, or chose to, let go of one trapeze bar before I had another firmly in my grip. Heck, I couldn't even see one swinging toward me! Admittedly, my husband was gainfully employed so I did at least have that safety net beneath my trapeze.

My husband Dave was supportive of my decision to leave my job. He knew the situation, as did my children, Dylan and Jenna. I realized this would be a surprise to many of my friends, family, and work colleagues. Most people don't just quit a job that is convenient and seems to be such a good fit, so there were questions and concerns.

Telling my class of students at the time went surprisingly well. It was their last year in the elementary building, and they would be at the middle school next year, so they were leaving, too. They wanted to know if I was moving. I reminded them that our daughter was still in high school and that we weren't going anywhere. They were content when I told them that sometimes people just need a change. I explained what retirement meant and that this would not be retirement for me. I hadn't even turned 50.

I met with a counselor and told her my story. She listened attentively to the unedited version and after about 30 minutes she shook her head back and forth indicating that she was trying to take it all in. She blurted out that my situation reminded her of a current news story where three young women in Ohio were held hostage in a man's basement. They were just stepping out into the world again after being cut off from society and were free to make a life of their own. They could choose where to go from there, but first needed to recover. So yes, an educated objective professional affirmed that I had been in a toxic environment. It was freeing to hear her confirm it was a healthy decision for me to leave.

There were several of us teachers that left Kalona Elementary that year. My teaching partner Emily moved to one of the other schools in our district, as did a couple of other teachers. A month into the following school year I was sitting at my daughter's high-school volleyball game when I got a call on my cell phone. It was the secretary at our central office looking for a substitute teacher for the next day. It usually was handled through an online service, which I had not signed up for.

The secretary explained to me that Emily's son had been injured at school that day, from a lunch table that fell on him. Emily needed a sub for the next day because she needed to be with her son. I did not want to take this on. I had no plans of subbing. I was exhausted by teaching, and I wanted to break away from the whole profession just to get my bearings straight.

I know what it is like, however, to need to be somewhere else and to worry about who is going to be in charge of your class. I knew it would give Emily peace of mind during a stressful time if I were to step in for her. Fifth-grade curriculum was second nature to me. I knew and liked the other fifth-grade teacher at her new building, so I felt I could help – just this once.

It turned out being a substitute teacher wasn't as bad as I had anticipated. It wasn't long before I officially put my name on the subbing list. I subbed for Emily's class at various times that year when she needed someone. I got to know her kids and didn't have to take any work home or be part of the staff politics that can go along with being a full-time teacher. I found it was energizing when I got to reconnect with some of my former fifth graders when I was in the middle school or high school buildings. Getting to touch base with past students has always been and continues to be one of the best things in my life.

Looking back, I see it was all a part of the groundwork God was laying. Had that subbing experience not happened, who knows – I might have instead been working at the front desk of Corridor Radiology. I went there for an appointment the previous year and was struck by the calming trickle of the water feature that served as a focal point on the wall in their office. I told the receptionist, "I want to work here, it's so peaceful," as I dramatically slumped myself down in the chair across from her to check in for my appointment.

Meanwhile, those of us who had gone on the Belize mission trip seemed to gel as we kept in touch after our meaningful experience together. Our church is always encouraging people to join small groups or community groups, and I wanted to keep that camaraderie going. I thought there was a much higher probability of us sticking with the group if we already knew each other and enjoyed spending time together. I sent an email to the adults from our trip asking if any of them would be interested in starting a small group.

Those of us who were interested agreed to gather on Sunday nights twice a month for Bible study while our kids attended activities at church for junior high and high school students. Chris and

Sarah Leyden, a couple Dave and I both enjoyed getting to know in Belize, graciously hosted at their beautiful home near the church. It worked well for us to meet at the same time as our kids since church was a 30-minute drive for my family. Some of the people changed over the years but the core group stayed together for the next 10 years. Pastor Doug and Natalie Fern were part of the group, so Doug knew I had been doing some subbing because I shared my experience with the group.

Once Faith Academy started operations and was more than halfway done with the school year, the first-grade teacher's wife had a baby a week ahead of her due date. When Doug saw me at church he asked if I would be available to sub at Faith Academy that week. He explained the situation, and that he wanted to give the new dad a week off to spend with his family. Dave and I were serving as greeters, so we were highly visible that week, which wasn't always the case. Typically, we could slip in and out of our big church without being noticed.

During that first year at Faith Academy when teachers needed to be absent, the staff would generally take turns covering the classes of eight to ten scholars from within. They made a point of calling their students "scholars" because it raises expectations for academic achievement. Since this absence was going to be an entire week, Doug thought he had better come up with a more structured plan. By then I had been subbing in our public school district at all levels, K-12, but I happened to have an unusually open week in front of me. I was available every day. As I paused to consider taking Doug up on his offer, I remembered how hard it is to find a substitute last minute. I also thought it would be interesting to see how it all works over there, so I agreed.

I had seen the scholars at Faith Academy in action once, as Dylan and I met them at the library downtown Iowa City to help with a field trip. The kids all wore school uniforms with khaki bottoms and navy logo shirts. And they called Doug "Mr. Fern." This shouldn't have surprised me, as he was in charge, but he is such a casual person that it did. I can't remember how I talked Dylan into going along with me. He was a sophomore at the University of Iowa in Iowa City so it's not like it was out of his way. But for him to show up to help supervise and interact with a bunch of five- and six-year-olds, was a bit of a stretch. He had enjoyed getting to know Doug in Belize and must have wanted to see what was up with this school as well.

The first morning I was there to sub, I got myself comfortable with the lesson plans, materials I would use, and all the other things a teacher needs to be familiar with to run a classroom for the day. After I felt somewhat situated, I walked out into the common area and Doug motioned me over. He mentioned circling up to pray, almost in passing. It wasn't much of a circle with just four staff members.

I soon discovered it was what we did every morning. Prior to the scholars' arrival, staff gathered in a circle. That simple daily ritual made a really big impression on me. Plus, someone had taken the time to buy a battery-operated milk frother for coffee and it was in the kitchen for everyone to use. It looked like it came from IKEA. What a fun gizmo to have around! That little detail left a positive impression on me.

I discovered that in addition to our spiritual focus, we spoke briefly about the particulars of the day ahead. It was a routine I came to cherish during my eight years at Faith Academy as a teacher, curriculum director, and principal. We also shared success stories from the previous day and then identified people and events that could be lifted up in prayer. There were times of great celebration and times of sadness.

Faith Academy opened with only two classes, kindergarten and first grade. The plan was to add one grade every year until it was a complete K-6 elementary school. This group of scholars that I substitute-taught for that week would always be the oldest at the school in their first six years. The public school in Iowa City went through sixth grade, so it was decided to have the same model. I knew that the following year the scholars who were currently in first grade would be the second grade class that would need a new teacher. *Should that be me?* About the third day I started visualizing me coming here every day and being a daily part of Faith Academy.

By the end of that week, I almost sheepishly asked Doug "Would it be weird if I applied to be the second-grade teacher here for next year?" His face lit up.

Why in the world would I want to teach second grade?

I knew that fourth and fifth grade was my sweet spot. However, the atmosphere at Faith Academy was completely different from any work environment I had ever known. Even though I knew the job would be challenging, it would be refreshing to be surrounded by encouraging, lighthearted people. As an elementary teacher it has always been easy to feel a sense of purpose in my role and that is a key factor in job satisfaction.

The difference I could detect here was in the leadership. I had already worked for six different principals with a wide variety of leadership styles. From my observations the factor that separated the great leaders from the rest was a healthy self-image as opposed to an inflated ego. Doug Fern was a healthy leader. He was not driven by power or status and would easily admit when he didn't know something or had done something wrong. He worked alongside his people and had created a positive workplace culture. I suspected this to be the case at that point. After eight years of working with him I knew this to be the case. The amount of laughter that took place among the staff at Faith Academy went a long way to relieving the stress that inevitably went with the territory of working in a school.

I interviewed, was offered, and accepted the job in the spring of 2014 as the Second Grade Teacher at Faith Academy. When I shared my news, I got a variety of reactions from people.

One reaction in particular caught me off guard. It was at a high-school graduation party. Graduation parties are key social events during May and June in our community. Being a former teacher and having our own kids around high school age, my husband and I were invited to a large number of parties for Mid-Prairie kids, which I loved. In catching up with one man from the community I hadn't seen in a while, I shared what I was going to be doing in the fall.

Knowing the part of Iowa City where Faith Academy was located, he asked, "Are you going to be packing?!" As in, are you going to carry a gun with you? "Man, some of the things I have seen at Waterfront HyVee … I try to avoid that place." And he went on to tell some stories of loud interactions he had witnessed there. That very HyVee supermarket became where I stopped most mornings to grab a pre-made salad for lunch at school or on my way home for some groceries. It became very familiar to me and I enjoyed shopping there.

"No, I don't think I'll need that," I answered uncomfortably with a laugh.

Another husband of a teacher commented with a pointed "Why!? Why there!?"

Admittedly, there were times I asked myself the same question. I didn't have my "elevator speech" ready yet. I'm not even sure how I responded at the time.

When I explained Faith Academy to my friend Susan over lunch at the Botanical Garden Cafe in Des Moines, she confidently said, "Jan, that sounds like a perfect fit for you." I was in Des Moines for our summer day of shopping. We taught together for five years in Ankeny. We had remained in touch, even though we now lived two hours apart.

*Susan Jones, left, my former teaching partner and I on one of our
many shopping day get-togethers in Des Moines*

Susan was the one who threw me a going-away party when Dave,
Dylan and I moved to Kalona in 1996 for a new job for Dave, where
we would be close to our families. Our friendship was the kind
where we were always able to start up right where we had left off,
even when it had been a while. Her affirmation was a breath of fresh
air coming from someone who knew me so well. On my two-hour
drive home that summer afternoon, I felt confident in my decision,
and was excited and at peace with the new direction in which God
was leading me. My mind was churning with possibilities. I was over
halfway home before I realized I hadn't even turned the radio on or
pushed in a CD to listen to.

CHAPTER 7

FOUR WALLS AND CONCRETE FLOORS

As she looked around at all the construction work needed to be done to get my classroom ready by the start of the school year, my friend Kim was concerned.

"Do you really think your class is going to be ready by the time school starts?"

Near the end of July 2014, I was giving some of my Kalona Elementary teacher friends a tour of Faith Academy. To have space for an additional classroom, some upgrades to the Faith Academy building on Cross Park Avenue were needed. The non-profit organization that was working out of the space directly next to Faith Academy moved out in the Spring of 2014. The timing was perfect, as it opened up an additional 3,000 square feet by simply cutting a doorway to connect the two spaces.

Walls in the additional space needed to be reconfigured to create four classrooms and the construction project was started with an optimistic date of having it ready to go by August 1, painting and carpeting included. As is often the case with major remodeling efforts, the project was running behind. I was excited to show my group of friends from Kalona Elementary where I was going to be working in the fall. They honestly were not all that impressed, however they tried to be excited for me. It was then that Kim, always the realist of the group, asked me if I really thought it was going to be ready to move in before school started.

I have remained connected with a group of teachers
from Kalona Elementary where I previously taught.
Here we are in 2015 celebrating Frank's 40th Birthday.
Kim Juilfs, Suzanne Yoder, Jill Hartsock, Frank Slabaugh, me,
Heather Herschberger and Emily Pennington

"Oh, sure it will!" I responded, practicing the optimism I was choosing to use for this new situation. It was hard to convince the group of teachers with the dust all over the area, sheets of plastic up, and gray concrete underfoot that I wasn't stressed about it. But I really wasn't. Doug seemed certain that it would be ready, and even if it wasn't I knew our little team would figure something out.

Before my classroom was completed, I was aware that in addition to needing the room to be finished, I would need to supply the room — with everything. The initial Visionary Team had already selected and ordered the curriculum. There were a few new things I could order, and others I did my best to find used. I got to select brand new student desks for the first time ever! My friend Jill, who had come along for the tour, was an experienced second grade teacher, so I asked her opinion on the type of desks that she would pick. Jill suggested I order a certain style of student desk, one that doesn't have a desktop that opens and shuts. I also got to order a new kidney-shaped table to use for small-group reading teaching. I made a trip to Parkview Church to place the order with the approval of the business manager of the church. The rest of the classroom was furnished with castoff chairs; my teacher desk was a castoff from the bank where my husband worked. They were happy to give it away to a good cause rather than having it take up space in their storage unit.

To see what additional treasures I might find for my new classroom, I waited in line for the doors to open at the University of Iowa Surplus store on sale day, which was an adventure. I had driven by this building many times in Iowa City and had no idea what it contained. Decisions had to be made quickly once I entered the building and saw something I was interested in, as other bargain hunters were eager to jump on a good deal for discarded university furniture. There wasn't time to debate over a purchase or it might be claimed out from under you. It was a little nerve-wracking, but I was up for the challenge.

DeDe Parker, my friend from our Belize trip who also taught music and art at Faith Academy, was experienced at this and accompanied me on my maiden voyage. It was well worth our time. I came away with three skinny tables and a metal cabinet. The cabinet even locked, but only after Dave figured out he could order a new key for it online by tracking the serial number etched inside the cabinet. I am grateful that husband of mine is always willing to investigate how to solve a problem for me.

But best of all, I purchased a blue, vinyl institutional sofa with drawers underneath for $5. Any experienced elementary school teacher knows not to have upholstered furniture in a classroom due to … potentially creating a haven for head lice. The reason it had been added to the surplus sale was a puncture on the sofa arm. I bought some fun colored duct tape, and we were good to go!

First day of teaching Second Grade at Faith Academy 2014 – including the prized sofa purchased from University Surplus

Throughout my career, every time I had moved into other classrooms there had been a lot of materials from the previous teacher. My first job was at Garton Elementary in Des Moines and the class cabinets and cupboards were so overflowing with papers and books from Mrs. Gundy before me that there was hardly any room for anything of my own. This was a bit extreme, but also a blessing as

I started. Since I didn't have many resources yet, I waited until the end of that first year and then did a big purge after determining what I actually used.

A classroom library was also something a new teacher could always depend on being in the room. It may have not contained the latest titles but it was at least a place to start. Not the case this time. I brought my own books with me, but most of mine were fifth-grade level. I made trips to The Crowded Closet, Goodwill, and other secondhand stores to start to build up an age-appropriate collection of books.

We often had families from church donate books once their children had outgrown their level. Teacher friends of mine also looked out for me and my class, letting me know any time they had books they were able to donate. This even included school furniture, sometimes reclaimed from beside the dumpster. In later years we could afford to be pickier with the books we accepted since we had grown to have an abundant collection in each classroom. As the libraries expanded, I continued to say, "At the beginning we were scrounging for children's books at every turn – it's great to be able to be a little choosy at this point!"

When I started teaching second grade in my first year at Faith Academy, I never expected to be there long enough to see us come to the point of having a generous amount of our own resources and materials! Yet, my journey at Faith Academy was just beginning, and would take me in directions I never anticipated.

CHAPTER 8
STARTING FRESH

*T*his is going to be different. Wow, starting the new school year with a family barbeque is something that can actually be pulled off with a small school like this. At my previous school, we held ice-cream socials with premade cups of soft-serve ice cream eaten at the lunchroom tables. The idea was the same – to welcome the families back to their school community for the fall and have a chance to reconnect with one another. But this was going to be taking it to a whole new level. Here, we would be interacting with all the families and even serving them dinner. This is going to really take some getting used to – but I am up for a change ... this is exciting.

In my experience of 22 years as a public-school teacher, the week leading up to school opening for the fall session is typically full of informational meetings and staff training with teachers throughout the district. Having worked in three different-sized districts, there were a variety of ways that week was structured. For example, the Des Moines Public School District (DMPSD) was so large we didn't have a district meeting and most meetings were conducted at our individual schools. As the teacher work-week before classes began approached, we looked forward to being able to eat lunch out at area restaurants, as we never had time for such a luxury once the school year was under way.

Another example was Ankeny Community School District (ACSD), a mid-size district I taught in for several years following DMPSD. ACSD was just north of Des Moines, and I taught fourth grade there from 1992-1996. The biggest reason I moved was that I felt changing from an urban district to a suburban district would be a way to reduce my stress level, as I was pregnant with our first child, Dylan.

The atmosphere at Ankeny was very different from where I worked previously. It didn't seem like we were operating in survival mode, which is how it felt when I was in DPMSD. When topics came up in the teacher's lounge that seemed like a big deal to the staff, I found myself wanting to let them know, "You have no idea how easy you have it compared to where I taught my first five years!"

Our fourth and fifth grade team of teachers in 1996 at Northwest Elementary in Ankeny: Doug Mackey, Mark Nordby, Susan Jones, and me — pregnant with Jenna

But I kept my mouth shut as I didn't want to point out that they had *little* to justifiably complain about. I didn't think making remarks like that would help me win friends and influence people as a teacher new to the district. It all turned out wonderfully, though, as I worked with some great teachers and became lifelong friends with Susan Jones, one of my fellow teachers during my time in Ankeny.

For years, Dave and I had many discussions about where we thought would be the best place to live when our children were growing up. We felt like each of us benefited from attending a smaller high school where we were able to participate in all the extracurricular activities. Even though we had good friends in the Des Moines area, we both liked our jobs, and we enjoyed the amenities of living in a city, but still felt something was missing.

We wanted to give our kids the same opportunities that we experienced by being a big fish in a small pond. We knew having grandparents in the same community was a big plus as well. Five years after starting at Ankeny, when Dylan was four, we made the decision to go back to my husband's hometown of Kalona. We moved during the school year because Dave got a job offer that started in October. Hills Bank had purchased an existing bank in Kalona and Dave was hired to be the branch manager. He would start when it opened under the new ownership. I stayed until the end of the first quarter to make the transition easier for my fourth-grade students, who would have a new teacher.

As I look back on our experiences, I have sometimes asked myself whether we would make the same decision today. I now realize both Dylan and Jenna would have been just fine and might have even thrived in a larger school atmosphere. But we did the best we could with the information we had at the time. We made our decision based on our own experiences growing up. As it turned out, by the time our kids were in high school there was only one grandparent left to watch them at their school events. When we moved to Kalona in 1996 all four of our parents were healthy.

Despite the less stressful environment working in Ankeny, I do remember feeling intimidated when district personnel were all gathered together for Professional Development or other meetings. My discomfort had to do with my relatively young age and inexperience and not knowing many people there. By the time I taught in the Mid-Prairie District in 2002, which included the towns of Wellman and Kalona, I had more experience, especially with my years as a student-teacher supervisor at the University of Iowa from 1997-2002. That supervisory position got me into countless elementary classrooms to observe and give feedback to college students in their last semester prior to graduating.

I was also a parent at that point, which made a big difference because I understood school concerns from a parental perspective. I was confident in my professional skills and knew the majority of the staff in the district. I felt comfortable and at home there, and I always looked forward to connecting with people at the district meetings who I didn't see on a regular basis. In Ankeny and Mid-Prairie both, we started with a large district meeting where we had inspiring speakers or videos to focus on remembering "why" we choose our profession as educators.

No matter the size of the district, I found preparing for school to start to be a fun week. It allowed me to be together with fellow educators after a summer of rejuvenation away from the teaching routine. The excitement was mixed with stress however, because I knew I had to get everything ready to hit the ground running once the students showed up. Most of us spent days at school ahead of that prep week getting our rooms ready. We didn't want to feel we were under the gun as back-to-school day approached. Nevertheless, it was typically a week of long hours, even though I always enjoyed it and looked forward to the experience.

Our back-to-school staff meeting for Faith Academy was held at Panera, a cafe in southeast Iowa City tucked away in a mall. Counting everyone, we were a cozy group of six. DeDe, who served as both our Art and Music teacher, was still on vacation, so Doug simply informed us he would bring her up to speed later. The casualness of it all felt so refreshing to me.

The main topic we covered was the plan for the upcoming Friday evening event, the Back-to-School Barbeque. All Faith Academy families were invited to meet the teachers and classmates and share in a meal of hamburgers and hot dogs the Friday before school started. They held the same event the previous year, which doubled as the grand opening of the school, and the other teachers and staff enthusiastically described what a hit it had been. Still, it made me wonder.

Are they really going to hold this on a Friday night this time of year? I guess it'll work for me – our family is past the stage of attending high school football games every Friday night in the fall when Dylan was playing.

I was the only new staff member, so I listened and enjoyed the camaraderie among the group. The meeting lasted less than two hours. I was amazed it was so short. It certainly wasn't what I was used to, but I liked it.

That's it? Sounds good to me! If there's something I don't know, I'll just ask.

I was a bit apprehensive leading up to the evening of the barbeque because I knew this would be a completely different environment for me to work in. I was now fully engaged in a private, faith-based school serving minority students instead of our neighborhood school where the families were similar to my own. It was all a bit overwhelming, but I was up for it. The meal was cooked and served by Faith Academy staff and volunteers and the event was held on the school grounds.

Before I even started, I knew I was going to have a more diverse group than I had ever taught before, with 90 percent students of color in my classes. I had Black and Hispanic students in Des Moines, but at most they totaled 40 percent of the class. I knew at Faith Academy this would be a huge difference.

In the end, the back-to-school barbeque was a great evening and I felt lucky to be joining this upbeat group of people who almost all seemed to know each other. It was apparent everyone enjoyed each other's company, as no one seemed to be rushing off at the end of the evening. I noticed some extended family members came along for the event as well. As much as I enjoyed the experience, I looked forward to when I would no longer be the new person and would have a sense of belonging within this group.

As I began the school year, I became aware I needed to make some adjustments in this new environment. I soon realized it may have been better for me to learn my new students' names by hearing the scholars and their families say them, so I could get the proper pronunciation down. Seeing the names in print and guessing how to pronounce them wasn't working for me at all. Names like Inaiyah and Adonijah threw me for a loop! Nevertheless, I did my best and I was thankful they were patient with me.

My commute was longer than I had experienced in my previous job at our neighborhood school, which was just three blocks from our house. In my new position, I drove 25 minutes to Iowa City every day. The drive to work was easy to get used to but when I was done after an exhausting day I just wanted to be home. I did not want to spend 25 more minutes in the car.

As I began again as a full-time teacher, I still carried a reluctance with me. I was going to be teaching second grade, which was not the grade level I felt best suited for. I cried on the way to school and on the way home from school almost every day for the first two weeks. There were parts of teaching I had always loved: establishing connections with the kids, showing students they were important by really listening to them, and playing a positive role in their learning.

I had, however, grown tired of cajoling them into doing what they needed to do. I did this simply because I wanted to prevent student-teacher confrontations from developing into a disruptive, oppressive classroom environment. Getting the scholars to do what they needed to do without push-back didn't come easy. It was exhausting and frustrating, even if there were only 11 scholars in my class. *Was this really what I was going to do all year?* Despite the frustration, I did love the kids and I did love the mission. Things got better.

I had previous experience teaching in the primary grades (Grades K-2) before Faith Academy, so I wasn't completely at a loss when I began with the second graders. In 1987, I got my first teaching job in the Des Moines Public School District as a first-grade teacher. Rather than interviewing for a specific position within the large district, the hiring process entailed candidates going through a videotaped interview with the Director of Human Resources and an elementary principal from within the district. The principals who needed teachers viewed the videos of the approved candidates and then selected the one they felt was the best fit for the opening in their building. As a result of this rather impersonal process, I ended up as a first-grade teacher in a very challenging, urban environment.

As I think back to my first few years of teaching, the situation I was getting into was much more than I had bargained for.

CHAPTER 9

FIRST YEAR TEACHER

I had had enough of my principal's gross lack of integrity and his inappropriate interactions with me and my colleagues, and I took it upon myself to act. I requested a meeting with the Assistant Superintendent of the Des Moines Public Schools to express our concerns. After hearing me out, he paused and spoke in a calm, measured voice as he chose his words carefully. He clearly just wanted to make this go away.

"The same code that protects John in this situation protects you and me."

That was basically it. My response to him was that I didn't need that type of protection. Even as I spoke what was in my heart, I began to wonder if I had made a serious mistake by bringing this to his attention.

Did I really just say this to the Assistant Superintendent?

My heart was pounding. I was stunned.

So, this is the way adults in positions of power handle conflict?

I met my principal for the first time when I drove two and a half hours from my parents' home in Wayland for a day trip to Des Moines during the summer prior to starting work at Garton Elementary.

The summer before I started at Garton, Dave and I married, and we moved to Des Moines for my job and Dave's new position in that city. He was able to transfer to one of the Des Moines branches of the financial services company he had been working for in Iowa City. At my first meeting with my new boss, I couldn't help but ask why, out of all the candidates available, was I hired for a first-grade teaching position? I wanted to be clear about my appreciation for being hired, as I was thrilled to have a job, so I waited until our initial meeting was almost over to approach the subject.

Why first grade?

For the first time in years, the number of new teachers in the job market increased, and there was more competition for each position. In an effort to attract and retain competent Iowa teachers, legislation was passed to increase teacher pay effective July 1, 1987. The minimum teaching salary was set at $18,000, so I got a raise before I even started. My initial contract was for a mere $13,600 a year — what great timing for me!

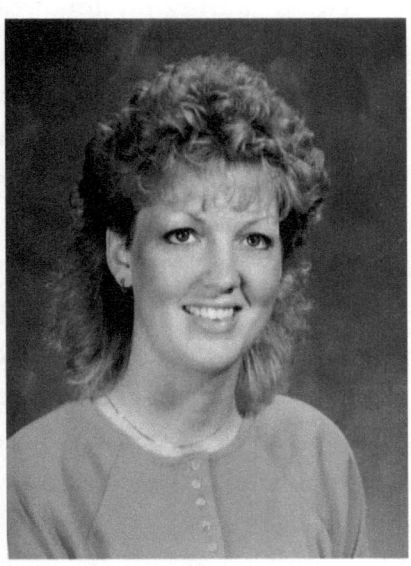

My first school picture as a teacher - Garton Elementary, 1987

I student-taught in third and fifth grades, and that was where I felt most comfortable. I also told the personnel director for the school district my preferences, so my expertise at those levels shouldn't have been a surprise to anyone. I had no experience teaching students younger than third grade. And first grade was a huge year as that is when most children learn to read.

"You're here because of me. I picked you," was my new boss's response when I asked him why I was chosen to be a first-grade teacher, given my experience at higher grades.

That was it. He offered no further explanation, which left me wondering why he didn't provide any specific justification. The reason for my selection became clearer when I met the other new teacher he had hired for Garton Elementary. She was young and attractive, too. While hiring two young women doesn't necessarily mean anything, it soon became apparent it was more than our teaching credentials that caught his eye.

His pattern of inappropriate comments and need to exert his authority over us played out during my four years there. He said and did things that would be considered sexual harassment today. Additionally, he had no skills as an instructional leader – and that is one of the main roles of an elementary school principal. I came to find out he had never taught elementary school. Instead, his teaching experience was solely as a social studies teacher at the secondary level.

Eventually, a group of female teachers and staff at the school got together and realized that several of us were having the same unpleasant experiences. Although everyone agreed, however, that no one was willing to take any action except to complain about it amongst ourselves. This was when I had my meeting with the district's Assistant Superintendent. As I described earlier, our meeting was extremely disappointing.

I could tell nothing useful was going to come out of our meeting, and I wanted to leave his office as soon as possible. Having done what I could, I also realized I had to either put up with the ongoing disrespect my principal subjected me to every day, or I could choose to request a transfer to another school within the district. I chose to request a transfer. Ultimately 14 staff members left the year I did and 11 more left the following year. It seemed obvious to me – and should have been obvious to district leadership – that there was some kind of problem with that high amount of turnover in a two-year period. Yet, the white male principal remained in his leadership role.

I was disappointed that a person who was incompetent at his job and demeaned those he supervised was allowed to stay despite his behavior. Worse, there was no indication anything would change. I had the naive expectation that once I graduated from college, the adult world would be a place where people were mature and worked openly to solve problems. As a 25-year-old, this was the first time in my life where I felt I was subjected to an injustice and needed to speak out. It would not be the last.

The school I transferred to was Findley Elementary in north Des Moines. Transfer requests were granted based strictly on seniority within the district. Needless to say, I didn't get my top request. Findley was considered an even more challenging environment to teach in than where I was previously, but not because of the atmosphere. It was because of the difficult Des Moines neighborhood where it was located.

It was a Godsend when my new boss, Bonnie Graeber, met me with open arms. Literally, she hugged me when we first met. She knew the school I was transferring from and the reputation of the principal there. She served as a mentor to me, and I learned a great deal in that year working for her. In addition to gaining new skills for teaching, I grew in my interactions with parents – especially with those of different cultural backgrounds than I had. I also observed examples of Bonnie's positive leadership.

Once as we were getting ready for end of day dismissal, a group of older boys came into the building — this was long before school buildings were routinely locked — and entered the area where the kids were getting things from their lockers. Several of us teachers saw this and were looking at each other with concerned glances.

So, what is this about? Which one of us should say something?

And before we knew it, Bonnie was on the scene. She stuck her hand out for a handshake introduction.

"I'm Bonnie Graeber, the principal here. How can I help you?"

The previously intimidating group of boys turned around and were walked back outside by our leader. This scene popped into my head more than once when I noticed people who were not supposed to be on our playground at Faith Academy. I walked up to them confidently, introduced myself and started up a conversation with them.

Whether it was intoxicated men from the homeless shelter down the street or older neighborhood kids there at the wrong time, I was always able to talk to them in a way that convinced them to leave the premises without a negative outcome. I also had the steady ability to de-escalate potentially volatile situations caused by upset parents who arrived unexpectedly in the office. I calmly listened to their concerns, as I validated their feelings, and we talked through possible solutions.

Thank you for being a strong female role model, Bonnie.

Looking back, in addition to having to work in a toxic environment in my job at Garton Elementary, I faced some real challenges in the classroom, too. As the children were arriving on my very first day as a teacher, a mother took me aside and let me know her child, Joshua, didn't belong in this class. He had been in Alternative Kindergarten at another school in the district and she failed to convince the administration that he should not advance to first grade.

She felt he should have been held back instead. It later became apparent that his teacher or principal should have recognized the extra year of kindergarten hadn't helped him progress. As a result, Joshua needed to be evaluated for special education assistance. We started that assessment process, and he eventually got the extra support he needed later that year. Thankfully, the outstanding special education teacher at Garton, Barb Spong, was passionate about getting students the help they needed. We administered assessments, put interventions into practice, and documented it all, with each of these steps taking a significant amount of effort and time.

Prior to all of that happening, I just did my best and started fresh each day. Everywhere we walked in the building I held Joshua's hand so he would make it from point A to point B without staying behind in the room or running off when we were in the hallway. He was a year older than most of his new classmates, yet he was smaller than they were. One day, as I was waiting for the rest of our class to line up, he jogged in place beside me, holding my hand while saying, "Gotta keep going, gotta keep going!" He seemed to have an interior motor that was always running. I didn't know it at the time, but behavior like this is one indication of attention deficit hyperactivity disorder (ADHD).

Joshua was not the only student who needed extra attention. There were at least four others I could have had directly by my side as well. I even had to walk backward as I led my class of 26 students in a line from one place to another so I could keep an eye on all of them. I needed to ensure we all made it safely from point to point, without losing anyone along the way. I was able to eventually get help from the district Behavior Consultant who placed three of my students on individual behavior plans. He offered numerous suggestions on how to help them, and I just kept saying yes to everything he presented because I wanted to help these children succeed. The idea of saying, "This is too much, I can't maintain this many individual plans...." never entered my mind.

It was exhausting. At the time, neither my college teacher-prep program nor student-teaching experience prepared me for how to handle this part of the job.

The time demands of special-needs students were apparent to me from the beginning of my career as a teacher. Following noon recess that very first day, as I was settling all my students down in front of me on the rug to read a story, I did a quick head count silently. *23, 24, 25 ... only 25? ... but I have 26 ...* I started to panic but had to keep calm in front of the class. About that time our secretary's voice came over the intercom in my room.

"Mrs. Hochstetler? We have Shumaine down here in the office."

I breathed a huge sigh of relief.

Thank goodness — I can't lose a kid on my first day!

A staff member on recess duty had taken him directly to the principal because he had gotten into trouble at recess — pretty big trouble. Even though no one in Shumaine's family had walked him into school that morning to tell me that he didn't belong, like Joshua's mom had, I easily recognized that he was another "big hitter." Big hitter was an unofficial term used to refer to students who are going to require a lot of time and attention from the teacher. I don't recall ever meeting Shumaine's mom. She never came to school or even to Parent-Teacher Conferences. As a result, the strategies we used to help him had to be carried out without support from home.

An incident from later in the year confirmed that Shumaine was on his own a lot. One day, he showed up at school wearing hot pink, fuzzy slippers made for an adult. When asked about it he simply stated that he noticed that it was such a nice morning outside he stepped into the slippers by the door and took his bike out for a ride. When he got home his mom had left and the door was locked, so there he was, stuck with those crazy-looking slippers. We were just glad he came to school. As it was, none of the kids gave him a hard time about wearing slippers all day. He was tall and tough for his age and the other kids were afraid of him. He was just one of the many challenges I faced as a brand-new teacher.

There was a big learning curve for me during my first years of teaching. Since I felt inadequately prepared to deal with many of the problems I faced, I relied on the mentoring I received from the experienced teachers in my building. My arrogant yet incompetent principal wasn't much help with academics or behavior. As an example of just how clueless my principal was, the only advice he had for me after my first evaluation was to post "North, East, South, and West" on the respective walls inside my classroom. I was dumbfounded. There were far more important issues I needed to receive guidance on as a novice educator.

As a first-year teacher it was protocol for my principal to observe me three times during the school year and provide helpful feedback. At our first post-observation conference, my principal opened his calendar and selected two random dates to falsely document he had been in my classroom for the other two observations he was required to perform. This completed his duties for the central office as far as he was concerned, and he sent the paperwork in.

Is this really happening right in front of me? Man, this guy is nervy – not to mention unethical!

This was my first full-time job after graduating college at the age of 22. When I compared notes with my friend, who had been hired at the same time as I, it was the same story. He made up her two other observations and even gave her the same advice on her written form – to hang signs to label North, East, South and West. At that point we didn't know what else to do but to accept the evaluations he had given us. We were both rated as above average in all categories. We put the labels up on our walls and moved on. At the same time, we both lost whatever respect we may have had left for our boss because of his dishonest behavior.

As difficult as it was, though, I am grateful I was placed in a challenging school with a diverse, urban population to start my career. Even though it was taxing, I had so many stories to tell my new husband every evening. Dave would push his plate back toward the middle of the table after he was done eating dinner and just listen to me as I excitedly – and exhaustively – told him about my day. He was such a trooper.

I taught first grade for two years at Garton and then requested to move to fourth grade when there was a vacancy, so I had only had a brief stint in the primary grades. As it turned out, my year of teaching in second grade at Faith Academy gave me a third year of experience teaching in the primary grades. That experience reminded me how the needs of the younger students varied greatly from those of the older students I had grown accustomed to working with.

I realized how valuable that year of teaching second grade was in helping me prepare for what was in store for me as the leader of all grades from kindergarten through sixth grade at Faith Academy! It confirmed my view that there should be a requirement for every school administrator to work as a teacher first — at the grade levels they are going to supervise — prior to taking charge of a school. It also helped that I experienced first-hand the benefits that came with the extra duties that were part of the school culture we created at Faith Academy. One of those requirements was Home Visits.

Working as partners with the parents was a key component of our outreach program at Faith Academy. One extra step we took was to build relationships with families by visiting each home in the fall. There were a great many challenges involved in performing this highly personal task. I needed to schedule times with families outside of school hours and find my way around various parts of Iowa City, Coralville, and North Liberty.

This was more challenging in the pre-Google Maps Era because I had to print out directions from MapQuest and hope they were accurate. As a result, it wasn't great when my carefully constructed schedule based on availability and location of the families had to be redone because something came up with the parents. It also wasn't great when I was drained after working a twelve-hour day and then had to be at school at 7:30 the next morning. What was great, though, was the connection I was able to make with the scholars and their families. My second graders couldn't have been more excited about the visits. It was so worth it.

"You're coming to my house tonight!"

"I'm going to show you my pet turtle!"

Being on their turf and getting to see where they lived and who they lived with was invaluable for better understanding our scholars. We were also diligent about not allowing our visit to turn into a Parent-Teacher conference. Our objective was to take an interest in their lives and show that Faith Academy and the parents were a team. Visiting the homes early in the year also enabled us to establish a united front in support of the child. We wanted the parents and the teacher to work in tandem, and to reinforce that all of us genuinely wanted what is best for the scholar. Issues are likely to crop up during the year and having a rapport with the parents helps the teacher to be able to make a call that might otherwise have potentially put parents on the defensive.

Along with that, it had always been part of my routine to make a positive phone call to each student's parents within the first week of school for that very reason. I never wanted my first phone call home to be a negative one. As a principal I required this of our teachers, as well. Best-selling author Stephen Covey refers to this as making a deposit in the person's emotional bank account – in this case it was the parents. If I needed to make a withdrawal, which would happen if I called home with a behavior incident to report, there would already be a positive balance. The hope is to not go "in the hole" by calling them only when there was a problem.

These visits made a big impact on me, too. Even to this day, I can still visualize every home I visited. There was one time where a student wanted to show me their bedroom. I glanced at the parent first to see if they were okay with that, and when they were, the child took me by the hand and proudly led me to their room. Their clothes and toys were neatly organized in Rubbermaid tubs. Wow – impressive. At another home, there was a mom who set up chairs right inside the front door when I came to visit. Message received – no need to go any further. We had a pleasant visit and I kept it brief.

A common theme I had noticed was TVs being on in every home, and not many books around. I get it – kids stay more engaged with a screen. It was something I had struggled with as a parent to my own kids. I don't know how many times I attempted to implement a "No TV during the week" policy at our house and the kids had a way of wearing us down. It was a topic we covered during subsequent Parent Connection Days.

Parent Connection Day was another activity that set us apart from other schools. It was initially called "Saturday School." Two times a year, on a Saturday morning, the parents would come to school along with their scholars. Families would all enjoy breakfast and lunch together and childcare was provided for preschoolers. We thought ahead to help identify potential roadblocks, like needing childcare and perhaps facing a lack of transportation to Faith Academy, and we did our best to eliminate them to increase the likelihood of success. Prior to registering for school months earlier, the parent(s) signed a covenant agreeing to participate in these specific extra events. The schedule for Saturday morning consisted of time in the classroom to hear from their scholar's teacher, a session in a large group with a guest speaker, a staff member or panel on a topic that pertained to parenting, and then a presentation from the scholars. The scholar presentation would always include some singing and a skit or scripture memorization performed by various classes.

During the parent presentation, the scholars got to do something fun with the teachers in their classrooms, which benefited those relationships. The parent presentation was also an opportunity for parents to get to know other parents from their scholar's class. I saw a noticeable difference in the response I got from my classroom parents from the first Saturday School in December to the second one held in April. Their initial sense of skepticism had changed to a forward-leaning excitement. I saw it in the parents' body language. Again, the extra effort that went into giving up a Saturday was worth it to be part of intentionally creating a meaningful, connected community working toward the same goals. It was especially important to create an environment where our scholars were excited to share their school with their families. Everyone also looked forward to what became a traditional box lunch from Chick-fil-A.

As staff, we also wanted to walk alongside parents and guardians and give them support, information, and encouragement to do the best job they can. An add-on in later years was door prizes. It was fun to pick out family games and sports equipment to give away. For example, when our theme for the day was "parenting in the age of social media," one winner went home with the Circle Home Plus, a Wi-Fi control device.

As a second-grade teacher during my first year at Faith Academy, I learned a great deal, including how much I missed several things that I took for granted at a public school. One thing I didn't realize was that I was going to teach at Faith Academy without the resources I had become accustomed to at a public school from our Area Educational Agency (AEA). This included things such as books, DVDs, streaming services, supplemental materials, and other resources we were able to borrow that were delivered free to school. I was also used to having access to the consultants and professional-development opportunities available through our AEA. Without an AEA, I remember thinking, *It's like teaching with one hand tied behind my back.*

While the lack of available resources was a challenge, the informal setting was refreshing and the revelations of working with families, students, and staff of color was expanding my mind. That was something I needed and wanted. Being able to talk about Jesus and the peace that He brings me, and being able to lean on His teachings to help in interactions with the scholars were new tools I hadn't been able to use in public-school teaching, and I was grateful for this new position I was in.

As much as I enjoyed being part of the Faith Academy staff, I was still exhausted by my duties as a front-line classroom teacher. Combined with the exhaustion I felt from my previous years of being an elementary teacher, I doubted whether I could do this yet again. Fortunately, God had other plans for me.

CHAPTER 10

"MOVIN' ON UP"

*T*his is emotionally exhausting. I have to be on high alert at every moment to prevent blow-ups from happening between these kids in my class.

What was I thinking when I agreed to teach second grade? I'm going to need to learn more strategies for teaching reading at this grade level. I liked it so much better teaching fifth grade where the students are able to work independently for longer periods.

I am not calm enough when things get crazy in class. I simply do not have the patience that I once did with kids. These 11 are a handful.

Still, the way we are connecting with these kids and their families at Faith Academy is what needs to happen for these children to make progress in their lives. It is what needs to happen in schools everywhere! They have opened up to me and I know their stories and individual needs. Having only 11 in my class is so refreshing and I care deeply about each one of them.

Doug's sense of humor has me laughing every day he's here. He keeps things light, yet is a great spiritual leader. I so appreciate working in the wonderful environment he created here at Faith Academy.

Singing with them every morning at Chapel is also my favorite part of the day. It's giving me the "music fix" I love. There are so many things about this place that I feel connected with.

This was the dialogue playing back and forth in my head for a couple of months during the middle of my first year at Faith Academy. I was conflicted on how to move forward. In February of 2015. I let Pastor Doug know I wasn't going to be returning as the second-grade teacher. Despite my best intentions, I needed to admit I dreaded signing up for another year as a classroom teacher. By telling Doug well before the end of the school year, I was able to give him ample time to look for a new teacher. At the time I made this difficult decision, I didn't know what I was going to do for a job. I just knew that it wasn't going to be teaching second grade. *Ugh – entering another phase of the unknown.*

I was disappointed to find myself in the same situation I was in just a year ago. The last thing I wanted to do was to let Doug down, and I felt I was doing that. It took a couple of weeks after I gave Doug the news for me to come up with the idea of staying at Faith Academy in a different role.

Because our low-tech network at that point was similar to that of a private home rather than a school, I inadvertently received an actual text message on my desktop computer at school that wasn't meant for me. Doug indicated he was considering asking a retired educator in our church if he might be interested in coming on board to help with administration at Faith Academy.

This got my wheels turning. Prior to seeing that text, I had no idea that staying at Faith Academy in a non-teaching position could be a consideration. I was inspired by the possibilities I imagined. I soon approached Doug with an open-ended proposal.

"You've got the Christian piece under control. I have quite a bit of experience in the educational world. How about I stick around to help out with the academics?"

"Sold!" was Doug's quick, emphatic response.

I was excited at the prospect of continuing on at Faith Academy. Because Doug so eagerly wanted me to stay, I felt respected, needed, and appreciated. I was excited by the prospect of being a key member of the school without having to be in charge of a classroom. It was ideal.

Doug was gifted in creating a vision and bringing people together for a common mission. Without his relationships with families in the neighborhood, built by years of commitment to the youth in the area, Faith Academy would have never gotten off the ground. He was smart and well-read. What he lacked was experience and training as a professional educator. While I was surprised he answered me on the spot, I wasn't shocked he was happy to investigate this possibility.

Soon, we came up with a plan for me to be the school's Director of Curriculum and Instruction. In this position, I would coach and evaluate teachers, coordinate student assessment, be in charge of developing the curriculum we used for all academic areas, and stay abreast of all student academic, social, and emotional needs. While we expected the scope of this new position would be wide-ranging, it soon became obvious there was much more to this role than we knew at that time.

One big hurdle to making this a reality, though, was money. Faith Academy wasn't able to pay for this new position in addition to adding the third-grade teacher for that next year as the school expanded. I was excited to use my expertise to stay engaged with Faith Academy in this new role, and I agreed to work on a part-time basis. As I suspected, the job turned out to be much more than part-time. On days I wasn't working at school, I was often on my laptop at home taking care of necessary paperwork or program planning.

Additionally, I was an avid reader, and this new position gave me the spark to explore recent research on teaching reading. To cover another area of concern, Doug had discovered Ross Greene's innovative *Lost at School* book about dealing with behavioral challenges at a school. I researched this approach in depth. Greene's program, known as Collaborative and Proactive Solutions, became the core approach we embodied at Faith Academy based on the premise that "all kids do well if they can." This approach centers around helping children learn how to behave appropriately so they are able to focus on learning. If they aren't doing well, it is because they are delayed in the development of crucial cognitive skills. I found the inspiring concept very thought-provoking.

I was rediscovering the joy of being an educator!

At the same time, I was moving into my new position at Faith Academy, my relationship with my daughter, Jenna, was going through some changes. This shift added some additional stress in my life. She had started her freshman year in college at Southeastern University in Lakeland, Florida in the fall of 2015. Being a part-time professional at Faith Academy worked out perfectly in being able to adjust to this major change while supporting Jenna's move away from home.

Doug was okay with me saving up a few of my days off and using them for our trips to Florida. I was excited for Jenna's new adventure and was actually the one who encouraged her to look at colleges in Florida. I was familiar with Florida and had some very pleasant memories from my time there. For 20 years, my parents had spent winters in Sarasota, Florida. Since I was their youngest and last to leave home, they started going south to get a break from the cold Iowa winters when I went away to college. The amount of time they spent in Sarasota got longer each year, until they were there for around five months a year.

My husband Dave and I took full advantage of having a place to stay with my parents for Spring Break trips when I was teaching, and we visited Sarasota frequently. Our family fell in love with the beach, and we inherited Mom's desire to catch the sunset over the water every chance she could.

While both my parents had passed away by the time Jenna decided to go to college in Florida, my family's fond recollections of our time there remained. Jenna was inspired by the Christian atmosphere and beauty of the Southeastern University campus in Lakeland, and she was brave enough to go there without knowing a soul. We had good family friends who lived just an hour and a half away, so that gave us both a little reassurance.

Nowadays, Jenna and I get along fabulously and talk every day. Back when she started college, moving-in day was extremely stressful, as four girls who didn't know each other attempted to make a three-person room accommodate all four of them as their new home. Dave and I observed Jenna always being the one to take the high road – "Oh, I don't mind sleeping on the top bunk" – which was admirable, but it was soon easy to see how this was all going to go. It was clear one of the girls was going to take the role of "mean queen bee" in the room and it certainly wasn't Jenna. We were concerned Jenna was going to be taken advantage of.

Jenna on move-in day her freshman year of college
with Dave in the background.

By the time we finished moving her in and having her push us away with her cranky attitude, Dave and I felt it was a good time to depart. Jenna was definitely feeling the stress of facing all the unknowns surrounding her new life at college in an unfamiliar place. As a result, we left campus earlier than we planned that Sunday to drive back home.

It was clear Jenna was ready to take on this new life on her own. We took a detour to spend some time on the beach about 90 minutes from Lakeland. A large pina colada at Frenchy's Rockaway Grill on the beach in Clearwater was exactly what I needed to toast with Dave to our new stage of life. Nonetheless, I did cry some on the drive home. I was both excited and scared for Jenna – and excited and sad for us.

Having experienced sending two kids to college by that point, I realized God has a way of preparing us for this detachment. The child who's leaving home becomes more difficult as the time to depart draws closer. While it hurt, we both knew it was all part of growing-up and tried not to take things personally. We knew it was time for them to become more independent and we were actually ready for them to move on due to the tension around the house. The beginning of this new chapter in my life added to the turmoil of starting in my expanded role at work, even as exciting as it was. In a way, this new position at Faith Academy was a real blessing, since it helped to have something to pour myself into. In that way, I wouldn't focus on our empty nest and lack of high-school activities on the calendar to attend.

Having each Wednesday off during the week at Faith Academy was also a blessing. It helped me to not get overwhelmed with the intensity of working with high-energy, five- to nine-year-old children, as I worked to create the best atmosphere possible for them. Despite appreciating the mid-week breather, I soon realized I didn't like missing out on the happenings on the days when I wasn't there, so I found myself sometimes going in to work anyway. I wanted to be involved with everything going on at Faith Academy. It was so energizing to be part of creating a new school as it grew, and I cared so deeply about doing everything I could to make it successful. As could have been predicted, the school board got much more from me than from an employee who only worked 32 hours a week.

Along with a challenging new job that far better suited my desires, I was excited to find out I actually got my own office when I became the Curriculum Director – not bad! There was an office space at the front of the building that Doug told me would be mine. Actually, DeDe first told me I needed to have my own office, and then Doug was brought up to speed. My new office had been used when the previous occupant leased the space but it hadn't been touched during the expansion.

At that time, we had six weeks of summer school for all scholars, and I was still the second-grade teacher through July, so I had limited time to get my new office painted and ready before the new school year rolled around. Dave helped install new shades and went to Mt Pleasant with me – an hour away – to pick up my free, used, desk from a Christian school which had recently been made aware of Faith Academy and our need for supplies of all kinds.

I would have liked to move the desk I brought with me to school last year from the bank, but I wanted the new teacher to have it. It was too big for my small office anyway. When our spunky bus driver and local church leader Elder Bernie saw my office for the first time before the beginning of the new school year, she started singing the theme song from the '70s TV show *The Jeffersons:*

"Well we're movin' on up ...

"To the east side ...

"To a deluxe apartment in the sky ..."

Elder Bernie would later become one of my best friends at Faith Academy. She joined the school when she saw Doug and Brandon

Parker – two of the driving forces behind establishing Faith Academy – walking around the neighborhood trying to find kids to come to a school that didn't yet exist. She figured if they did *that* in the hot summer months, then she wanted to see how she could help out at this new school. So, she became the "bus driver." To start with, she drove the old clunky white van that Parkview Church used for The Spot, the after-school program Faith Academy grew out of. God had more in mind for her as well. She later earned her degree in social work and became our Family Liaison.

Elder Bernie and I outside my office – I had complimented her on a new dress and the next day I found a gift bag on my desk with a new one for me! When I tried to pay her for it, she said, "You are not taking away my blessing!" What a generous friend.

Her full name is Bernadine Franks, and she goes by Elder Bernie due to her position as an elder in her church. Her sister was the pastor at their church and Elder Bernie referred to her as Pastor Boyer rather than Sylvia. I learned that most Black churches used these terms for people out of respect, both in and out of church. Elder Bernie didn't attend Parkview Church where my husband and I worshiped. It wasn't likely she would have attended a church that didn't allow women to be elders, let alone pastors.

If I had realized the stance on women in leadership at Parkview Church, we wouldn't have started going there, either. As it was, I sat through more than one Mother's Day sermon by the longtime lead pastor that left me infuriated. One sermon in particular made me so mad I was at the point of crying in a bathroom stall afterwards. At the end of another one, I noticed a mother I knew – who was a doctor – sitting near us. I asked her incredulously, "Does this type of sermon not bother you?"

"Oh, I've just gotten used to it," she said almost as if in passing. The gist of the pastor's messages was how important it was to be a stay-at-home mom instead of a working mother, and I resented the implications of what he was saying. I had always worked as a teacher when my kids were growing up, except for the five years I worked part time as a student teacher supervisor at the University of Iowa. The wisdom I gained from that supervisory job gave me another skill set that prepared me for eventually assuming the role of principal at Faith Academy.

Dave and I agreed to not attend church on Mother's Day when that particular pastor was preaching. We didn't talk about leaving the church at that time, but we never committed to becoming members. We understood that no church is perfect. Our kids had friends there and were benefitting from the youth programs. The reason we stayed at Parkview came to me later.

God wanted us at that church for our family to be part of that life-changing Belize mission trip, for us to meet Doug, and ultimately for me to become a leader at Faith Academy.

I'm grateful God orchestrated this, as going on that mission trip sent my life on a new trajectory. As a result, I have been blessed with friends and experiences that otherwise wouldn't have been possible.

Once Doug decided to offer me the new position, we immediately recognized two of the most important tasks we had to tackle. We had to find a replacement for me as the second-grade teacher and find a new third-grade teacher. As we were faced with not knowing who would take my role as the second-grade teacher, we weren't sure where to begin to look. As it turned out, the perfect candidate was soon placed in my path. Surprisingly, it was someone I already knew, had worked with, and respected.

CHAPTER 11

LEFT ALONE TO LEAD

From the start, Doug wanted to offer a competitive wage for teachers at Faith Academy. His approach won my respect immediately. As a result of his emphasis, we were able to implement competitive starting salaries, but it was more of a challenge when the teacher came with experience, me included. To find a teacher who was willing to work at a school where they made less than a public-school teacher, even though the job was at least as challenging, was not an easy task. Along with full-time teaching responsibilities, there were additional job-related expectations that Faith Academy required teachers and staff to fulfill. In hindsight, it's clear many of the teachers who came to Faith Academy arrived via paths that could only have been orchestrated by God. The hiring of the woman who replaced me as the second-grade teacher was a prime example.

Joni Beachy had been my student teacher for my fifth-grade class at Kalona Elementary in 2008. The exact year is easy for me to remember as it was the year that Dave's dad died unexpectedly. Don and Marvel, my in-laws, came home to Iowa for a brief visit in February to see a dear friend of theirs who was in serious condition in the hospital. Like my parents, they were snowbirds, but their destination was the Rio Grande Valley in Texas, instead of Sarasota. Typically, Dave's parents stayed there from November through April. During their unexpected visit to Iowa, they were here for less than a week.

Grandpa Don, Dylan, Jenna and Grandma Marvel in front of their place in Pharr, Texas 1999

At that stage of my life, there wasn't much time in the margins for us due to Dave and me working full-time. When combined with the amount of time we spent with our kids supporting their activities, there was little left to spare. I coached Jenna's fifth-grade basketball team and Dave was coaching a 15-and-under Amateur Athletic Union (AAU) basketball team for Dylan that included boys who had been pulled together from a variety of area schools. These guys were serious about developing their basketball skills and it required a lot of time from Dave and Dylan both.

When Don and Marvel made their trip up to Iowa from Texas it happened to be during the week that Joni was doing her "head teaching" in my classroom. This was the week the university designated for the student teacher to take the reins — being completely in charge of the classroom. This meant Joni was responsible for planning and teaching all subjects. She also had to perform all required duties for my fifth-grade class. I was in and out of the classroom to give her space to be in charge, yet I didn't want to abandon her if something should come up.

I used the time to plan for the rest of the year and do research on new ideas to use with my students. It was a treat to not come home exhausted at the end of the day that week. Teachers see this part of the student-teacher experience as the payoff for all the extra work that having a student teacher requires from them the rest of the time. It was then I invited Don and Marvel to our home for a homemade meal. They came over on a school night, and after dinner we enjoyed an evening of playing dominoes with the kids. Dylan especially loved playing games with his grandparents as he has always had a competitive nature. This dinner is something I know I would not have initiated if it hadn't been for Joni's help at school. All of us considered that a special bonus night together, having no idea that within the month Don would pass away unexpectedly from a heart attack on the golf course in Texas.

Joni did very well as my student teacher. She was open to learning from feedback and cared a great deal for the students. I knew she was going to be an outstanding teacher when she got her own classroom. She took a job in the Des Moines Public School District after graduating, the same district where I started my teaching career. I was impressed that she was choosing to broaden her experience base, as DMPSD is the largest district in the state of Iowa. Periodically, I would run into her parents around town, as she was from Kalona where I taught, and they would always update me on her teaching career and her life.

I received a text from her on a Sunday afternoon during the spring of 2015. She was planning on moving from Des Moines back to the Kalona area and wondered if I knew of any teaching jobs. I called her right away. Having recently gotten engaged, it was where she and her fiancé were choosing to live, and he was going to move to the area from Montana. She thought that I was still teaching at Kalona, so was surprised to hear of my change.

I couldn't believe the timing. I was excited she had reached out to me, as I thought she would be perfect for the second-grade teaching role I was about to vacate. I knew she had a strong Christian faith, was a competent teacher, and was very flexible. When describing Faith Academy to her, the best analogy I could think of was that we were building the airplane as it flies. I told her if she was up for that, we would be thrilled to interview her. This conversation took place when I was hanging out in the car while Dave was looking around at Men's Wearhouse in Coralville after church. Since church was 30 minutes from home, we would usually eat lunch and run errands while in town. When Dave got back to the car, I couldn't wait to fill him in.

"You're never going to believe this!" I blurted out.

I was ecstatic to tell him all about my conversation with Joni. After a formal interview, Joni was hired and started in the fall. She was thrilled that we were willing to work with her to give her time off at the beginning of the school year for her wedding and honeymoon, since the date had already been set. This type of schedule flexibility is typically not allowed in a public school. We were fortunate in that we had an experienced sub who was willing to start the year for her, which made it less stressful for Joni. Joni is one of the examples of how God arranges things to work out perfectly for everyone when it is part of His plan. It was also another sign showing how God was blessing Faith Academy.

Making my transition from teacher to a leadership position was tricky at times. I had the experience to know what needed to happen at an elementary school, but I hadn't considered things from every angle. Doug had also just hired Doreen, an experienced school secretary, to run the office. He knew Doreen from church, and I had worked with her at Kalona Elementary. She was willing and excited to make the change to Faith Academy after 18 years in her previous job. She was able to turn our humble office – an office that started with only a few hanging files that Brandon had created and the church's copy machine -- into a real school office. Her background was invaluable, and she was all-in when it came to our mission. Like me, she was a recent empty nester, so was willing to give it the extra time it took.

I also had to deal with many of my own preconceived notions. For example, overly confident people irritate me so much that I find myself reluctant to be a "take charge" type of person. I discovered my new position was a balancing act, as Doug and I needed to perform like a team. In some situations, he had the final say, but there were times when I was the go-to person.

One of my most profound and unanticipated "go-to" moments happened in the fall of 2015. Doug and his wife Natalie were expecting a baby in October that year. At the time, they had four children, ranging from kindergarten through high school. Their family was so excited about this new baby. The day when Doug left school to rush to the hospital to be with his wife during delivery is etched in my mind forever.

Within an hour or two, I got a text from Doug, simply stating, "We lost the baby." My heart dropped and I was overcome with sadness for Doug and Natalie. I knew the excitement and joy that Doug was feeling just hours before. As crushed as I was, I needed to somehow kick into leader mode and tell the necessary people and make sure that Doug's own children, who were in kindergarten and second grade, didn't find out about the loss while at school. They knew their mom had gone to the hospital to have their baby sister and were anxiously waiting to hear about her arrival. When I told the few adults that needed to know, I made sure that I didn't do this when there were scholars present. There is no script for a tragedy such as this, and we all did the best we could with what we knew at the time.

This is Doug's story to tell, so I will not go into more detail. He appropriately took two weeks off to be at home with Natalie, where they could grieve after the funeral of little Lila Marie. Our Faith Academy family stepped up and surrounded their family with love and support. Parents of the scholars sent flowers and came to the funeral. Our small group that had been formed after our Belize mission trip had a tree planted at the Ferns' home in baby Lila's memory with a personalized memorial stone placed beneath it. We, their school and church family, delivered meals to their family for weeks. It was an unusual position for Doug and Natalie to be in, as they were always the ones who were serving and caring for others.

Life had to go on at school. I led the "circle up" times every morning with staff. Wanting to respect Doug's time with his family, I made any decisions that needed to be made without bothering him. One event loomed particularly large on the calendar. In September we had agreed to take our scholars to be part of the American College Testing (ACT) annual meeting as part of their presentation to kick off the gathering. Iowa City-based ACT, Inc is widely known for creating and managing college entrance exams.

Finalizing our school's participation in this meeting would happen while Doug was on leave. It was my responsibility to coordinate and execute the details of that morning. It wouldn't have happened without our small team of teachers and staff working together. I was heartbroken for the Ferns and there was a sadness that blanketed our school for a time. In addition to him being the Head of School, his own children's classmates were grieving for their loss.

The idea for our scholars to be part of the ACT annual meeting was sparked at an open house held at Faith Academy. Our scholars were always charming when guests came to our open houses or visited for short periods of time. During the early years we had open houses each month or upon request. This was a time when guests came in for a tour, a presentation by the scholars, and then a question-and-answer time with Doug and me. These open houses were very important since we needed to raise awareness of our existence. We had no signage outside and were located in a nondescript building on the backside of a strip mall.

We flew below the radar getting started, but we needed donors as well as students. We knew we had started a meaningful mission and wanted to make people aware of our school and the special opportunity we offered. Our goal was to offer a high-quality education at an affordable price to families in the part of town that is often neglected. That relatively small contribution from scholars' families was necessary to make them feel committed to their children's education and the success of the school. The rest of the cost needed to be picked up by donors.

Word of mouth and advertising on the big screen and bulletin at Parkview Church were how people were finding out about Faith Academy to that point. Often people who already knew about us would extend an invitation to a friend or colleague to come check us out. A couple of people from ACT came to an open house after receiving a personal invitation from a co-worker who had been on the initial committee at church to get the school started. They were impressed with what they learned about our school.

One of the aspects of the school they liked the most was our Declaration that described our values and goals. Our scholars memorized and repeated it every morning during Chapel. The ACT visitors were inspired when they heard our scholars recite the Declaration:

We go to Faith Academy, a Kingdom School. We exalt the name of Jesus. We recognize his presence here. We believe in God the Father, God the Son, and God the Holy Spirit. We believe the Bible to be God's holy word, to be complete truth, a guide for our feet.

I am created in the image of God, and He loves me beyond my imagination. God calls me to love and serve the Lord Jesus Christ— to listen and obey. To listen and obey the first time, not the second time, not the third time, but the first time.

To use words with kindness; to respect God's creation and all authority; to not seek harm against another; to love and encourage others; and to serve my community.

For I can do all things through Christ who gives me strength. I can be a teacher, a lawyer, a parent, a missionary, a doctor, a musician, a coach, a business owner, a computer programmer, or a poet.

We will display a crown of beauty instead of ashes; the oil of gladness instead of mourning; a garment of praise instead of despair. We will be called oaks of righteousness, a planting for the Lord for the display of his splendor.

Jim Hussey, an executive at ACT, was one of the people who attended that open house. I knew him as a parent of a former fifth-grade student, and also as the president of our Mid-Prairie School Board. He contacted me shortly after having been there and asked if we would consider bringing our scholars to their ACT Annual Meeting. He thought having their group of approximately 800 employees from across the U.S. meet our scholars would be an extraordinary opportunity for both Faith Academy and ACT. They would hear our scholars recite our five-verse declaration and it would blow them away as a powerful kick-off to their all-day meeting.

The gathering would also serve as an introduction of their organization's new CEO from the Netherlands. It was to be held in October at the Marriott in nearby Coralville. ACT would provide transportation by sending a chartered bus to pick us all up at school. The scholars felt like royalty that day! It was a 20-minute trip across town to a new hotel and convention center. We needed to have our declaration polished and be ready to recite from memory. In addition, they wanted us to stay around so they could bring us back out at the end of the morning session. They could then ask the scholars a few questions and present us with a donation to support our educational endeavors.

My biggest fear was keeping the kids under control in a new and stimulating environment for that lengthy period. With this in mind, I was relieved to see a note that a certain behaviorally challenged student, Keshwan, had a dental appointment and was going to be gone that morning. His behavior was so unpredictable that I was already planning to have one staff member assigned to keep him safe, and in the right place, for the morning. Finding out Keshwan wasn't going to be able to attend was good news to me.

Whew – one less thing to worry about.

When his mom arrived to pick him up for his appointment, the secretary mentioned that she was sad he was going to have to miss the outing. My heart dropped.

Shhhhh, no! I remember thinking.

I almost said it out loud. After Keshwan's mom heard that he would miss the event, she willingly let him reschedule his appointment to go along on our trip.

Are you kidding me?!

I didn't want to have anything go wrong on this very important day that could have far-reaching effects for the future of our school. The last thing any of us needed was Keshwan misbehaving in front of all those influential people.

It was a bit of a concession when his mom said she would go along with us. I knew she would genuinely help keep him in line. This is in contrast with what I have experienced from a few parents during my career. Sometimes, their presence actually made things worse. At least I didn't have to come up with the one-on-one staff member at the last minute, as everyone had their specific roles determined for the morning.

The joke was on me. Here I was trying to hold this kid out and it became evident that God wanted him to be part of the morning. While the ACT staff was holding the bulk of their meeting, our group had an activity planned in another area of the convention center. It would be far enough away for noise to not be a factor.

The scholars were asked to draw a detailed picture of themselves and write what they were going to be when they grew up. We had sketched up a template for them to write and color upon. It was designed to look like an employee ID worn on a lanyard. I walked around and glanced at the scholars' drawings as they were working. Teachers and staff were on high alert and did a great job keeping the peace among the scholars.

Teachers Joni Stoltzfus, front, and Tracy Reichter, back, work with scholars behind the scenes at the ACT Annual Meeting

The agenda was packed. There were so many scheduling and logistic considerations to keep track of that morning, including snacks, drinks, and a restroom break. I felt it was most important to make sure our scholars' behavior did not escalate in a negative manner. We had 45 scholars at that point and rarely a day went by that we didn't have a conflict arise, whether that was between scholars or even a scholar-teacher situation. Often these situations needed extra support from another adult in addition to the classroom teacher. Faith Academy was not a typical private school.

When we walked back into the ballroom and on stage, I spoke briefly with the emcee to indicate which of the scholars he should call on to ask what they hoped to be when they grew up. The presentation began. Each time the microphone was placed in front of a scholar, I tensed up. I didn't know for sure what they were going to say. This was a big stage, literally and figuratively, where Faith Academy was being introduced to 800 people who had the potential to make an important, perhaps far-reaching judgment. They would bring their thoughts and opinions back into the community with them. The scholars gave typical answers, such as wanting to become a teacher and animal doctor and when they were asked follow-up questions, the scholars answered appropriately. Every time the emcee went back to the scholars there was one hand that eagerly waved above the others wanting to be selected, and that was Keshwan.

No way. Don't pick him. Too much of a wild card.

Annnnnnd ... the emcee picked him.

"What would you like to be when you grow up, young man?"

"I want to be a missionary so I can tell people about God," Keshwan confidently stated.

And the camera zoomed in on his employee badge he had drawn. There it was, shown over the large screen to all the conference members. Keshwan beamed with pride, as did his mom who was sitting in the front row with the teachers.

A collective, "Ahhhhhhh" was voiced from the audience.

Oh - my - goodness. Lesson learned.

I was humbled. Sometimes we think we've created the best plan for something to be successful, but God has His own course of action to make things play out in the way it should happen. This interaction with Keshwan clearly went according to His plan, not mine.

CHAPTER 12
CELEBRATING FAITH

ow are we supposed to get a decent fourth grade teacher if we can't even advertise until the end of April?? Spring graduates start looking for jobs as soon as January and the good ones get snatched up. I've been trying to communicate this to the board in a way that isn't too assertive, yet one reason I'm on this board is because of my experience hiring, recruiting, and working with new teachers. Are we really not going to continue adding a grade unless we have a substantial fundraising event? And so late in the school year?! I am not in favor of having combination classrooms, containing more than one grade, as had been suggested. Having one teacher serve two grade levels is not the best way to meet the needs of our scholars.

Money was always going to be a concern for Faith Academy, using the business model we chose. I have faith that God will provide, but we can't just sit around waiting for that to happen. There's a parable I often think of when conflicting feelings arise between having faith that God will provide for our school and working hard to get the money to come in:

A storm descends on a small town, and the downpour soon turns into a flood. As the waters rise, the local preacher kneels in prayer on the church porch, surrounded by water. By and by, one of the townsfolk comes up the street in a canoe.

"Better get in, Preacher. The waters are rising fast."

"No," says the preacher. "I have faith in the Lord. He will save me."

Still the waters rise. Now the preacher is up on the balcony, wringing his hands in supplication, when another guy zips up in a motorboat.

"Come on, Preacher. We need to get you out of here. The levee's gonna break any minute."

Once again, the preacher is unmoved. "I shall remain. The Lord will see me through."

After a while the levee breaks, and the flood rushes over the church until only the steeple remains above water. The preacher is up there, clinging to the cross, when a helicopter descends out of the clouds, and a state trooper calls down to him through a megaphone.

"Grab the ladder, Preacher. This is your last chance."

Once again, the preacher insists the Lord will deliver him.

And, predictably, he drowns.

The preacher goes to heaven. After a while he gets an interview with God, and he asks the Almighty, "Lord, I had unwavering faith in you. Why didn't you deliver me from that flood?"

God shakes his head. "What did you want from me? I sent you two boats and a helicopter."

When Faith Academy opened, in addition to large and small contributions from individual donors, we were financed through Parkview Church. Our paychecks were run through the church and the building lease was paid for by the church. We will always be grateful they acknowledged the need for the school and supported it financially for the first several years. Despite the uncertainty we lived with, I chose not to make the nearly constant concern surrounding raising money my all-consuming focus. Even when the idea would flit through my brain, I put my Dale Carnegie skills from "How to Stop Worrying and Start Living" into practice.

What is the worst thing that could happen? *Well, Faith Academy could have to close due to lack of funding.*

Choose to make peace with that. *If we close, I am marketable and will get another job. Plus, it sure seems that God brought me to this mission. He's got me.*

I read the Dale Carnegie book for the first time in 2002. This was about the same time I read *The Purpose Driven Life* by Rick Warren. Both were life-changing for me. It was soon after my mom had passed away from cancer, and I was struggling to come to terms with my kids not getting to have their grandma see them grow up. She was their number one fan, as well as mine. This life-changing loss forced me to mature in a way that I likely would not have otherwise.

Being in a job at Faith Academy with this much uncertainty was something that I wouldn't have been able to do in my 20s or 30s. It required trusting in God on a new level. A situation that seems impossible as measured against human standards is simply an opportunity for God.

As a board, we knew it was necessary to get other streams of income. Since our fees were unusually low, only about ten percent of what was needed to operate was generated from tuition. We knew the school we modeled ourselves after in Minneapolis held a yearly fundraising banquet, so we decided to follow their lead and hold our first banquet in April 2016, which was toward the end of our third year.

Wow. As per usual, we jumped in with both feet and just did what we needed to do to make it happen. What an exhausting undertaking, but what an amazing feeling afterwards when we pulled it off. It took many people volunteering their time and talents to make it happen. The chairperson of our school board at the time, who had been heavily involved with the Catholic school in town, was familiar with private-school fundraising events. When it was all over and the proceeds were counted, he was in awe of what we achieved that evening, despite the fact we hadn't even served booze.

Starting in January of that year, a group of people – mainly from the church – started meeting regularly with Doug and Doreen, our secretary, to plan and support the event. It soon became apparent there were a great many details that needed to be taken care of. Meal planning, creating the desired atmosphere, setting up the church, serving the meals, and a million other things had to be addressed. We had to plan everything happening behind the scenes to have a successful event. Mailings went out to churches and area businesses to promote the banquet. Doug and I worked together to lay out the program for that evening. All Faith Academy staff members were also encouraged to host a table of potential donors at the banquet.

That last part bothered me. I was not a fan of putting pressure on our teachers to ask their people for donations for our school – wasn't working here enough? I know there are missionaries who have to do their own fundraising, but they have time built in for it and they knew that when they signed up. Protecting the teachers and staff from the brutal truth of our financial situation was the way I felt most comfortable operating. Doug didn't discuss the urgent need for school funding with them either, for the most part. I wanted the school staff to be able to focus on taking care of the day-to-day operations with the scholars and creating a positive environment for them, not think about our finances. It was, however, a reality we needed to face.

At every board meeting the topic that occupied the majority of our time was how we were going to bring in money. We firmly believed God had orchestrated the creation of Faith Academy. But as the parable makes clear, we had to take advantage of the opportunities we were presented with and do the work. This meant we needed to use our skills to come up with the financial means to keep our school open. We were operating in the red the first few years and Parkview

Church would cover our school expenses until we could pay them back after we collected donations from our big fundraisers. We were grateful for this flexibility but knew that this was not sustainable. Doug was the one who spent time meeting with people to encourage them to support us, as we didn't have a development director at that point. Board members also graciously helped with that task.

There was an unspoken tension among the school staff, as we always knew our budget was very limited. It takes supplies to run a school. The basics were provided, but every staff member knew in the early stages they would need to come up with any extras on their own. It has always bothered me that teachers anywhere would have to supply items for their own classroom. It shouldn't be that way. Our staff sometimes took this a step further by supplying materials, paint and even tables in their classrooms when they wanted a particular item.

Several times community groups from supporting churches wanted to bless us and asked if there was anything we needed. Sometimes it was a work project and sometimes it was a financial gift. On one occasion, our first-grade teacher requested a set of Rigby Leveled Readers. He had used them with struggling readers in a reading practicum at the university recently. These readers allowed children to practice their newly learned reading skills with real stories. Doing this was crucial to their reading development, and quality readers on that level weren't easy to come by. As an educator, I agreed it was needed. I just didn't know where the thousand dollars to purchase them was going to come from. The timing of the church group's offer was perfect, and they were happy to cover the expense of a specific request. We were thrilled to see so many scholars benefit from them, as they were stored in a common location and shared among the grades.

Another time, our kindergarten teacher wanted a set of blocks for her scholars to build with during free choice time. To get a quality set that could be used for many years wasn't cheap and I didn't want her to have to purchase it herself. I reached out to my newly retired brother-in-law, Steve, who had a whole line of woodworking equipment in his garage. Within a week, he delivered a beautiful set of wooden blocks, complete with non-toxic oil protection. He even built a wooden box with handles to use for storing them. Retired people proved to be a golden asset for Faith Academy!

The idea behind hosting a table at our fundraising event meant getting "butts in chairs." The table host was simply responsible for filling their table with people they knew. Of course, the underlying assumption was that the people we invited were potential donors and might be influential among their friends. It felt a bit awkward at first, as I got friends and family involved in the event, knowing it was ultimately a fundraiser and we were going to be asking for donations at the end of the evening. I had conflicting feelings as I was truly passionate about our mission at Faith Academy, and I wanted my people to be there to learn more about it.

This was a huge event for me, but I found it hard to invite people. This was especially true that first year, not knowing how the evening was going to look. Of course, I sincerely appreciated the willingness of my friends and family members who did attend the banquet. It also became obvious to me which staff members had been blessed with the gift of "sales" and which ones shied away from getting people to attend the banquet with them.

I was relieved when the day finally arrived.

Even though we knew it was going to be a challenge, we held both Parent Connection Day and the banquet on the same Saturday. Since we were going to the expense of paying a speaker to come in, we would use their expertise with both the parents of our scholars in the morning and the potential donors in the evening. Faith Academy is not located in or near Parkview Church. They are in different neighborhoods of Iowa City, 15 minutes apart. While Parkview had a huge building that sat empty all week, as most churches do, no one brought up trying to house the school at Parkview. We decided early on we wanted the school to be in the same neighborhood as the families we were serving.

As a result, teachers needed to transport many items across town in their own cars after the morning was done at the school to set up for the evening banquet. This just added to the chaos of an already hectic day. Still, working with a group of people who enjoyed each other, as our team did, on an endeavor we deeply believed in, was energizing! Several of our spouses showed up to help, too. It was always a family affair when we had a big event.

By the time the fundraiser began, the worship center at the church had been transformed into a grand dining room with over 30 tables set up with elegant centerpieces. The committee had been busy working that morning as we were spending time with our scholars, their parents, and our guest speakers at Faith Academy. To leave the crowded, loud school environment with concrete floors and beige metal folding chairs with dents in many of them, and arrive in this large, carpeted space so tastefully decorated at church was quite a shift. It felt like going from being in the garage to the living room. This was the juxtaposition that existed between our life at Faith Academy and the peaceful environment of the founding church.

Doug used his Spot connections to arrange for our guest speaker, Dana Thomas and his wife Bridget. Doug had met them through Kids Across America, or KAA. KAA was a camp that ministered to urban youth and their youth workers. Doug, DeDe, and others had taken groups of kids to KAA over the years. A group of us went out to dinner with the Thomases on Friday night after Doug picked them up from the airport. My husband and I enjoyed being part of that intimate group hosting the Thomases and getting to know them prior to the big events on Saturday. We also came to find out their son was attending SEU in Florida, the same university as our daughter Jenna.

The morning of our Super Saturday, as we referred to it, Dana and Bridget gave a powerful presentation to the parents on raising children in our world today and the content was spot on. It was thought provoking and was well received by our parents. Being Black and originally from Chicago, they had immediate credibility with our group of parents — especially after Dana started talking about Portillo's, a popular restaurant in Chicago famous for their Italian beef sandwiches!

It was my role at the banquet to give an update on how things were going academically at Faith. Doug had put together statistics for the first couple of years for a pamphlet advertising the school. I then updated it and reported the new information to everyone. Wisdom, Doug's friend who taught P.E. at Faith Academy, welcomed everyone to open the evening. Wisdom has a great sense of humor and was very comfortable with a microphone. It did make us all a bit nervous when he was on stage as we never knew what jokes or funny stories he was going to come up with. Even though everyone was dressed in semi-formal attire, he set the tone for the evening as fun and energetic, yet relaxed.

After dinner, Doug took over to begin the official program of the evening. He talked a bit and then welcomed me up to the stage. His introduction of me was complimentary, talking about the value that I added to the school. Coming from the guy who is more often humorous or sarcastic, I'll take it.

My heart was pounding as I made my way from my seat at our table up to the stage to stand behind a narrow podium to deliver my short speech. Our statistics were impressive: the reading scores were above those of area schools with comparative demographics, we had a high retention rate, and our student to teacher ratio was an impressive 12 to 1 on average.

Even though it was part of my new role to embrace the data, it was more natural for me to focus on nurturing the relationships with the scholars and their families. I was able to sneak in a few stories we heard from the parents such as "I can't believe the way our daughter can pray! She wanted to ask the blessing at our big Thanksgiving meal ... in front of cousins and everything."

Once my portion on stage was finished, I found I could enjoy the rest of the evening without the distraction of nervously awaiting my speech in front of the large audience. Every year, putting on the fundraiser and my participation on stage became easier. In time, I looked forward to the evening, as I interacted with the audience, shared heartwarming stories, and described our academic progress from the past year.

Dana gave the keynote address that evening on the unique opportunity to reach children and families with the academically-driven Christian education Faith Academy was providing. When I listened to Dana, I was amazed at the way he confidently gave a passionate endorsement for the work happening at our new school. When involved in the hustle of day-to-day activities, I seldom took much time to reflect on what a unique mission I had become involved with. This reminder was uplifting, and I was recharged after his message.

But the extra vote of confidence came at the end of the evening. Doreen had gathered a group of people, including my husband Dave, who were responsible for counting the donations. It reminded me of a Jerry Lewis Labor Day Telethon. The suspense built as we milled about visiting with guests while the group hurriedly tabulated the checks and pledges behind closed doors.

It was unbelievable – and thrilling – when the announcement was made prior to everyone heading home for the night. The result of the evening – the first time we attempted such an event – had been to raise $127,000! None of us knew what to expect and we were shocked at the generosity of the people in attendance. It was an uplifting night for everyone involved. It had been exhausting, but after that overwhelming response, and while basking in the energy, support, and love generated by friends and family of Faith Academy, it was a gratifying end to a highly successful evening.

I soon saw that people felt good about supporting us financially. I learned to embrace that we were giving them a chance to be part of this life-changing ministry happening right here in Iowa City. I was humbled to see the gifts that came in. During my time at Faith Academy, we have had private donations of up to $50,000 on more than one occasion. As a board, it was an honor to be trusted to steward very large donations that represented an individual's legacy provided to the school.

Donations were what kept our doors open. I happen to be the one working in the office a time or two when one young man would stop in and write out his monthly check. He was a contractor, and he was so casual about it. He would say things like, "Hey, Man.... the way God has blessed me - this is the least I can do." He was typically dressed in his casual work clothes as he gifted us with his generous donation.

At an open house where we were conducting the initial group tour for people who were the key contributors to our school expansion in 2022, he joined the tour when it was already in progress, as he was running a little bit late. One of the other donors asked him, "Were you on the construction crew that did this?"

"Ah, no – just wanted to see the project." was his humble response. *If you only knew the depths of his generosity.*

Scholars in the early years with small playground set behind them

At one board meeting in particular, I shared, yet again, about the need for there to be more for the scholars to do at recess. The playground equipment had been fine when we had a younger and smaller student body. It had been donated by a local wood structure company and we were thrilled for it at the time, and it had gotten lots of use. But there was now a need for more equipment that was especially suitable for older children. One board member was inspired by my request and acted upon it. She took it upon herself to purchase a Goalsetter basketball hoop and have it professionally installed. It was an in-ground pole, and the height was adjustable, a top-of-the-line piece of equipment. What a gift! The kids loved it. I was thrilled to have another option for recess and our physical education teacher was even more pleased. Kids in the neighborhood came and used it after school hours.

Our Goalsetter adjustable basketball hoop is complete!
The look improved after a local artist was hired by the donor,
Julie Dancer, to paint a mural on the building

Another donor witnessed firsthand the worn-out state of the 15-passenger van that Elder Bernie drove. Bernie used it to pick up our donated sandwiches that served as the main course for lunch for the week, as well as to transport our scholars. Over the summer the donor purchased a Ford Transit van that was only a year or two old! Unbeknownst to the donor, that exact week he purchased the van, Doug was driving a rented van with a group of teens from church, as he took them to a camp out of state.

As he drove the teens around, Doug sent up a prayer. "God, it would be amazing if Faith Academy could have a van just like this to use." The air conditioning in the rented van actually blew cold air, all the windows went all the way up, and unlike our current van, it felt luxurious. When Doug returned back to Iowa City, he was flabbergasted to hear the amazing news! Soon we were handed the keys to our nearly new van. It was the same model and make as the one Doug had been driving when he sent up that prayer. All of us recognized the amazing, divine timing.

We were definitely not doing this hard work alone… nor **could** we.

CHAPTER 13

FORMING A TEAM

Dedicated teachers are the heartbeat of a dynamic school. I've shared the unique story of how Joni, who had been my student teacher, and will share in the next chapter how Joan, whose mom was in my Iowa Principal's Leadership Academy, came to be teachers at Faith Academy. There are many more stories of how Faith Academy and our wonderful teachers were drawn to each other. This is a bigger story than just us and our school, though.

Veritas Church, one of the larger churches in the Iowa City area, has an active program for college-age students who meet once a week. We were blessed in our school's second year when a connection was made with them, and the college kids wanted to volunteer at Faith Academy. These energetic students served in many roles, mostly as helpers in the classrooms, until the pandemic curtailed that. From that partnership with Salt Company, three teachers emerged and were later hired as our initial fourth-, fifth- and sixth-grade teachers. I always jokingly said, "They spent a lot of time volunteering here and STILL wanted to come work for us!"

One of the most unlikely teachers God sent us was Mandy DeLange. Mandy had been a Mormon from birth until the middle of her college years. Her husband was going to start law school at the University of Iowa. They came to visit from Utah and since the two of them had recently left the Mormon Church, finding a new church home in the town they would be moving was of great importance to them.

On Sunday afternoon toward the end of their visit, they stopped by the Parkview Church campus on Dubuque Street. The main building was open, as activities were going on at the time, and they walked in to find out more about the church and what it had to offer. One of the first people they ran into was the head pastor at the time, Doug Schillinger, a big proponent of Faith Academy. They introduced themselves, told him what they were doing in town and remarked they were looking for a church to belong to. When they were almost ready to part ways, the pastor turned to Mandy and asked, "And what do you do?"

"I'm looking for a teaching job."

This immediately got Pastor Schillinger's wheels turning.

Me with our teaching crew in 2017
From left: Me, Tracy Reichter, Mandy DeLange,
Crystal Johnson, Hannah Shetler
Back Row: Laurie Thompson, Char Jacobsen, Trevor Johnson

"Hey, I happen to know of an opening at our Christian school on the other side of town. I believe it's third grade. You should really check it out."

He let Doug Fern know this had transpired, and Doug let me know to expect their visit, as he wouldn't be at school.

The next day, Mandy and her husband Matt stopped by the school and met me to have a look around. I immediately got a good vibe from her. She was upbeat, easy to converse with. and you could pick up on her sincere interest in our scholars. During our meeting, I asked when they were leaving town, hoping I could have another opportunity to follow-up with Mandy if that was needed. When they told me they were departing the next morning, that increased the urgency.

On the spot, our casual meeting turned into a job interview. We later had a formal interview over Zoom so Doug could be a part of the process. We also requested a video recording of her teaching so we could see her in action. We knew this could be easily obtained during her current student-teaching experience. We were thrilled. and she ended up becoming our next third-grade teacher! Showcasing the supportive and helpful staff at Faith Academy, we all showed up to move her and her husband into their apartment when they arrived with their moving pod at the end of that summer.

Something that sticks with me from our experience with Mandy was a phrase that was coined when she was praying at Circle Up one morning.

"Dear Lord. help us to see these scholars the way you see them."

From then on, this became an unofficial motto that we often used. It was a sincere prayer meant from the heart. She was asking God to help us to see these children in the same light that He sees them, and to care about and love them unconditionally. We know that we can start each day new with God, because He will forgive us of past mistakes. In turn, we want to allow our scholars to start each day fresh with us.

Another example of how God helped us find the perfect teacher came in 2017. By the end of May we had done our hiring for the following year, and I was feeling great about having that all taken care of. Suddenly, we discovered that one of our new hires who was going to teach first grade was telling people at Bible School she wasn't going to work at Faith Academy after all. This was quite a shock and finding that out through the grapevine was a sign – to me at least – that she wouldn't be a good fit for us. In the end I was grateful for the way things ultimately worked out, but at the time it happened we were scrambling to find a replacement.

As soon as it was confirmed that this teacher had changed her mind, a name popped into my head as a potential teacher. A woman named Laurie Thompson had applied the previous year, but we had already committed to hiring another candidate. I had filed Laurie's application away in the chance that I might want to contact her if something came open. Even though we had never met, we knew several of the same people and they spoke highly of her, including one of our classroom volunteers. This was the perfect opportunity. I called her and asked if she might be available to interview for a position with us.

"This is so weird!" she responded. "I have the contract for my current school on my dining room table and I have had all intentions of signing it and sending it back in, but I just keep walking by it. Don't know why… and yes! I'd love to interview at Faith Academy."

By now, Laurie had a year's experience teaching a combined classroom of first and second graders in a public school, and a first-grade teacher was exactly what we needed! As it turned out, Laurie brought a lot of valuable experience with her. In addition to teaching the same grade level we wanted to hire her for, she had worked as an associate for many years in a neighboring district where she lived. In that role, she specifically helped students learn how to read. We were similar in age, and she offered wisdom to our young staff. She also added a bright spot, as she always told her stories in an animated way.

Her impact went far beyond the classroom, too. One year she gave two siblings a ride home once a week so she could keep them after school and teach them how to cook for themselves. She used the kitchen at the school and spent her own money on the ingredients. The boy was in her class and his older sister didn't really like to spend time with him. This project of Mrs. Thompson's served a dual purpose. It was a way for them to have a positive experience together, as well as to learn how to prepare healthy meals, which was not happening at home. During their time together she would talk with them about everything from her horses to God.

She planted many seeds and simply loved her scholars. She went to the effort of taking her class to her farm every spring for a field trip. Her husband and their neighbor were enlisted as helpers for the day. It was a highlight of the year for these six-year-olds to get to spend the day outside with animals. They spent time brushing the horses and feeding them treats. They also watched her husband trim a hoof or work in the forge to make a horseshoe. They each got a keepsake horseshoe to take with them. They collected chicken eggs and observed bees at work in their beehive. Some had never been on a gravel road before, so that was even an experience to remember from the special field trip to Mrs. Thompson's rural home.

I eventually got to the point where I wouldn't even be stressed when we had a teacher vacancy. I knew that God always provided the right person at the right time. Despite my faith, there were a few times I became a little nervous as vacancies had yet to be filled right up until the eleventh hour. For example, one time it was getting to the end of one summer and we still did not have a fourth-grade teacher.

A young man from the Des Moines area saw our ad on TeachIowa. org and applied for the position.

It was the first time I had used that site to advertise. It turned out he knew a family whose son was going to be in his class. He came on board just in time to start the school year. We were so appreciative because he had a heart for God and a flexible demeanor. His year was cut short when COVID closed us down, though. He moved to the east coast after getting married that summer. As a result, we once more found ourselves looking for a fourth-grade teacher.

I thought surely there would be a year when we didn't have to hire a new teacher. Due to the transient population of Iowa City, being a university town, that was never the case during my tenure at Faith Academy.

Our sixth-grade teacher, Shay, let me know that she knew of a teacher at her church who had become disenchanted working in the ICCSD. He had taught fourth grade for several years. Shay let him know about our opening and encouraged him to apply. After she talked with him, she told me that he seemed very interested.

Brian came on board with us for the 2020-21 school year. It was great to get a teacher who had years of experience teaching the very grade level for which we had an opening. I could sense that he needed the same type of "building back up" that I did when I was recovering from a teaching experience that had been tense. After getting to know him better, I sensed that "toxic" was the word that describes the work setting he had endured. It was great to see him appreciate the positive and supportive workplace environment we had created at Faith Academy, and it reinforced what we had been striving for as one of our goals. As we met for our weekly one-on-one sessions in my office, he would open up more and more.

"I just love working here – you have no idea," he would often state with a grin.

"And we love having you here!" I responded.

It makes me smile when I think of the way he would walk into my office with an idea or a request. I loved that he felt so open to come to me with them.

"Okay ... feel free to say no to this, but..." he would say —and then he would continue with his innovative thought.

There was a bonus to having staff members who had experienced working at other places. Almost without exception, they were grateful to work in an environment where, even though the day-to-day work was exhausting, it was a light-hearted atmosphere where people cared about each other. Everyone was willing to help one another and put in the energy it took to accomplish our goal of doing the best we could for the scholars.

Even after I announced that I wasn't going to be returning I was able to see another teacher come to us in ways that seemed unexplainable to her. After our banquet in April, 2022, I received a call from Kristy Delashaw asking if we could meet to talk about our opening for a third-grade teacher. She wasn't sure she wanted to apply, but someone from her church told her about the job opportunity and thought it would be a perfect fit for her. Currently she was working in a part-time position for the public school system. It was really ideal for their family, and she wasn't looking for anything else.

When she came over to our school, I could sense her openness to God's calling and she said more than once, "I don't really know what I'm doing here,"

My response to her was to point my finger to the sky and say, "It's God ... you would be amazed to hear some of our staff stories."

She was an experienced teacher with grown children of her own. An adopted special needs child was also part of their family. When she spoke of him, I could sense her compassion for children who struggled. I was delighted in her interest, as it is always helpful to have a variety of ages and experience levels among the staff.

As we were arranging for her official interview, Doug and I received this email from her:

As I shared with Jan on Monday, I am not sure what God is doing, but He is doing something!

When my family packed our bags to leave Washington State and come all the way to Iowa, a state we had only visited the weekend of my husband's interview, I had no idea what was in store for us. But, God is good and our journey is only beginning. Jesus brought us to Iowa City so that my husband, Paul, could pour his life and faith into the lives of college students through Young Life. And God brought me here so that I could love his children, in any way possible.

As Doreen walked me through your amazing school, I had to blink back tears multiple times. Seeing kids celebrated, supported, and loved, all in the name of Jesus, was an honor to witness. God is at work.

When I reached out to Kristy recently, I asked how everything is going for her now. She responded by letting me know, "God has used my time here in mighty ways. The work is hard, but the blessings are many."

My final story includes a person from my hometown of Wayland, who I knew of but didn't know personally. Knowing there was a kindergarten position open, Alicia Wenger stopped by to see if she might be interested in working at the school, having just moved to Iowa City. She had been a public school teacher in Wayland for 13 years. Doreen apologized for Crystal not being able to give her a tour as she was absent that day due to having sick kids at home.

"I've been around awhile – I can give you a tour," said a slender woman standing behind the secretary, Alicia remembered.

During the tour, both the woman and Alicia got emotional talking about the mission of Faith Academy and the way it had evolved over the last ten years. Alicia could already feel what a special place this school was.

The woman who humbly addressed Alicia and gave her the tour was Elder Bernie, who would be in charge of the school five months later – stepping in as Head of School.

When she got in her car after the tour, she called her mom, sobbing.

"I don't know why I'm crying," she told her mother. "I have never felt so much joy and peace in one place! What about my retirement, my consulting options, my friends, my family, my Wayland home? It means leaving! I think I'm supposed to work here but it would take a miracle of God's provision!"

One week after her interview she was hired as the fifth-grade teacher for the 2023-24 school year. The initial posting of a kindergarten position changed to a fifth grade job as a staff member within changed grade levels.

I visited with her recently – at a funeral at Sugar Creek – a familiar scene for me to catch up with people from Wayland, past and present. She was telling me how much she loves her students and was talking about them by name, as they were previously my crew.

"You don't know how happy that makes my heart!" I told her. "You are the perfect kind of person to work there — one who knows how to roll with it when things don't go as planned or anticipated and who loves our scholars just as they are!"

She commented how she no longer uses the words "something went wrong today" but instead refers to changes and roadblocks as opportunities for God to show us what He wants us to do.

I shook my head in agreement as one of the phrases I frequently used was, "This just gives us a chance to exercise our flexibility." And it was during those times when beautiful things had the opportunity to take place and would often play out.

Alicia's example was, "The internet is down this morning? Well, I guess we can have an extra 30 minutes of Bible time and you can ask any questions you've been wondering about!"

The timing was also perfect for Alicia to become a proud resident of South District Iowa City since she no longer had her own children at home. I know it is not easy moving schools — especially to a new grade level – because it requires a lot of prep work outside of school hours. She shared that she is at peace when she is working with her scholars and knows she is exactly where God has called her to be.

It has truly been astounding to see God pull together this amazing team. I love how these inspiring teachers have come to us in so many different ways. They are the reason Faith Academy has thrived, even during difficult times. While I have only told a few stories in this chapter, many of our Faith Academy teachers have come to work in this remarkable place in their own unique and God-inspired way.

CHAPTER 14

GOT TIME FOR A TOUR?

As I was working at my desk after school when most people had gone home, I saw a figure go by my office window. Next, I heard the front door being tugged at in an attempt to open it. I peeked out my blinds to see who was trying to get in. I was surprised and pleased to see who it was as I recognized him immediately. I went to the entryway to let him in. "Dwight! Good to see you! What are you doing here?"

Dwight was our son's first Sunday-school teacher at First Mennonite Church when we moved to the Iowa City area in 1996. Most people in the area know him for his unprecedented success as a high school basketball coach at Iowa Mennonite School (IMS). It has since been renamed Hillcrest Academy.

"Is this the Kingdom Center? I'm actually looking for Fred."

"No, it's Faith Academy. You knew I work here, right?"

We exchanged pleasantries and caught up a bit. Our daughters are the same age and knew each other, but were now in college, both out of state.

"Since you're here, do you have time for a tour?"

I had seen our secretary do that so many times, it was just natural for me to extend the offer. The more people who learned about Faith Academy, the better. This was especially true for someone like Dwight who was involved in Christian education, and a guidance counselor at IMS where he coached.

When we got to the gym at the end of the tour, I asked him what he had been up to. Anything new? He told me he was finishing up getting his Administrative Degree and would be officially licensed in the fall to be a principal at a K-12 school.

Wow. I didn't know he would be interested in doing that at this point in his career. He's older than I am.

I wanted to hear more about it. I had toyed with getting my administrator's certificate in case Faith Academy ever wanted to get accredited. I already had a master's degree and a post-graduate reading endorsement, so I wasn't sure it would be worth the large amount of effort it would take. Even though I loved learning and taking classes, the thought of having someone look over my transcripts to determine what I would need to take to get the official certification kind of made my stomach turn.

Dwight proceeded to tell me about the certification program he was in. It was called the Iowa Principal Leadership Academy (IPLA). It was offered through the area education agency. The program was designed for educators who had already earned their master's degree and had a minimum of four years' teaching experience. He described how the coursework thoroughly covered the six standards created in Iowa to serve as the framework for school leaders.

I couldn't believe I was hearing that such a program existed. It seemed tailor-made for me. Educators attend all-day workshops once a month on a Saturday. They also hear from faculty around the state with expertise in different areas. He told me there was a lot of outside class work to complete as well, but that it had all been very practical. He found it interesting, and exactly what he needed to know, since it didn't spend time on theory. He added that during the summer there is a weeklong class that focused on Evaluators Training that had to be attended in person.

Wow - that sounds exactly like something that might work for me!

"So, you just go up to Cedar Rapids once a month for two years and the rest of the work is done in between, except for the weeklong class that you need to go to every day?" I asked to clarify.

"Oh no, it's in Elkader. They don't offer one at our AEA."

Dwight could tell my bubble was burst.

"Elkader? How far away is that? Our AEA in Cedar Rapids really doesn't offer it?!"

I was disappointed. What seemed like a perfect idea just became a lot less appealing. A two hour and fifteen-minute drive. Each way. Year round. For two years. By myself. This suddenly sounded like a lot of hassle. But I didn't want to rule it out before I had thoroughly investigated it.

The tour ended and Dwight went on his way to see if Fred could be found at his new location down the street from Faith Academy. He did follow up with an email.

Hi Jan!

Thanks for the awesome tour today, was really neat to see what you are doing! Very cool to hear your passion for what you are doing, and neat to see Joni and the kids and other staff there!

I checked in with Harold Knutson, the facilitator of our program and below is his response. Let me know if you have questions, and I hope this might meet your needs! Great timing, with May 1 the deadline!

. . . .

Response from Harold:

We are asking those who are interested to fill out the necessary application material by May 1st. We plan on starting another class in

September if we get enough students. If the person wants to apply, please have him or her contact me via my email address and I will forward it to Pat Heidersheit at AEA 1. Pat will then send the necessary information. Thanks.

. . . .

They were starting a new cohort, a group of colleagues who would go through the program together, and it looked like I had only a couple of weeks to decide if I wanted to pursue it and get all the necessary paperwork – including letters of recommendation — together to meet the application deadline. I knew going through the program would require some personal sacrifice. After some conversation with Dave, he was supportive. What a trooper. Doug was in favor of it as well, knowing that my having the credentials to serve as principal for Faith Academy would really help us as a school. I decided to go for it!

Even though the four-and-a-half hours of driving in a day sounded overwhelming when Dwight mentioned it, I got used to my monthly trips to Elkader. It was in a beautiful part of Iowa and other than one slippery trip of white-knuckled driving in the winter, it was a scenic and enjoyable drive. When I walked into the first class meeting, I remember thinking, *Who am I going to connect with out of this group?*

There was a group of 14 educators from a variety of districts across the state. And sure enough, I met Lora Kester and she ended up being my "class best friend." Lora and I connected the very first week. She was my person. We were about the same age and had been long-time elementary teachers, had a similar style, and each had two adult children. We also discovered both of our college-age daughters were living in Florida at the time, not far from each other.

I looked forward to catching up with her every month. We sometimes would communicate between our monthly classes, particularly when we were working on a project together. I was continually impressed by her willingness to share with me and others in class. Her area of expertise was reading instruction and literacy. She was a gold mine of information.

Part of the requirement of the program was to select a current principal to serve as a mentor. I was fortunate that Chris Gibson from Alexander Elementary School in Iowa City agreed to fill that role for me. She was well respected in the district and loved by those I knew on her staff. Alexander was the public school in our neighborhood of Iowa City, so I had already interacted with her as the principal of that building. We shared some of our students already, due to special-education programming. Along with that, I knew she was a Christian. She had even attended our first fundraising banquet. It couldn't have been a more perfect match. I was grateful for the time I was able to spend in meaningful conversation with her and for the many ideas and wisdom I gleaned from her. She shared that it can be a lonely position and we both found our time together encouraging.

Our clientele was from the same area, and I always felt that our buildings were in partnership, never in competition. There were times when people I interacted with at Faith Academy wanted to bash the public schools. I was not about that. I will never be about that. As we worked together to improve our community, our common mantra was, "We can use all the help we can get!" I never felt a spirit of competition. As a result of her being my mentor, we often had teachers from Faith Academy observe her staff to get ideas. Faith Academy is a small school compared to the much bigger public schools in the area. Due to our small enrollment, we only had one section for each grade level. One disadvantage to this setup was that our teachers didn't have a grade-level partner to bounce ideas off of. I highly valued the relationship we had with our nearby public school. It was a relationship I hadn't anticipated being so positive when I started at Faith – what a pleasant surprise.

I love to learn and the information that was being delivered in the IPLA program was exactly what I needed to better serve in my leadership role as Director of Curriculum and Instruction right then! The timing was amazing on so many levels.

For example, just when I learned I was going to have to go through the process of filing all the paperwork for our English Language Learners (ELLs), that month's guest speaker at IPLA would be an expert on ELL. When a Faith Academy board member mentioned starting a preschool, at my next class we heard from the Director of Preschool Programming at the Iowa Department of Education.

Along with that, the director of IPLA was a retired superintendent who had many connections across the state with leaders in their fields. I learned about an innovative reading curriculum, "Reading Side by Side," through one of our guest speakers. We later adopted that curriculum as our third- to sixth-grade reading curriculum. And we even gained a new teacher at Faith Academy from the connections I had at IPLA.

One Saturday when Lora and I were catching up before class started, she asked me if we had any job openings. Her Florida daughter would be moving to Iowa City for her husband to start medical school in the fall and she was looking for a teaching job.

Yes, but would she want to work in a challenging school like ours? And it's a Christian school — how would that line up?

Lora knew that, though, so I doubted she would bring up the possibility of Faith Academy if that weren't okay.

"Actually, we have a Kindergarten opening," I informed her in a hopeful manner.

"That's what she teaches now. And her Christian faith is really important to her!"

It was as if Lora were reading my mind.

I arranged an interview after receiving her daughter's application. Doug and I interviewed her over Zoom the next month. Lora's daughter would become our next Kindergarten teacher.

During this two-year stretch, I found that I actually took that one day off a week from school, as was allotted in my contract. It was a chance for me to work on assignments for class. One important class assignment I needed to stay on top of was reading and summarizing ten journal articles for each standard relating to the work of an educational administrator. This amounted to 60 total articles.

This was my favorite assignment. I love to stay informed about current research and I had found an outstanding resource called The Marshall Memo. Kim Marshall had curated ideas and research from the best of more than 60 magazines and journals. His tag line was "A weekly round-up of important ideas and research in K-12 Education." The target audience for his articles was made up of principals, instructional coaches, superintendents, and teachers. Marshall would narrow his selections down to six to eight particularly informative, inspiring as well as applicable articles a week. I would select mine from there to thoroughly read and review. Even after I completed my program, I listened to his podcast on a weekly basis. I still subscribe today and highly recommend it.

Over the two years, Dave made the trip with me a couple of times and we made a fun weekend of it. Lora and her husband Dan joined us for one of those adventures and we stayed in an Airbnb together. Our husbands enjoyed spending the day watching Iowa football in a sports bar and sightseeing in Dan's Jeep Wrangler while Lora and I were in class. On the downside, I had to leave a family reunion to go to class once, missed a wedding where my daughter was maid of honor out of state, and couldn't make another wedding of a cousin in Des Moines. In the end, I appreciate it was a short chapter and a meaningful time of growth that God laid in my lap for the benefit of Faith Academy. It was well worth it for the connections I made, and knowledge I gained. Ultimately, this credential was essential to my being chosen to serve as the first principal for Faith Academy. This was not a position that was on my radar just a few short years before I started the program. God had directed every step.

CHAPTER 15

THE POWER OF MUSIC

My mother and I had a close relationship. I am her only daughter, and I was heartbroken when she died of cancer in 2001. I was only 36 at the time she passed, and I felt the loss profoundly. Prior to that I had not closely known anyone who had gone through cancer, so I was navigating an unknown terrain. I know it is true that a heart that is broken is a heart that's been loved, so I realize even now I was a lucky daughter to have her as my mother.

We had just moved back to Dave's hometown of Kalona in late 1996 and were excited to be closer to my parents. So rather than a two-and-a-half-hour drive from Des Moines, it was now about a 30-minute drive to Wayland where my parents lived. We moved so that our kids could grow up around their grandparents. I was devastated when only four years later I was living there without my mom. It was certainly not the life I had envisioned when we made the decision to move back home. Dylan was in second grade and Jenna was only four.

The holidays of Christmas and Easter have never been more special to me than during my years at Faith Academy. Long before becoming a teacher there, I had been given a nativity scene by my mom that she told me was sturdy enough for my son Dylan to play with as a child. She purchased it at the Crowded Closet thrift store, which had a section called "10,000 Villages" that specialized in products from third-world countries. In this case, the nativity scene was made of exotic wood. It had been part of her Christmas decorations for years.

A scholar plays with the nativity scene from my mom in my office.

At Faith Academy, I was proud to bring that keepsake nativity scene to my classroom – something that wouldn't have been appropriate to do in public school. I also soon discovered, starting with this wonderful gift from my mother, how much I deeply loved being able to share my faith with my scholars through the wonderful music and profoundly spiritual environment at Faith Academy. My faith grew even stronger as a result.

After I brought the nativity scene to Faith Academy for the first time, I started to notice one of the boys in my class as he moved the pieces around. Damion frequently stood around the shelf where I had the scene displayed, and I asked him to tell me about it. From being in chapel and listening to the Bible stories I had read in class, he told me – in his own second grade words – the entire story of

Jesus coming into the world. I couldn't help but tear up to think how pleased Mom would be to know her gift was being used in my classroom as a teaching instrument for a boy who was learning about the real meaning of Christmas – possibly for the first time.

Being in chapel with my scholars and learning about the events leading up to Easter was heartwarming as well. They were sincerely disturbed when they discovered that two of Jesus's closest friends turned away from Him toward the end of His time on earth. They had just learned about Judas – who betrayed Jesus – and Peter, who acted like he didn't even know Him. "How could they do that?!" they wondered out loud.

Coming back to school on the Monday after Easter, our class talked about how special it was to celebrate the day of Jesus rising from the grave. Starting in 2016, Parkview East, an extended campus of Parkview Church that founded Faith Academy, had weekly Sunday services in our school building. Doug Fern was the main pastor.

The hope was that our families who were unaffiliated with a specific church would attend here. Dave and I started attending Parkview East as I thought it would be meaningful for our Faith Academy families to see familiar faces when they visited there in hopes that our presence would help them feel comfortable. It was exciting to be part of the growth. We would set up and tear down folding chairs in the gym every week.

A few years after Parkview East began holding services at Faith Academy, a Congolese Church started using our facility as well, holding services following ours. Soon a Hispanic church met in our building. We could leave the gym set up and they would tear down the stage and chairs. With a remodeling project in 2019, we were able to expand into an area that had previously been a secondhand store. Part of the space was set up as a permanent chapel as well as the Worship Center for Parkview East. No more setting up and tearing down every weekend!

During our Easter Sunday services, we invited all scholars who were available and interested to come and perform during the church service. Having learned the song "Up from the Grave He Arose" in Chapel, it was the perfect song to share on Easter Sunday. As I led the song and accompanied the congregants on the piano, I loved being very dramatic with the scholars – quietly singing the verses and then belting out the chorus with gusto. I discovered it's amazing what I can get kids to go along with when I'm having fun with it myself. The congregation and parents were treated to a more enjoyable version of a traditional hymn than most were accustomed to. Some had never heard this song. There was no requirement for our parents to be Christians to enroll at Faith Academy.

Seeing our scholars in their Sunday best, rather than the school uniforms they were required to wear day after day, was a treat for me. When I complimented kids on what they were wearing, I almost always emphasized "But it is what's on the inside that matters!" because I didn't want them to think their worth comes from how they look. Many of them told me their clothes were new. This clearly indicated that having them up front at church was a big deal to their parents. It confirmed in my mind that it definitely was a good idea to have our scholars perform songs at our church Easter service. I left the service on a high.

Music was an important part of Chapel and I got involved with leading it by default. A couple of days into my first week working at Faith Academy, I was brave enough to tell them I played piano, as I walked over and played along with one of the songs we were singing. I was able to play by ear, so although I wasn't a polished pianist, I could pick up almost any song. Brandon Parker was one of Doug's friends who was in on getting the school up and running. His job at the school those first couple of years was a "catch-all" position running the small office, communicating with parents, supervising recess, being the emcee of Chapel, and "other duties as assigned."

Brandon would get us started every morning with music. At first, we were limited to the songs we already knew such as "Jesus on the Main Line." We worked together on coming up with what we would sing, and Doug definitely had his opinions. As I embraced my role as music leader, I eventually took full responsibility for the singing portion of Chapel. The scholars would walk in to music playing over the speakers. Most often the song was "Good Morning, Wake up to a Brand New Day" by Mandisa. The original staff told me that song was played every single morning during the school's first year! It was great to finally get a variety going. In subsequent years, Doug liked to blast Earth, Wind and Fire's "September" every day of that month. After I retired in 2022, I texted him on September 1 at 7:51 a.m. to make sure he remembered the tradition.

Me leading singing in the original Chapel space
in 2018 with adults in the background
From left, they are Joan Thanupakorn, and Laurie Thompson,
with Collin Bockelman ("Mr. B") in the sound booth.
There were scholars lining three sides of the room.

Another Chapel tradition of those early years when we had a small student body was to sing when it was someone's birthday. "Ice Cream and Cake" was played from the sound system, and everyone would dance along. "Ride with your boy now slip and slide…" Big smiles would come on even the shyest of scholar's faces when they were dancing to that. As our school grew, that song had to be saved for a rarer occasion such as a Golden Birthday – as when a scholar turns 10 on the 10th of the month – or a significant birthday for a staff member.

Scholars would request songs and that made my heart happy knowing which songs meant the most to them. Dallas always wanted to sing "Diamonds;" Faith requested "Ever Be;" CJ loved singing "Three in One;" and Abraham's favorite song was "Help Is On the Way." I will forever think of those children when I hear those songs. As principal, I greeted the scholars every morning at the door as they arrived. That was when the requests started rolling in – and I loved it. We sang hymns, current praise songs, kid's songs such as "Father Abraham," sing-and-response songs and many a capella songs. Some songs were enhanced by accessories such as a paper mâché "P" for emphasis. I purchased it at Hobby Lobby to hold up during "I Am a Promise" – a song from my own childhood. One scholar would stand up front and hoist the letter into the air when we sang the lyrics, "I am a promise…with a capital P!"

We broke out a tambourine for "I Saw the Light." Since so many scholars raised their hands to be the one to play it, everyone knew it was a crowd favorite. One day a new tradition was established. Without being asked, one of the scholars passed the tambourine along to the person next to them so they could get a turn. It would often just go on down the line throughout the song. Seeing the scholars put into practice the concepts we were all striving to teach them, such as being concerned with others, sharing, and enjoying each other's company in a healthy way, was rewarding beyond measure.

There was one song that enabled me, as an adult in my 50's, to finally understand the idea of the Holy Spirit. "There is a Redeemer" is a song I taught the scholars. We sang it often, particularly during the Easter season. The line, **"Thank you Oh my Father, for giving us your Son ... and leaving your spirit 'til the work on Earth is done"** meant a great deal to me because it explained that God left a spirit on earth to help us in times of need, like an advocate. Prior to Jesus ascending into Heaven, it was different. It was after He ascended that the Holy Spirit was able to dwell in Christ followers. I had gone to church all my life and hadn't fully grasped that concept until I was singing that song over and over with the scholars.

As a teacher at Faith Academy, I was reminded there are many bits of info I was able to recall because of learning them through a song. For example, thanks to the television shorts "Schoolhouse Rock," I can recite the preamble to our constitution as well as explain how a bill becomes a law. Because of the music leaders I had growing up at Sugar Creek Mennonite Church, outside Wayland, I can sing the books of the Old and New Testaments in order.

I know children retain information in a variety of ways. When I was out and around in the building, I would inevitably hear scholars singing or humming chapel songs. More than once I walked into the girls' restroom and was greeted with a song wafting out from the stall. A young scholar told me once that she was singing chapel songs over at her grandma's and it made her grandma cry. I knew it was likely her grandma was touched with the message of the lyrics, or it was a song she already knew and was moved that her granddaughter was singing it. The songs we sang together in Chapel encouraged an understanding of the gospel I'm hoping will stick with our scholars for a lifetime.

A profound memory I carry with me from my high-school days is also one of the most perplexing. As a senior looking forward to college, my high-school music teacher discouraged me from pursuing music education as a major. It was devastating to hear that from her. Despite this bucket of cold water being thrown on my young dreams, I reawakened that dream of teaching music in my time at Faith Academy and I loved it.

CHAPTER 16

A Christmas Miracle

I was excited. I felt confident that I had decided what I wanted to do with my life as I approached going to college the next year. I could hardly wait to tell my high-school music teacher, as I knew she would be excited for me, since I would be following in her footsteps. As I approached her, I was proud of the path I was going to take.

"I've been thinking that I might want to major in music education and become a music teacher!"

Her dismissive response surprised me.

"Oh, I doubt you would like it – there's all the music theory classes and everything."

Why would she say that?! I've played the piano since elementary school. I've also played violin and flute. I participate in the Band and Choir and go to all the competitions. I've competed as part of small groups, and even solo. I've been in our high school's musical every year and had the lead my senior year. I was in the Swing Choir and sang a duet at our Pops Concert. And you think I can't handle a little "Music Theory?!"

So much for that idea.

I realize that I wasn't as serious as I could have been about my studies in high school, as I was always more about having a good time. But that interaction took the wind out of my sails. I didn't tell my mom or friends or anyone about it – I was actually embarrassed. As much as I loved music, I took a big step back and decided that maybe I should focus on something else to study. In the end, I did become a teacher, as I wanted. Instead of teaching music, though, I taught elementary school.

A part of me also learned something else that day. I learned how powerful a teacher's words can be. I learned how they can lift a student up to inspire her to achieve more than she thought she was capable of. Or they can crush dreams. From that moment on, consciously or unconsciously, I decided I wanted to be the type of teacher who inspires her students to be the best version of themselves. And even though I chose not to become a music teacher, my love of music burned brightly within me. It still does.

Parkview Church had a tradition of performing a children's musical every year in the Fall. Beth Noeller was the director of the drama and she had someone else do the music portion of it. I met Beth at a Women's Bible Study held at our church during the year I was subbing part time prior to coming onboard at Faith Academy. It was the first time ever that I had been able to participate in a daytime event at church due to always working full time.

The women at the Bible study were a different type than I was used to being around. The most notable difference was the much larger number of stay-at-home moms or retired women.

Beth was a spunky older lady who had worked in a professional role at Pearson, a testing company, for years. When we split into study groups after all of us viewed the Bible Study video, Beth and I ended up in the same small group. Beth was the energetic type of woman that I hoped to be when I eventually retired. We had gotten to know each other a bit through that experience, so she wasn't just a person off the street when she came into my office a couple of years later with what I first thought of as an irrational idea.

"Natalie Fern has asked if I would be willing to do a musical with the kids here at Faith Academy. What do you think?"

What do I think or what am I going to say out loud? Are you kidding, Beth, these kids will eat you alive. You have no idea what you are getting yourself into. They are so different from your quiet, cooperative church kids.

Instead, I kept my doubts to myself and decided to venture into the scary unknown.

"That sounds like a fun idea – let's give it a try!"

DeDe was our music teacher at Faith Academy, and she directed the music portion of the production by practicing with the scholars during music class. I helped Beth get everything else rolling. As much as I had my doubts regarding whether this was going to be a success, I wasn't just going to throw her in to lead our kids when she didn't know them. I knew that once a relationship with them was established, interactions would be much smoother.

Beth Noeller and I at the Faith Academy banquet 2022

As we started moving forward with this grand project, different things needed to happen. Assigning roles, communicating with parents, and lining up practices, for example, all needed to be done. The scholars who had speaking parts stayed after school on our "early out" days so that parents wouldn't need to bring them back in the evenings for practice. Instead, they could simply remain at school and practice between 2:30 and 4:00 p.m. with Beth. That 90-minute period was the weekly time for staff meetings or Professional Development as the scholars went home an hour early. I found myself becoming anxious after only one week. I kept thinking this had the potential for becoming a huge disaster.

If only I could be in two places at once – I'd really like to help Beth and keep our scholars corralled so she could accomplish what she wanted to every week, making it a positive experience for everyone.

But it wasn't possible, as I was in charge of our staff meetings and training. It was a rough start, but Beth found an assistant to come with her every week. Our secretary often found herself staying late in the office with the remaining kids whose parents hadn't picked them up promptly. Beth wanted all scholars to memorize their lines. I saw this as an admirable goal, but again I was skeptical.

Meanwhile, I made copy upon copy of lost scripts because we didn't want anyone to get in trouble when Miss Beth found out. To be honest, we were all kind of scared of her, including Doug and I! To help out, I got the blessing from our teachers to pull kids from class to work with them on memorizing their lines. We all realized it was a lot to expect for them to find the time to memorize their lines at home. Ultimately, Beth was right, and I was glad she insisted they commit their lines to memory. The play was much more professional and the sense of accomplishment our scholars felt was immense as a result.

It definitely required an "all hands on deck" attitude to pull off the musical. That first year's performance reminded me of the 1983 movie *The Best Christmas Pageant Ever* where no one had any idea what some of the actors were going to do or if they were going to remember any of the things they had been practicing. But just like in the movie, the kids came through in the end, and it turned out much better than expected.

Beth and I in the lower right corner directing one of our Christmas musicals - Annie behind the microphone ready to sing a solo!

We were excited and relieved at the same time. Beth must have been surprised, too. After the closing number, Beth stood up, turned to the audience and shouted, "It's a Christmas miracle!" Her honesty cracked me up. She almost immediately started talking about how we would do things next year.

This didn't put her over the edge? She's willing to do it again!

The following year I took over the music portion of the production, as DeDe felt it took too much time away from her curriculum in music class, which I could see. I had plenty of other tasks in my job description, but I realized this was a chance for our scholars to be part of a production they would likely remember for the rest of their lives. And, it was my chance to be a music teacher, sort of.

Since I led music in Chapel anyway, we worked on the musical songs during Chapel. We also sent CDs of the music home for the kids to get familiar with. In one case, I had to send home a CD player as well, as they were becoming more extinct. Everyone was pretty much singing their parts in their sleep before it was over every year. Elder Bernie played the music in her van as she picked up and delivered scholars. The parents did their part, too. I was outside when a dad was dropping off their scholar in the middle of the day after an appointment. As they opened the door, the music from our musical drifted out from the car.

Yes! I love it! Thank you for helping to get this music in their head!!

I enjoyed teaming with Beth on the project. We complemented each other well. She was organized way ahead of time, and I offered the flexibility and encouragement that made our scholars feel comfortable. The success from the fruits of our collective labor was experienced by our scholars and it was amazing.

No one could replicate such a feeling for them. The scholars had to do the hard work themselves and they felt the satisfaction of accomplishing something difficult – a job well done. They had to memorize lines and the music and some even performed solos or duets. Everyone was involved. Over the years we went from singing everything in unison to adding harmony. One of the musical scores even included polyphony, where the scholars split into two groups and sang different melodies at the same time. I chuckled as I thought back to my high-school music teacher and realized that might have been something that would have been covered in music education classes.

One year we had a fifth grader assigned the lead in the musical. He was a great singer but had previously shown signs of anxiety. I was thrilled, and a little surprised, when he agreed to take the part. DeDe advised us of who had strong voices in music class, and he was our guy. He practiced for weeks and was nailing every part of his role – he had his lines memorized and everything. We decided to run through some of the rough patches during school the morning of the performance. He was about to sing his solo and just froze.

The audience was empty except for the teachers who would always graciously sacrifice some class time during December to support the scholars during practice as asked. Scholars were off to the side as part of the performing choir and saw what happened, too. My heart dropped. He had been doing so well! I was helping someone with a costume in the back of the gym when it happened. He ran down from the stage and fell into his teacher's arms. His teacher calmly talked to him, as they ended up walking out of the gym together. We carried on and practiced other portions for the rest of our allotted time. All of us adults gave each other knowing, worried glances as we passed each other in the hall for the next few hours before the performance. It was going to start at 1:00 p.m.

There had been announcements at church, fliers had gone home, emails were sent, and blurbs were posted on social media. This musical would happen with or without him. All of us really wanted it to be with him, as he had practiced so hard to be such an important part of this musical. We also realized this was another opportunity to turn the situation over to God. Our scholar had taken the role seriously and spent a lot of time working on his lines and would willingly work on his solos whenever I asked him to. He even sought me out a time or two and asked to practice his lines. The staff I was able to talk with ahead of the performance all said the same thing to each other – pray for our reluctant scholar. We did.

In the end, he was magnificent. His mom had asked off work to be able to come see him during the day – and she was sitting there in her work uniform whooping it up. "That's my boy!" Best. Day. Ever.

Beth selected a different musical each year. The younger scholars anticipated getting to be involved with a speaking part as they got older and couldn't wait for their chance. Beth came up with props and sound effects that put the icing on the cake for the production. I can still see Dallas and a group of kids enthusiastically carrying a big "tree" up the aisle to start building Noah's Ark on stage as part of "Christmas in Reverse." There was significant help from volunteers with costumes, along with playing the piano and other instruments. Some years cookies and lemonade were served afterwards.

We all got to share the joy that the scholars and their families felt when the musical was finally presented. There were solos that gave us goosebumps. It became a tradition to perform it the last afternoon before everyone left for Christmas break. The positive energy that filled the gym – or in later years the Worship Center – was the best way to celebrate Christ's birth and send everyone off for Christmas break.

For years to come, certain songs from the Christmas Musical stayed with us as the scholars requested that we sing them in Chapel. I was thrilled to oblige. "The Perfect Ten" enabled them all to memorize the Ten Commandments, paraphrased appropriately for kids. "Three in One" is a song that explains the Trinity – Father, Son, and Holy Spirit. This was again sung in words that kids can make sense of.

After our new music teacher, Mrs. Ankrum, came onboard she naturally became involved. She agreed to be in charge of the music portion of the musical for the following year. A new tradition of having our families from other countries share their customs in celebrating the birth of Christ was started as she put in the effort of writing a script herself for the musical. This time, it was not a play with characters like we had done in the past.

God's timing for the passing of the baton was again perfect. I had contracted COVID in December of 2020, and had to miss the whole week of school leading up to the musical. Since I had been working one-on-one in my office with a scholar who needed to work on his memorization, he had to be quarantined due to exposure. This was prior to the vaccine and we had strict guidelines to follow even though I had been wearing a mask. Our scholar missed a week of school as well and couldn't take part in the musical. I felt terrible about that. I was no longer in charge and Mrs. Ankrum and Beth did fabulously, even having to divvy up the boy's verses to other scholars.

There were so many highlights from the musicals over the years for me. One of the most meaningful moments has to do with a text that I received on a Friday night when I was gathered with a group of teacher friends from my days at Kalona Elementary, hosted by my friend Emily. Our old teacher friend group were all finally on Christmas Break and took time to gather before family activities took over. As we were just calling it a night, a mom from Faith Academy sent me a short video with a message:

"Omg Mrs. H - I'm laying here in my bed and I hear the boys singing a church song from school and it brought tears to my eyes." Heart emojis.

It was a song we had sung in the musical.

Among the Legos and game controllers, the boys had taken the initiative to find one of the songs that we sang in the musical that day on YouTube and had it playing on their TV and they were all singing along. The mom had been sweet enough to send me a video of it.

Jesus Christ, shine into our night
Drive our dark away
Till Your glory fills our eyes
Jesus Christ, shine into our night
Bind us to Your cross, where we find life
We find life Lord
Still we often go astray
We chase the world, forget Your grace
But You have never failed to bring us back
Reveal the depths of what You've done
The death You died, the vict'ry won
You made a way for us to know Your love

I was able to show the video to my friends and they shared that special moment with me. I was reassured that all of this hard work is so worth it!

I may have never become an official music teacher, but God enabled me to use my musical interests and gifts in a way that honored Him. This happened at a time when many children could showcase their beautiful voices, and their families and other audience members would be moved by their children's expression of joy and love in song and music. His plan is perfect.

CHAPTER 17

BRINGING IN TANAGER

"I know my child — I am his mother. He does not need to have a counselor. He needs to be told what to do and he will do it."

Ten minutes into our meeting, Omari's mother was adamant. She didn't want to have anything to do with what we were suggesting. She did not want Omari (not his real name) to go into counseling brought on by his extreme behavioral issues.

Despite her strong reluctance, I was feeling tense but confident in the task that was ahead of us. Had I not had years of experience communicating with parents as an educator, it would have been a very intimidating setting. Around the table was our highly competent and caring team: Doug, Elder Bernie, Omari's teacher, and both his parents. Fortunately, I felt very comfortable with Omari's father, as he had been to school many times and had even made it a point to thank us for our work with Omari. Most recently, he had been there to take Omari home after another explosive episode where he saw first-hand the behaviors we were discussing with the two of them. As I leaned forward to speak, I wanted to reassure Omari's mother that all of us were on her side and we wanted the best for everyone involved, especially Omari.

"I understand and agree that you know him better than anyone."

Our meeting had opened with prayer from Doug asking for guidance and wisdom as we talked through the next steps on how to best help Omari. He stressed that we were a team all wanting the same positive results.

To set the stage, people around the table recapped recent incidents and the numerous steps taken to keep Omari calm and to prevent such outbursts from happening. All of us could feel the sincerity and concern we had surrounding Omari. His dad nodded his head in agreement as we recalled the most recent outburst he witnessed when he arrived at school. I remember Omari's father looked so exhausted and sad to be talking about his son and the desperate state Omari was currently experiencing. It was clear that Omari's two parents were not on the same page when it came to their son's needs. Several of us reiterated how hard it was to see Omari when he gets overwhelmed and lashes out because he can be such a sweet and encouraging child otherwise. As much as we hadn't wanted it to come to this, though, our staff felt the situation required us to take a bold step, and I spoke up.

"In order for Omari to remain at Faith Academy we need you to allow him to see our therapist. To this point you have not accepted that help. We cannot move forward and continue to have him as one of our scholars if he doesn't do this – his behavior is far too disruptive and it's affecting all of us, including other students. Omari will have to go to another school, unless we are able to use every tool in our tool belt, and that includes our licensed therapist."

There was no immediate response to my statement. I didn't expect instant agreement, but I was somewhat pleased when Omari's mother at least didn't say no.

"Our therapist is in the building now and you can meet her and ask any questions you have. This way, you can be fully informed before making a decision in the next day or two."

Miss Dawn had been standing by in hopes of being able to meet the parents. Once she received the message and came to the meeting, the rest of us left the room so Omari's parents could talk openly with Miss Dawn. I trusted her completely. Dawn was an experienced therapist who knew her trade and put Omari's parents at ease through her professional and caring conversation with them. After thoroughly explaining the packet of paperwork with Omari's parents, they took it home.

All we could do at that point was pray and prepare to accept their decision.

The next morning Omari met me at the door when he arrived for school, stopped on the spot, and started digging in his backpack.

"Mrs. H, they said I can meet with Miss Dawn!" he announced happily as he handed me the folder full of the filled-out papers.

Thank you, Jesus! Oh, I can't wait to tell the others!

All the kids loved Miss Dawn and looked forward to going with her when she picked one of them up from class for their session. They knew they could choose from her shelf of cool toys when they spent time with her as she utilized play therapy. Play therapy is a means of counseling where the child chooses from toys and games to explore feelings, thoughts, behaviors, and experiences through play. It is developmentally appropriate and feels safe for children.

The results with Omari were nothing short of miraculous. Omari grew so much through his interactions with Miss Dawn that his problems began to lessen in short order. Over time the meltdowns subsided. Teachers and other staff were informed of his specific needs and were part of his success plan. Conflicts no longer sent him into a rage as he developed coping strategies and learned emotional regulation. It was a huge win for the child's life. I am grateful we were able to provide the help he needed, especially since we didn't always *have* this resource to offer.

In the fall of 2016, I was starting my second year as the Director of Curriculum and Instruction at Faith Academy. I knew that with all of the stresses associated with teaching in a modern, results-driven environment, classroom management can be an overwhelming issue. While classroom management refers to skills and techniques teachers use to keep students organized, orderly, focused, attentive, and academically productive in class, it is also a very nebulous and loosely defined notion. In particular, potential solutions to behavioral problems are all over the map. Answers vary widely, depending on who is talking.

Despite our challenges, I felt confident about many aspects of Faith Academy. Our growing team was hard-working and dedicated. The families of our scholars were on board with the mission. Our curriculum continued to improve as we honed in on our scholars' needs. Our biggest frustration was dealing with our scholars' disruptive actions. There were too many conflicts among the scholars and too many times when seemingly minor issues blew up into major outbursts. Finding a solution to this problem was among our daily prayer concerns.

While there are many books and theories about how to get students to behave so that they and other students can learn effectively, we desired more than simple compliance during instruction. We were learning as a team from reading a book by Ross Green, *Lost at School*. The central theme was that kids will do well if they have the tools to cope with problems that arise. This is because they generally do not want to behave incorrectly. Just like when we teach math to them, we can't expect the scholars to solve math problems if they have never been taught how – and we wouldn't be upset with them for not knowing. By that same reasoning, we certainly shouldn't get mad at students for not knowing how to conduct themselves in a classroom and in social settings if they never learned how to express what they are feeling in a constructive manner.

As a school staff, teaching children important subject matter was obviously high on our list of goals, but there's much more that we wanted to accomplish. Theodore Roosevelt summed it up well when he said, "People don't care how much you know until they know how much you care." Building relationships with our scholars would always be a top priority. The children who attended Faith Academy knew they had many adults in our building who cared a great deal for them.

Our desire was for school to be a peaceful place for them. We didn't want it to be a place where they were berated by frustrated adults. We wanted to understand their challenging behaviors and the reasons behind them. Using what we learned from Ross Green, our staff worked together diligently to help change our scholars' patterns of behavior. As we began to make progress, it became apparent that many of our scholars would benefit from seeing a counselor on an individual basis.

At that point we were still existing hand-to-mouth financially, so there was no budget for a guidance counselor to be on site. Along with that, even if we had the funding, there were relatively few guidance counselors who had the training and skill required to provide the professional level of assistance many of our scholars needed. Trying my best to find a solution that worked for everyone, I spent time the previous school year researching and making phone calls looking for professional help. I reached out to mental-health departments at the University of Iowa, and to several local therapists I knew had positive reviews.

One great candidate was also a Christian, so her values lined up with what the scholars were learning from us. We felt that match would be ideal. She did us a favor by changing her schedule to get a scholar and her mom in to be seen during a critical situation for a session or two. However, getting to regularly scheduled appointments

25 minutes away was too burdensome. This became a barrier to continuing service, so that didn't work out in the long run.

I also reached out to other social-service agencies who might have professionals who could assist our scholars. As I contacted each of these agencies, I first had to determine if they served children. If they did, I needed to know if they accepted Medicaid. If they met both those criteria, the answer was almost always the same: there was a months-long wait to get an appointment. As had already been shown, it would likely be very difficult for our families to adjust their schedules to get their children to these appointments away from school. Many of our parents work at jobs with hourly pay and missing work to get their child to an appointment meant not being paid for those hours. The type of therapy that was needed takes more than one session to make progress, so the child would require ongoing appointments.

Despite the frustration involved with running into countless obstacles, we continued to look for a solution where our scholars would get the help they need at an affordable cost. It was also important the therapy be conducted on campus so parents wouldn't need to take time off from work to drive children to appointments. Finally, our answer to prayer came in a most unlikely setting — when I was in the chair getting my hair cut!

Ever since my niece, Morgan, earned her degree as a cosmetologist, I had been going to her for my hair. Even though I need to drive almost an hour for hair appointments, it was well worth it. This regular appointment guaranteed a chance to connect with my niece almost monthly. I even followed her through ten salon moves. We have such a close bond, we can jump right into conversations about the deep stuff.

My niece Morgan and I at her sister's wedding reception

I was sitting in her chair in Cedar Rapids when she casually mentioned a program her son was involved in at his school. I soon realized that this revelation regarding a resource that could be used for Faith Academy was a potential game changer. And it was exactly when we were ready for it.

She was talking about the counselor her son was seeing at school. I said curiously, "So you mean the guidance counselor, right?"

"No. The counselor is from Tanager Place in Cedar Rapids. They have a licensed therapist who comes to the school. The one my son has is great for him," she said.

I learned Tanager Place is a human-service agency that serves children. It was only a bit more than 30 minutes north of Faith Academy. I set out to investigate!

Within a week I was sitting around the table in Doug's office with Tonya Hotchkin and her supervisor, both from Tanager Place. They were describing their school-based services and how they worked. The possibility of expanding into the Iowa City area was exciting to them.

A few months after that initial meeting with Tanager, it looked as if we would have our very own therapist in house! Andrew was our first therapist to come on board and help us work out the kinks in this new position. At first, the paperwork associated with getting a child into the program was a major task. Because of our small staff at that point, I took the lead. This onboarding process involved copying, distributing, and following up on the complicated and lengthy forms required. The forms weren't even started until after the initial contact had been made to explain what we were offering.

I would contact the parents in person and carefully formulate my words to communicate that we think their child would benefit from therapy. Knowing that we were offering an opportunity for children to meet with a professional to learn how to deal with their emotions and work through issues felt like we were providing exceptional service. I was ecstatic to finally be able to offer something like this to our families. I also knew it had to be seen by the parents as something that was worthwhile to them, as well.

I realized it could be overwhelming for a parent to hear that our school staff thinks their child needs therapy. I soon learned that reactions varied widely from "Oh good, that would be amazing to have a professional help them develop skills to deal with their emotions," to simply, "No, my child doesn't need that," and everywhere in between.

As teaching professionals, we routinely help children react appropriately to challenging or unfamiliar situations. As we enlisted parents' help in bringing this counseling assistance to their child, we needed to slow down and remember that this can be something the parents had not realized was such a major issue until we brought it to their attention. As a guiding principle, I also wanted us to remember to treat each case with the sensitivity it deserved.

Some parents also held the belief that we are too easy on their children at school. They feel if their children were to just be disciplined, they would do what is right. "They don't do this at home – they know I don't play," summed up the attitude some parents held. Of course, this approach just stressed public behavior and didn't address the root cause for why the child was acting out.

As a part of this process, we soon learned what hot-button words to avoid when talking with parents. For example, we learned to say counseling instead of therapy. We found it was also important to communicate to parents that their child was not the only scholar who was able to benefit from these services. That way they would know their child was not singled out.

In the end, it felt rewarding to be able to offer something truly special to parents to help their children learn skills that would lead to more positive social interactions and self-control. I also created a concise introduction to what the school offered, which included the following:

"Fortunately, we have the privilege of being able to have your child meet with a counselor during the school day, so you won't need to drive them to appointments. There is typically little or no cost to your family as your family's insurance usually covers the portion you would be responsible for. Tanager also accepts Medicaid."

To make this happen the school paid the agency a portion of the therapist's salary. This was a much better deal financially for everyone involved rather than trying to independently hire someone ourselves. And we were also getting many additional benefits in partnering with Tanager. We were given ongoing training for our staff, while Tanager provided supervision and insurance coverage for the therapist. Tanager and their therapists were also easily accessible to work as a team with the scholar's teacher and other staff to benefit the scholar. As part of the counseling services provided, the therapist was also in communication with the scholar's family.

The staff training Tanager provided was eye-opening for our teachers. We had a great deal to learn about new research regarding positive ways to interact with children. We also discovered how critical it was that we were all on the same page with methods and terminology. I was thrilled with the amount of help and knowledge we were getting from our new partnership.

When we took on Tanager Place as our consulting service, we got so much more than we had contracted for. Tonya, the supervisor of the School Based Services program, gave me her cell phone number and more than once she talked me through how to deal with intense problems we were having with a particular student. Much of this happened during the time when we had agreed to a partnership with Tanager, but our first therapist had not yet started. To have an expert guide us through some of our most challenging behavior issues early on was a Godsend.

That following summer we had the privilege of learning about Trauma Informed Care from Tonya and her staff. This new approach was revolutionary. Tonya introduced us to *Help for Billy* by Heather Forbes and we did a book-study on it. This methodology was so successful it became required reading for new staff. It coincided with the book we had been studying the year before, and it was evident that our philosophies matched up.

Later our designated therapist provided ongoing training for our staff. She led round-table discussions personalized to our needs, concerns, and questions. New vocabulary became common lingo among our staff. When a child became upset about something, they were in a condition referred to as their "downstairs brain." This meant they were not thinking rationally, and they needed some time to calm down – to become regulated and move back into their "upstairs brain." The guiding principle behind this distinction is that children cannot be reasoned with or taught when they are in their downstairs brain. It's only after they've calmed down and moved to their upstairs brain that they can react objectively and learn from their experience. The same theory is true for adults. I recall a time or two when I said to a scholar, "I'm in my downstairs brain right now – I'm going to need a bit of time to calm down before I talk to you about this." Humbly modeling our use of the philosophy proved to be a great way to let the scholars know that we were in this together and it was always well received.

The principle that particularly stuck with me is that the chance to make things right will still be available when the child calms down – even if it is tomorrow. There is no need to demand a child apologize when they are still upset about something that happened. It might satisfy the adult, making them feel like the problem has been taken care of, but that insistence will evoke a statement the child does not mean. A child only learns the consequences of their actions when they are able to absorb the lesson we want to teach them. That doesn't happen if a child is too upset to internalize what we're trying to say.

Changing our mindset to this new way of dealing with children took a considerable amount of time and willingness to incorporate. Asking why a child did something was rephrased to asking a child "what's up" or "what's going on" when they were struggling. The simple rephrasing of how we spoke to our scholars significantly changed our interactions with them. We no longer were willing to risk false harmony at the expense of doing the right thing to help the child. In other words, we had to accept the methods we were using and communicate with each other about how we were using them to shape our scholars' actions. This meant we needed to let other staff members know when they were going down the counterproductive path of punitive punishments. We also needed to be vulnerable and willing to admit when we were the ones using an ineffective method. This new way of approaching these situations helped us realize punishment relates to personal suffering, not learning how and why to change an undesirable action.

As might have been anticipated with such a major change to our approach, a few people still had a hard time accepting it was okay if a child didn't obey an adult as soon as they were told to do something. This resistance, of course, wasn't what we wanted, but we were learning not to react as if the child were guilty of the ultimate wrongdoing. Would it go smoother for that child if they *did* what they were asked? Yes. Would the classroom be calmer if everyone did what they were asked? Of course. In varying degrees, schools everywhere have students who walk in every day with a whole lot of baggage that impedes them from being willing and ready to learn. And we knew many of our kids were experiencing trauma in their lives and they were simply trying to seek control in one area of their life by acting out.

Frustratingly enough, one of the people who couldn't quit using the word "obey" was someone who didn't even work at our school. It was one of our volunteers. After all the progress we made as a staff, it was so upsetting for me to witness this. Rather than asking questions of the scholars to understand what may have caused their actions, she continued to use the old-school philosophy of "do what I say because you are a kid". She was continually backing kids into a corner and making them upset — causing them to be in their downstairs brain.

In the end, I felt I needed to stand up for our scholars. I simply could not accept our kids being upset by words the woman said that didn't agree with our philosophy as a school.

I had a conversation with her and invited her to some of our in-service training sessions where we were learning about Trauma Informed Care and other topics. In this way, she would be learning along with us and would be able to interact with kids more positively. Unfortunately, I learned that even though she was there at our training sessions, it didn't mean she agreed with what she was taught, much less put any of it into practice. In the end, her interactions didn't change. It was frustrating and unfortunate. Needless to say, I was relieved when the volunteer did not return the following year.

Our relationship with Tanager Place, the social services agency providing an onsite therapist for Faith Academy, remains intact today. Things are even better now. The whole paperwork process was streamlined and taken on by the therapist. Tanager has provided us with two fabulous women, Laura Greening and Dawn Neff, who have cared for our scholars as well as staff in my time at Faith Academy. We saw them as part of our school family in every way. I respected them and leaned on them heavily for their expertise, especially when confronted with difficult circumstances. They each worked closely with our Family Liaison, Elder Bernie, and the relationship was one of mutual respect and admiration.

When Laura told me she was moving out of state due to her husband's job, I was devastated. She was so upbeat to work with, loved our scholars, and it was clear that they were making positive gains by working with her. She had also become my confidant. In Laura, I had a person who I was able to connect with when I discussed sensitive subjects. I think it helped that I wasn't her supervisor. She was very wise and caring.

Before she left, she guaranteed her replacement would be just as good. I found that hard to believe – but thankfully, it was true. When Dawn came on board it took her minimal time to get the lay of the land and pick things up just where Laura left off. Times were even more challenging for all of us through the pandemic and she was everyone's counselor! Above all else, she served as an advocate for all her scholars always going to bat for them and reminding us of their needs. Dawn is a fun co-worker and is a bulldog when she needs to stand up for what is best for her kids. I found another close friend and confidant in Dawn.

The Tanager team spent countless hours training us, counseling us on how to best work with our scholars, meeting with families, and intervening during times of crisis during the school day. We have witnessed scholars who were unable to get through a single school day without a blow-up become successful. They learned and practiced the skills needed to respond appropriately to conflicts and disappointments through therapy. It took all of us working together to create a safe environment where this learning could be practiced. I often referred to our school as a laboratory where everyone was learning how to interact with each other under the care and supervision of wise, well-trained professionals. We acknowledged we weren't perfect, either. We sought Christ's guidance and lots of ongoing training and prayers.

The changes at our school were amazing – and the work needed to continue. God is the one who brought this game-changing service to Faith Academy. He knew what we were facing at the time and it was evident that He wanted us to be able to help the children and their families. He aligned everything perfectly for us to learn about Tanager Place and the services they offered. And it all started randomly right there with me sitting in Morgan's salon chair! I have learned however, that with God, nothing is random.

CHAPTER 18
CULTURAL COMPETENCY

"*I was weeping for all of history's incredible atrocities against fellow men, which seems to be mankind's greatest flaw....*" Alex Haley, author of *Roots: The Saga of an American Family.*

In 1977, an epic cultural event happened on television. *Roots*, a book written by Alex Haley about a Black family spanning generations, came out on network TV as a mini-series. It dominated the primetime airwaves for eight days, and it received nine Emmy Awards. Keep in mind this was a time when cable TV didn't exist and most people had only three channels, plus the public broadcasting channel – that's it. Even though it premiered at a time when the country had many fewer people than it does now, *Roots* still holds a prominent place as one of the most-watched television series in history.

I was in the sixth grade when as a family we sat together in our living room and were mesmerized as we watched the eight episodes. Watching *Roots* was my introduction to slavery and my memory of it is vivid, as it was told in a very impactful and compelling way.

With the exception of the impression that *Roots* and a couple of other television shows left on me, most of what I know about history I learned as an adult. I was not that intrigued by history when I was in school growing up. Unfortunately, I was not much of a reader as a student, either. For the most part, I only read what I was assigned to complete my classes. I was much more interested in what was going on around me with people. In other words, my focus was on socializing. My life-changing love for reading came later.

The Poisonwood Bible was the first significant book I read of my own choosing. I just made myself stick with it, as it was an Oprah Winfrey Book Club pick. I was determined to complete it so I could have the feeling of accomplishment as I watched the show when Oprah talked about it. My mom and I shared a love of Oprah and would discuss topics after they had been on the show.

While I didn't think that much about Oprah's personal life, my mother had a strong opinion on one thing regarding her. Mom thought Oprah and her longtime romantic partner Stedman Graham should just get married – she didn't like it that they were living together. I think Mom just wanted to be sure I knew that she didn't approve of their arrangement. I subscribed to *O* magazine and would give the copy to Mom as soon as I was done reading it. Once I became a mother, Mom was always recommending different parenting articles or shows that she may have seen in the magazine or elsewhere. After Mom's death, the magazines just piled up in my house and were a reminder of the loss of my confidant and the wonderful friend my mom had become in my adult years.

I learned a lot of things from being a teacher over the years that I may have missed during my own education. When a person teaches about a topic, it requires learning it on a deeper level, which I have benefited greatly from in my chosen profession. As a fifth-grade social studies teacher, I was responsible for teaching U.S. history. Having found textbooks to be dry and unengaging, I wanted to make the learning stick for my students better than it had for me. To do this, I needed a way to make it more interesting to them.

The Waltons and *Little House on the Prairie* were TV series I watched growing up, and this is where I learned about those time periods. They were stories of families and what they went through in an earlier America. *The Waltons* portrayed life in the 1930's and 40's in rural Virginia, and *Little House on the Prairie* was set in the 1870's in Minnesota. Those TV series formed the backdrop for anything I read about that was even remotely close to those time periods. They were the settings I visualized, and it helped me to relate to what was happening. As a teacher, I realized I wasn't the only one who learned that way, so I set out to teach social studies by reading engaging stories with my students or viewing and discussing stories rather than by having them only read a dull textbook. One example of viewing a story was when we watched Disney's *Pocahontas* and sorted out the fact from fiction.

It was during my upper elementary years that my family watched *Roots*. In addition to the powerful story it told, I'm sure it made such a big impact on me because it was in story format. Thinking back, I'm thankful that my mom made watching it a priority for us. The only other time I recall her gathering us in the living room to watch something on TV together was when Billy Graham crusades were on – and I can't say I remember much from those. I can still recall intense scenes from *Roots* as an adult. In teaching, to help my students comprehend what a slave auction was, I used a scene from that series that I found on YouTube all those years later.

Realizing that I could repeat song lyrics verbatim was another way I learned history in elementary school. I reached out to my childhood friend, Shari, to see if she could help me find a resource I was looking for that had made history stick for me. Sure enough, she had a discarded copy of the musical script, *My Country 'Tis of Thee*. It was a musical we performed in fifth grade, and the same show was done every year. Since the oldest kids in the elementary school had the honor of performing it, it was an event we anticipated as we moved through elementary school.

This was not unlike our Christmas musical at Faith Academy, where the older kids were the ones who got the speaking parts. We even sang the songs on our daily bus ride home, so we had them memorized by the time our turn finally arrived. Later in life, I sang the songs, "Going West in a Covered Wagon," "Don't Forget to Dot the 'I' — for the Inventors," and others with my fifth graders. This was another way of providing them with information in a fun way that they might be able to remember.

I also found children's novels set in the time periods that covered the fifth-grade social studies curriculum set by our district. There were so many excellent books we could read that we would not have time for them all. I loved it when my passion for historical fiction would strike a chord with a student and open up a whole new genre for them. I changed up books I read with classes or small groups over the years, but one that I used, *Roll of Thunder Hear My Cry*, by Mildred Taylor, left a lasting impact on me, and my students who read it.

It was set in the 1930's in Mississippi and tells of a Black family who owned the land they lived on, which was not common in that era. The main character is a confident ten-year-old named Cassie. She learns what it is like to grow up in a place where the white people were doing everything possible to not allow any Black family to be successful. When I read about the mistreatment that occurred as seen through the eyes of this intelligent and outspoken young girl, it left an indelible mark on me and my students.

There was one situation where Cassie's grandma forced her to apologize for bumping into a white girl on the sidewalk when it was clearly an accident. The white girl's father made a huge deal out of it and Grandma could see that apologizing was the only way out. The author did a great job of conveying the humiliation felt by Cassie due to the injustice of her own grandma not standing up for her. It was clear her grandmother was used to this demeaning way of life and had just accepted it.

To read this with 10- and 11-year-olds who could easily see the injustice caused emotional reactions from all of us. I learned when emotions are triggered in our brains, our reactions help us store our recollections more effectively, resulting in stronger memories. That is why these stories stick with us – we feel and remember the emotions the characters are experiencing. Reading a textbook rarely evokes the same kind of emotion, making the material easily forgettable.

When I learned *Roll of Thunder Hear My Cry* was recently placed on a list of books banned for racism and explicit language, I was seriously disappointed. As I read the book to my students and I ran across a word that was unacceptable to use in the classroom – the n-word used in historical context – I called it out ahead of time.

"This is not a word that we use. Why do you suppose it might be used in a book that we read at school?"

I can think of a couple other books over the years where I needed to use the same approach, but with different words.

My students understood the author was attempting to be true to the setting and the time period to educate the reader and to make a point about how profoundly unfair and disturbing this was. I would also stress to my students it is still not acceptable for us to use those words. End of discussion. And as for the topic of racism, I know those who do not understand history are doomed to repeat it. Of course, racism is described explicitly in the book – the point is to show how Black people were treated at that time. It helps us to understand the Black plight. If people don't understand the root cause of a problem, how can we ever solve it? These are lived experiences of Black and Brown people in America.

After researching it, I learned that the author of *Roll of Thunder*, a Black woman, wrote the book based on stories she heard growing up. She used to spend time visiting her grandfather's house and it was there she heard these stories. These family stories made a huge impact on her as a child and became the basis for her book.

Much later, after I had been teaching for a number of years, I had a desire to understand history even better myself. Being part of a book club helped to expand my reading selections. It was helpful to discuss books with friends after reading them.

A mechanism I used to enable my students to talk about books they were reading was "Dine and Discuss." It was similar in concept to being part of Book Club. I would select a book and put a sign up on the bulletin board encouraging students to get one of six to eight spots to have lunch with me and we would discuss the selected book. Their only requirement was to read the book. I did nothing more than have them bring their school lunches back to my classroom and we would talk about different elements of the book as we ate together. I would find out if they liked it and if there were questions they had or if they wanted to share any reactions they were having.

I made sure to select books that stretched my students – something they wouldn't just breeze through on their own. My role as an educator was to introduce them to quality literature – and I embraced that. Through my conversations with students, I noticed there were times when students missed crucial points in books such as *The Boy in the Striped Pajamas* or *Out of the Dust*, both historical novels. That motivated me to intentionally discuss what they were reading with my students.

I had forgotten about "Dine and Discuss" until I recently was going through a box of artifacts from my teaching days and was reading letters from the students. Many of them mentioned loving that activity. One even stated, "Because of you I can't put books down!"

Starting at Faith Academy, I knew I would be working closely with Black children, families, and staff members. I wanted to be more aware of different cultural beliefs and values. I wanted to be sensitive and honor our differences as I interacted with the community.

I needed to further develop my cultural competency. One of my favorite sayings about this comes from a presenter on the *Leader in Me* podcast. "When you open a book, you open the mind and the heart of another human being, and you can't help but be changed by the encounter."

Doug had created a list of useful books for us to understand the community we worked with at Faith Academy. I was thrilled to have these recommendations. I wanted to be the best leader I could be in this setting, and I knew this would help. Once I got the list I dug in!

The saying "the more you know, the more you realize you don't know" described my situation when I started reading the books on our professional reading list. I listened to audiobooks on my drive to and from school as well as reading some of the other books recommended to me in my time away from school. I wanted to be able to take part in the discussions we had as a staff, not only because I was interested in the subject, but because I wanted to lead by example.

One book in particular that enlightened my understanding of Black culture in America was *The New Jim Crow: Mass Incarceration in the Age of Colorblindness* by Michelle Alexander.

The New Jim Crow revealed to me how some influential white people had created laws that enabled them to keep Black people at an unfair disadvantage. For example, I had never heard of Redlining, the discriminatory practice that allowed banks to exclude loaning money to residents of certain areas of towns based on the race or ethnicity of the people living in those areas. Redlining was part of a system that made it nearly impossible for most Blacks to own homes. Long-term home ownership is the main way many Americans build wealth.

I also became aware of the mass incarceration of African Americans, and that it had been made possible by discriminatory policies established over the years. Longer sentencing for minor crimes is just one example. Learning that the injustices facing people of color in the 1930's and even earlier, were being continued using a different strategy, was eye opening.

Just because the 13th Amendment was passed making slavery illegal in 1865 and the Civil Rights Act was passed in 1964 prohibiting segregation and racial discrimination, doesn't mean things changed like a switch had been flipped. I learned about systemic racism.

While reading *The Warmth of Other Suns* by Isabel Wilkerson I learned more about The Great Migration. Between 1915 and 1970, millions of Blacks left the South to escape the brutality of Jim Crow laws to find safety, better pay, and more freedom. I thought back to what I learned in the social-studies book I taught from in previous years. It acknowledged this trend, but without giving it the name The Great Migration. The book I taught from simply said workers were needed in the factories up north and that is why many Blacks chose to move out of the South.

It didn't acknowledge that the racial violence Blacks experienced in the South drove them to move away. This persecution even resulted in the brutal death of countless victims. The textbook only described what Blacks were moving toward, without mentioning the misery they wanted to get away from. As I learned the truth, I knew I had inadvertently only been teaching part of the story. I wanted to gather all my former students and share this new awareness with them.

As Maya Angelou is known for saying, "Do the best you can until you know better. When you know better, do better." I will continue to learn and grow all of my life. My desire to improve and be the best I can be will always be part of who I am. This awareness enables me to not beat myself up over things I could have done better, particularly when it comes to my teaching career.

We used our Cultural Competency booklist – the combined list Doug and I felt would be useful for our understanding of Black culture and history — as part of our Staff Professional Development plan every year. In the spring, each staff member would report back on the book they had selected from the list with what they learned and how it affected them. We set aside two sessions and dedicated the 90-minute meetings to learning from each other and open discussion. It was a great exercise – one I looked forward to every year. Many staff members would then take their peers' recommendations when they decided what book they would read next.

We knew these books were not "light reading for enjoyment." Being a predominantly white staff, we knew we had to educate ourselves on the things we almost certainly didn't understand due to our different experiences growing up. I cannot change that I was born into a white family with both a mom and a dad — but I can become more aware of the Black people's plight by seeking to become educated on topics of which there is always more to learn. Reading these profound books was a way to help us begin to understand another person's life experiences.

Even with acknowledging the need for white staff members to be more aware of Black history, implicit bias and all, we did have an incident where a Black parent brought a difficult situation to my attention. She reported that a white teacher had said something she found offensive. My initial response was to thank her for bringing this up to me. I respected her for this as I would much rather she brought it to school where we could deal with it, rather than talking about it only with her friends in the community.

A teacher had referred to "Negro Spirituals" in class and more than one scholar went home and told their parents about use of this phrase, as they were uncomfortable with her using the word "Negro." I knew that the teacher who said it was very aware of social justice issues and had taken the time to educate herself more than many teachers regarding cultural competency. I was confident we were going to be able to work through this by coming together for a conversation. We then arranged for a time to gather all the parties together. Elder Bernie, our family liaison, opened our discussion with prayer.

"Most gracious Master, we thank you — for everyone's willingness today to come together and talk about the hurt that has been experienced. We pray that our time together will be positive and fruitful and that we can learn from each other as we all care about these scholars at Faith Academy. Just guide our conversation. In Your holy and precious name, Amen."

The four of us then had a very honest conversation about what occurred. Elder Bernie and I had already established a relationship through previous interactions with this mom and knew her well, so even though it was uncomfortable to start with, I valued everyone around the table and wanted us to be able to come out stronger on the other side of this conversation. A turning point in the conversation took place when Elder Bernie shared that she had only recently learned the difference between using the phrases African American, Black, and Negro from a book she read from our Cultural Competency booklist. "And I'm Black and didn't realize it!" she shared. We were all able to laugh and lighten the mood.

That eased the tension and we realized we would all need to continue to learn from each other and keep open lines of communication. I had heard Jemar Tisby – a renowned podcast host and author of *The Color of Compromise,* a book on our list — say that "white spaces often valued Black people's presence but not their perspective." I was adamant about that not being the case at Faith Academy. I was so pleased that everyone was willing to meet to discuss the incident from their different points of view, as that is exactly what we preach to our scholars. Our honest and sensitive meeting reinforced the value of talking out our differences.

As we were closing, the teacher let us know there was one more thing she would like to do. She wanted the student to come to the office and hear about how the talk went. By taking this additional step, our scholar would learn that her mom and her teacher had each explained their perceptions about the incident and had reconciled.

YES! Great idea. I'm happy to bring this full circle.

I went and got the child out of class. I could tell she was apprehensive as she knew her mom was having this meeting today. I chatted with her all the way to the office letting her know that we had met and talked through things and that everyone was good. I told her I would let her teacher and her mom explain what they had talked about. Elder Bernie and I left the three of them alone for the conversation. As they finished and the door opened, the mom and the teacher were hugging, and I was overcome with emotion. Our scholar was there to witness this beautiful example of conflict resolution.

I am forever grateful to that parent for being willing to bring this to our attention and come in to talk about it. I am also grateful to that teacher who I knew wanted to do what was right by our scholars and was always seeking to learn.

And to have my remarkable friend Elder Bernie, serving as our Family Liaison, as the one able to facilitate the working relationship between home and school? Especially at a point where race is an issue, and an extra dose of sensitivity is required? Priceless.

CHAPTER 19

RACIAL INJUSTICE

Reading about racial injustice and discrimination is valuable on so many levels. Yet, it's all too easy to compartmentalize those stories as something that happened years ago in a place very different from where we now live. It's easy to tell ourselves we know better and things have improved so much since then. It's rarely that simple, though. Sadly, some ugly events taking place in our country recently gained national attention and revealed that things hadn't improved as much as we once thought. Two experiences during my tenure at Faith Academy stand out as profound examples of racial discrimination as it continues to happen. Worse than that, I can see our relationships with each other aren't nearly as close as they need to be.

One particular morning we were clicking along, enjoying the sun shining in the front windows to the south of our offices at Faith Academy. Our secretary, Doreen, was clearly shaken when she came in and told me that Nia, the woman who worked part-time as our receptionist at school, had been in a car accident and wouldn't be in this morning, or at least not on time if she was able to come at all.

Oh, what a hassle for her – I hope there's not much damage.

Nia was a mom to one of our sixth-grade scholars. I recall Nia brought her daughter Aisha to school for the very first time to visit as a prospective student the week I was subbing in first grade back in 2014. They were living out of state at the time but were planning a move to Iowa City. I remember being impressed with this beautiful little girl who came to hang out with the class to see what it was like. Her mom had a bubbly personality, and it was easy to see that her daughter was her world.

Little Aisha's hair was intricately woven into a new and impressive style, and it was accentuated with a beautiful bow. She was well received by the other kids and the girls especially made a big fuss about her the day she visited. As it turned out, Nia and I would get to know each other extremely well in the following years. First in a teacher-parent relationship as I was Aisha's teacher when she came to Faith Academy as a second grader. In subsequent years, we developed a principal-parent connection. Later, when Nia helped out in the office, we had a boss-employee relationship. We also attended church together, so we knew each other outside of school, too. Both Nia and Aisha had spunky personalities and we always knew where we stood with each of them.

Nia worked in our front office at Faith Academy on a part-time basis for a couple of years. She greeted people with an energetic "Good Mornin'," and the office was always brighter when she was around. Her sense of humor and animated way of talking were endearing to me as I find I connect more easily with people with whom I can laugh. I also knew she was a single mom working on her nursing degree and didn't have much down time, to say the least.

On the day of the car accident, I sent her a quick text letting her know we were glad she wasn't hurt and that I would see her when she got here. I told her to take her time. I saw when she walked through the front door she was not her typical bouncy self. Her demeanor was far more reserved. I came out of my office to see how she was doing and to find out what happened.

After she set down her things, she proceeded to tell Doreen and me about the accident. Nia described how a young girl ran her car into Nia's car at an intersection. There was damage done to both vehicles. When they got out of their cars, Nia could see the girl was young and had no idea how to handle a traffic accident. Nia was concerned about her and asked if she was hurt. They talked and the girl immediately apologized. She told Nia it had been her fault. Nia reassured her and said that it was going to be okay and that everything could be fixed.

Once the police arrived, they wanted to take the girl's story and move through the process as usual. Nia put on her "mom" hat and told the officer the girl had called her mother and that she thought it would be best to wait for the girl's mom to get there. Nia knew that if her daughter Aisha was to find herself in a situation like this someday, she would want to be there with her before statements were taken and things got official. Nia had a big heart that way.

When the mom arrived on the scene, she saw that Nia was Black. Both the mother and the girl who said she was responsible for the accident were white. The mother told her daughter it was not her fault. The mom convinced her daughter to change her story – and all this happened right in front of Nia's eyes.

I couldn't believe what I was hearing – that someone who lives right there in Iowa City would behave like this. Nia had shown the courtesy to ask the police officer to wait for the girl's mother to arrive, as she knew if the roles were reversed, that is the way she would want her daughter to be treated. Doreen and I didn't have adequate words to comfort Nia regarding the injustice that she experienced that morning. We did what we often found ourselves doing at Faith Academy. We stopped and prayed. Doreen prayed a calming prayer, thanking God that no one was hurt, and then asking Him to comfort Nia and to soften the heart of the mom involved.

At the time I was optimistic the truth would eventually prevail, and that the teenage girl would tell her mom what she knew to be true and that Nia could get her car fixed without her insurance company having to pay for repairs.

That was not the case. The girl's mom kept pressing with her story – her lie. Nia was ticketed and her insurance company had to pay. It is one thing to hear a story like this. It is another to know it happened to a person of color whom I loved. I was indignant. I saw this is an example of the way that younger generations are taught to blatantly discriminate based solely on someone's skin color. The daughter originally intended to do the right thing, but learned from her mom that when the other person involved is Black, they deserve to be treated differently. It still sickens me to think of our hard-working, fun-loving Nia being mistreated like this.

I witnessed another incident through the eyes of a Black friend on January 6, 2021. That day, we had to pick up a school van. It wasn't unusual for us to run errands like this during the school day. Even though I wasn't typically involved, no one else was available, and I was happy to get out and about during the workday, especially if it meant spending time with Elder Bernie. In this case, one of our vans needed to be picked up at a trusted local mechanic who did work for us. As I was putting on my coat to take Elder Bernie over to pick up the van, we got ready to leave together. I couldn't help but notice she was not her typical upbeat, joking self.

"Mrs. H – have you heard what is going on at the Capitol?"

"No, I haven't. Doesn't sound good from the look on your face," I cautiously replied. I could tell it was a serious matter to her.

She proceeded to tell me about the insurrection that was taking place at the Capitol building in Washington D.C. It wasn't being referred to as an insurrection yet, but what was happening was so significant that I soon realized it was a major event in the history of our country. I also knew I would always be able to recall where I was when I learned about it, just like people of an older era say they remember where they were when they heard John F. Kennedy had been shot.

When we got into my car, I turned a news channel on. We listened intently. Elder Bernie's mood was anything but light-hearted, so I took special notice. She looked over at me and talked to me directly with a tone of disbelief.

"Mrs. H – if Black people were charging into the Capitol that way they would have been shot by now. You know it. No one has ever treated our Capitol in such a way – at least not Americans! And the guards are just getting pushed aside. Sounds like some have been shot." She was shocked and overwhelmingly sad. (No police or guards were shot, but at least one died later and four other people died as a result of the riots).

My mind immediately went to a scene from years ago when I was in our state capitol in Des Moines on a field trip with our fifth graders from Kalona Elementary. The legislators weren't in session at the time of our visit, and it was a more relaxed tour. As we were listening to our tour guide speak in the Senate, one of our girls sat down in a chair where a senator typically sits when they are working. She was simply taking a seat to listen as the guide was talking. The tour guide glanced over and saw that she was in the chair and came unglued.

"Oh no, no – you can't sit there, that is only for our senators. Get up!"

The tour guide treated the chair as if we were in the Pope's private area at the Vatican or something. I felt bad for our student as she didn't realize it was such a big deal. I made my way over to her and whispered in her ear.

"It's okay, you didn't know. I'm sorry that happened. Now we know."

I told that story, in an abbreviated version, to Elder Bernie to emphasize how unacceptable this outrageous mob at the Capitol was behaving. What I experienced was a trivial event and it had just been at the state level, yet the people involved were so picky about treating our lawmakers' furnishings with such reverence. I couldn't believe that these people in Washington were swarming all over our national Capitol building with the violent level of disrespect that was being reported. Elder Bernie agreed, and as we listened to the news, I could see the hurt in her eyes. What's more, it came to light that the mob wanted to harm people, and not just property.

In the coming weeks and months as I listened to discussions and heard the various points of view on what took place that day, I was glad I had been with Elder Bernie to see the situation through the eyes of my friend who has her own, very different vantage point. It was clear to me the way this group of almost all white people, fueled by misinformation about the 2020 election, was responded to was radically different from the way any group of Blacks had ever been treated during a protest.

I describe these experiences because they were distinct lessons for me. I saw that what I had been reading was not just an academic discussion about something that happened a long time ago in a far different place and time. What was happening now wasn't from a book or a TV series this time. It wasn't even from a news report about current events. I had a front-row seat to my Black friends' experiences of injustice. It confirmed this unfair treatment continues to happen in my lifetime to people I care about, and I am sadly disappointed.

CHAPTER 20

A WEEKEND IN NATURE

As Elder Bernie and I drove up the lane to the retreat lodge at Crooked Creek Christian Camp for our Faith Academy staff retreat, she commented on the surroundings.

"These red barns and beautiful green trees and fields …."

They were pastures to me, but she called them fields, as "pasture" is evidently too rural a term for a city girl like her to know.

"They look like the pictures from the jigsaw puzzles that me and my sister, Pastor Boyer, you know her, put together as kids in the projects – the projects in St. Louis where we grew up. I don't think either one of us actually thought we would see them in real life. It is beautiful out here!"

In the spring of 2016, I knew I was going into a leadership role for the fall and was thinking about our staff needs at Faith Academy. Teaching is a demanding profession, like many others. It is important that we approach our jobs with the understanding of who we are as a team as we acknowledge and respect the reliance we have on each other. When we work as closely with each other as we did, there are going to be times of conflict. It's less likely that we would get upset with someone when we like and understand them. Spending time away from work together is a good way to get to know other team members better.

I felt we needed a bonding and planning experience, and I suggested that we have a summer staff retreat. This would be especially helpful for us because many of our staff are part-time and don't cross paths with each other during the workday. A retreat would enable us all to gather and better understand each other as we plan for the following year. Doug wholeheartedly agreed. We couldn't just keep running one step ahead of things, putting out fires, or "building the airplane as it flies."

It seemed to work best to have the retreat on a weekend at a time when we were all still in town due to Summer School. The first couple of years we held six weeks of morning summer school to provide our scholars with structure, consistency and to keep them engaged in academic skills. It also gave us a chance to implement extra things such as baking, camping, and other extension activities. We later adjusted it to four weeks. Staff liked the idea of a retreat, too, and we were excited to do some reflecting, planning, and bonding.

When Dave and I were youth-group sponsors at First Mennonite Church in the late 1990s, we had our planning retreats at his parents' cabin near their pond, and that worked really well. That property had moved on to the next generation, though, so I needed to think beyond that. Adults required more comfortable accommodations than teenagers. I knew of a Mennonite camp down by Wayland (God's country, where I grew up) that would be the perfect setting for it. It was named Crooked Creek Christian Camp, and we could use the Shepherd's Inn, which was the newest building on the property. The Inn had nine bedrooms and was set among trees with deer and other wildlife. I was excited when I found it was available right when we wanted to hold our retreat.

As we were there in June, it was not yet too hot and outside everything was still green. We spent most of the time getting to know our new staff, sharing dreams for the future of Faith Academy, planning things we wanted to happen in the upcoming year, and just having fun together. Finding out about each other's interests and personal stories was a huge part of the weekend.

We all discovered that Shay, our sixth grade teacher, was a huge nature buff when she brought her own hammock along and slept overnight hanging between the trees outside. The following year, our new first-grade teacher joined Shay in that outdoor adventure. We also discovered how much Elder Bernie did NOT care for the outdoors, except to look at it through the windows. She walked straight from the car to the cabin and back out again the next day. No nature for her. Mr. B and DeDe made a huge Costco run and took care of all our cooking needs.

Some of our time was designated for Bible reading and private devotions. Several people took advantage of being outside to commune with nature in the beautiful setting. We spent time deciding on priorities for various programs, and planning events for the following year.

We played games and laughed so hard my stomach muscles hurt the next day. "One Hop" was Doug's favorite game, and it was obvious that those who had served on The Spot ministry with him were already experienced in it. It was a game that used any available table, a ping pong ball, and whatever objects we found lying around to use for paddles. The competitive ones among us loved it and if Doug didn't win, he always seemed to finish in the top two.

At the Inn, we played One Hop on the screened-in porch and just yelled and laughed as loud as we wanted. There was no shortage of trash talk, either. By that point in the retreat, we were definitely comfortable with each other. We also knew that for miles around, there was no one around to hear. Others chose to politely excuse themselves ahead of the games. Some broke into one-on-one conversations or some went off to bed.

An energetic game of "snaps" at a later staff retreat. Staff members -
Trevor Johnson in the cap, Doug Fern, Brian Scott, Char Jacobson,
Shay Rausch, Elli Kloewer, and Laura Ankrum with her back to us

In subsequent years we always took a personality test to help us
become more self-aware and to better understand our co-workers.
We did the DISC, Myers-Briggs and the Enneagram in different years, but never more than one at a time. DISC stands for
"Dominance-Influence-Steadiness-Conscientious" and is an assessment
used for determining behavioral tendencies. Myers-Briggs is a personality type assessment, and Enneagram is another personality-typing
tool. Each of these can be very useful in giving us insight into why
we behave the way we do, and it also helps us to understand each
other's behaviors. As leaders it was a way to develop our people by
giving them tools to gain clarity and direction to assist with goals
and self-growth.

We took these personality tests ahead of time and then learned
what the scores meant at the retreat – at times having trainers join

us for that portion. We took time to share our results as a group. It was interesting to see who was surprised by the results and who was already aware of their tendencies. We assured everyone that no one type was superior to another. The goal was to enable us to work better together and for us to understand the way people respond differently to the same situation, according to their natural inclinations. While we didn't want it to be used as an excuse for certain behaviors, we did see it as a way to increase our ability to collaborate effectively with our diverse team.

This was a profound experience for me. I remember having some "A-ha moments," particularly as I learned that several team members were typed as the "D" in the DISC assessment. Being assessed as a "D" indicates the person is most comfortable being the driver or dominant personality. People with this personality type tend to be assertive and capable of putting themselves forward boldly. They also tend to be resistant to influence from others. We had three "Ds" on our small team that first year and neither Doug nor I were among them. Knowing this enabled us to better understand interactions among the school staff and to help us guide the team in a productive way.

There were insights I gained from the other assessments as well. Knowing that Shay was an introvert from her Myers-Briggs score enabled me to not stress as much about her being the one teacher who had a classroom that was physically distanced from the rest of the teachers for a couple of years. She was energized by time alone and didn't need to be in the midst of everyone else to be content.

Being aware of enneagram styles guided my leadership as well. It affirmed my inclination to ask one teacher to be a mentor to a new staff member when I found out that she was a "2," indicating she is a person who finds joy in helping others. When I became aware our kitchen supervisor was a "9" enneagram, it raised my level of concern with a situation that commonly took place. Knowing she is a peacemaker who avoids conflict at all costs, I counseled her on phrases to use when it appeared that a staff member was taking unfair advantage of her easy-going personality.

Being a leader in an organization requires being able to affect others' behaviors, keeping the team focused on a goal, and motivating them to achieve it. Understanding a team's communication styles and what drives each of them is crucial to bringing about success. The personality tests we took enlightened us in many ways, as the realization they provided opened doors for more effective interactions. Bringing an awareness to how others might perceive their actions is a huge first step for people who have not had this type of training before.

The activity I looked forward to the most every year at our retreat was a team-building session that Doug led. We began by taking the time to have each person share their story – where they're from, interesting things about their life, and what brought them to Faith Academy. We then were asked to say what we needed from the rest of the staff during the next school year. We wanted to find ways that our team members could help each other.

The answers could be general – "I need you to encourage me to take care of myself as I know I can't run on empty all the time." Or they could be specific: "I need you to pause at my doorway before coming into my office to enable me to finish my thought before we start talking so that I can remember what I was doing when I try to get back to it." The result of this brilliant exercise was we became closer as a team by allowing ourselves to be vulnerable and admitting what we needed from each other. We were also able to operate more effectively day to day.

After each person shared, we would take turns highlighting specific traits or things that the person has done that we appreciated about them. Everyone heard feedback from four to six people before we moved on. It was uplifting for all of us. To this day, I can remember specific things people noticed and appreciated about me and I'm sure other staff remember theirs as well. I found myself making sure I continued to reflect the positive behaviors on which I had been complimented. We wanted to fill each other's buckets at the retreat, as we are in a stressful and important line of work. Of course, our overriding goal was that we wanted to make a positive difference in the lives of the children we teach and their families.

We left the camp with fresh ideas and our priorities aligned for the following school year, which was a satisfying feeling. The retreat was an amazing opportunity to unwind and have a good time as a staff, and the experience brought us closer. I found this kind of event to be life-giving for me and I know it was a highlight for the others as well. Research shows that job satisfaction is highest when the employees have a sense of purpose and belonging. Our weekend retreats certainly made it clear that both of these were a high priority at Faith Academy. These very focused weekends also helped me remember God cares just as much about the people doing the mission as He does about the mission itself.

CHAPTER 21

COMMUNITY

S oon after it started, it became apparent that Faith Academy was more than just a school. It was clear we had a positive impact on those around us, affecting people who didn't even come through our doors. From the beginning, we shared ideas on how to make meaningful connections in the community. Most of them didn't get to the implementation stage because we were primarily focused on "putting out fires" in our initial stages of becoming a school. And then of course Covid-19 put a halt to all outside interactions, including field trips.

One community project did come to fruition, though, and it was highly successful. Elsa, a mom of one of our scholars, worked at Legacy Senior Living, located not far from Faith Academy in Iowa City. Their staff had been challenged by the center's Activities Director to present ideas for their residents to interact with people from the community. Elsa immediately thought of Faith Academy.

"Wouldn't it be amazing if Faith Academy brought some of the scholars in to do something with the residents? Is that something you would consider?" she asked me over the phone.

I was excited as I gave my energetic response.

"This is the exact kind of thing that has been on my heart for a while now – it just hadn't gotten to the top of my list yet. Thanks for asking! Yes — we can definitely work something out!"

We selected the third-grade class to serve as the pilot class. We got permission from all the parents and made a plan. Mandy, the third-grade teacher, and I decided upon some songs from Chapel that we thought the scholars sang well and then we let the scholars choose which ones they wanted. They narrowed it down to three songs. I accompanied them on the piano in Chapel and I wanted to go along to the senior center anyway, so it worked out perfectly.

I drove the class and their teacher to the facility in our newest van on a frigid day in February of 2019. The kids were super excited on the way over and had a lot to say. Once inside, they were more tentative but did a great job following directions and were a little more comfortable once they were greeted by Elsa's familiar face, as they recognized her as the mom of one of our scholars. I remember it was easy to detect which scholars were used to being around older people and which of them were uncomfortable in this new setting.

As we were moving the piano up front in the meeting room at the nursing home so that I could lead the scholars in singing, I felt like I recognized the resident with a beautiful smile sitting in the front row. It suddenly clicked. She had been one of my professors at the University of Iowa when I worked on my Reading Endorsement in the early 2000s. Dr. Fielding was someone I admired for being very smart, articulate, and also a sharp dresser.

I remembered trying to earn favor with her when she called me up front in a large lecture hall to ask me to share the method I used to hold Reading Conferences with fourth-grade students when I taught in Ankeny. She had learned about it from reading one of my journal entries for her class. Her course was one of the only times I took a class as a grad student that was a mix of graduate and undergraduate students. Because it was so large, I was a bit nervous.

I distinctly remember this was the first time I experienced using an Elmo projector – the instrument that would eventually replace the overhead projector that often left the side of a teacher's hand all blue from the Vis-a-vis pen. It was a welcome advancement. I easily slid the paper under the projector for everyone in the hall to read from. Feeling honored that she wanted me to present my strategies, I remember how I appreciated her kindness and understanding as she asked me clarifying questions, was encouraging, and treated me with respect in front of everyone.

A flood of emotion came over me as I realized this was *that* professor. I wanted to be able to share all that I had done in education since the last time I saw her. I knew she would be interested and I'm sure would have found the whole premise of Faith Academy intriguing. But it soon became clear to me this was not the way things would develop as she sat there that day. It was apparent that she was failing cognitively – perhaps she had Alzheimer's. She seemed to be completely fine physically. The difference in how she appeared sitting there and the vibrant professor I remembered was a stark contrast. It didn't seem that long ago at the time, but I calculated later that it had been around 18 years.

That experience spoke to me how the playing field all levels out toward the end of life. Despite her extraordinary career where she impacted so many of us in inspiring ways, she simply blended in with everyone else at the senior center, appearing to be just like all the other residents she was sitting among.

I glanced up at one of the nursing assistants and commented, "I'm pretty sure I know her – was she a professor at the U?"

"Do you hear that, Linda? This lady knows you from the university!" the caregiver lovingly informed her.

Dr. Fielding responded politely – smiling and nodding. But nothing she said indicated that she understood that I recognized her from her prestigious role as a professor from the College of Education.

I bet our scholars will see her as just another "old person,".

I wanted to stop everything and explain to everyone that this is a precious person who has her own, very impressive story – which I knew only a fraction of.

In this way, I realized there is a parallel to an elementary school, where every child has his or her own story, is precious and deserves to be valued. I remember acknowledging another parallel when my dad was living in the nursing home at Wayland and my siblings and I went in for a "care conference" where we discussed the progress and shared concerns we had about Dad. It was eerily similar to parent-teacher conferences I conducted.

But it was time to sing, and I had to pull it together.

Focus.

Our plan was to sing two songs, share a Bible verse the scholars had memorized, sing one more song, and recite our declaration – the five verses that they committed to memory and said as a school every day in Chapel.

As we were sharing the last song, our scholars sang the very moving words from Chris Tomlin's *Good, Good Father.*

Oh, and I've seen many searching for answers far and wide
But I know we're all searching for answers only You provide
'Cause You know just what we need before we say a word
You're a good, good Father
It's who You are, it's who You are, it's who You are
And I'm loved by You
It's who I am, it's who I am, it's who I am

I had to stop singing and just focus on my piano playing because I got choked up. It's not unusual for me to get emotional when I hear kids singing these beautiful words and melodies, but something else tugged at my heart this time.

When I glanced up from the piano, I noticed one of the center's employees standing in the back of the room with tears streaming down her cheeks. She was clearly touched by the beautiful singing that was filling the room from our scholars. I hoped that whatever was going on in her life, like the words the scholars were singing, no matter what she was searching for, she could sense God has the answers, and that she realized there are some solutions only He can provide. My prayer was that this was a meaningful experience for her.

After the singing, our kids presented valentine cards they made for the residents and then spent time reading with them. This was when I saw my former professor kick into gear. I noticed she was more alert and leaned in. She was in her element and her memory of her love of reading and children must have been sparked. This was in her wheelhouse.

Time spent reading with residents of the nursing home – third grade teacher, Mandy DeLange (on the left) – looks on.
My former professor is on the right.

Our scholars are the recipients of so much generosity. All of us realized they would not be attending Faith Academy if it were not for our generous donors. We saw this was a way we could have them take part in giving back to the community. We also saw how we could touch others, many of whom may not even have a connection with the school. And in this case, from the reaction of the employees, to my emotional, thought-provoking reaction to my former professor, I knew it wasn't only the residents who were blessed.

Everyone involved was pleased with how our visit to the nursing facility played out. Our scholars got a lot of affirmation from the residents and staff as we were putting on our coats to leave.

"That was awesome ..."

"Please come again ..."

I had the mother of one of the scholars tell me the next time I saw her that her son couldn't stop talking about the visit that evening at home.

"He felt like the old people really enjoyed the visit from them. I could tell he was quite pleased about the way his class helped someone else."

We were hoping to arrange another visit the following year, but our outings came to a halt due to Covid.

Intergenerational interactions benefit both sides. It was clear that it brightened the residents' days to have all this young energy come in to sing and interact with them. It was good for our scholars to see that everything doesn't have to be about them, that they can give of their time to uplift someone else's day. My hope is that a relationship with a senior-living facility can be rekindled at Faith Academy – and that this could spark an inspiration for a similar relationship elsewhere.

CHAPTER 22

It's Hard to Hate Up Close

"You don't care! You're not my family!"

This was Jaxon's response to me when I talked with him about why he was in my office (his name and all the children's names in this chapter are not their real names). It was clear he was upset, but to hear that cutting comment hurt me.

I have known Jaxon for several years now. The love I have shown and the "benefits of the doubt" I have given him have been huge. And this is how he responds to me?

We gave him time to cool off. At that point, I decided it would be smart to call his grandmother. When I reached her on the phone, I explained we were just calling her to let her know what was going on with him that day. I also emphasized we were partners in doing what is best for our children.

I had learned that it was always better to get ahead of stories going home rather than have the child's potentially one-sided perspective being the first thing told to parents. Plus, with siblings in the building, any incidents at school would be talked about at home, whether or not they were trying to get their brother in or out of trouble. We wanted to be the first to describe what happened.

"I'll be right over," she declared as she hung up the phone.

I knew Jaxon's grandmother hadn't been in the best of health, so I was concerned. It was not my intention to interrupt her day and have her expend her energy in walking over to school.

We were in my office discussing what happened when I let her know the specific comment Jaxon had made. I reiterated that he wasn't in trouble for it, of course. I just thought it was worth mentioning, as it revealed that he was either seeing or creating a disconnect from what we intended. Grandma immediately spoke up. She was upset.

"Stop, right there. Jaxon, look at me. She is your family. These people – Pastor Doug, Elder Bernie, Mrs. H – they are your family. They are my family, too. They care about us so much – believe that – they all want what is best for you. **They are helping you.**"

Jaxon looked at her. He looked at me. And then he looked down. I could tell it was soaking in. He respected Grandma. He loved her. I also knew Jaxon enjoyed spending time at his grandma's house. It was a loving environment, and he knew what to expect when he was there.

Jaxon's attitude took a positive turn after that day. When we had conversations with him, he responded much more quickly without getting as angry as he had in the past. Knowing that we had the support of his grandmother carried a lot of weight with him.

This same lovely woman gave a testimonial for Faith Academy at one of our open houses. She shared that it was when her grandkids started attending our school that she came back to her faith and started living for Jesus. Her life had been changed from that point forward. Hers was another uplifting story where the effects of Faith Academy are broader than simply what we teach the children who are enrolled. Her story brought me and several other staff members to tears as we had no idea her experience had been so profound.

On another occasion, there was a dad who for several years had a strong desire for his son to attend Faith Academy. His ex-wife had primary custody of their son and would not agree to having him enroll at Faith. Once they had experienced online learning at a different school for an entire year in 2020-21, the bottom dropped out for their son, Jeremiah. He refused to turn his camera on during Zoom meetings and was essentially making no progress in school. He was at a low point emotionally as well. When his father first called to see if we were accepting new students, his words were inspiring to me.

"I've seen what you do with kids – it's just incredible."

Because they were concerned with Jeremiah's lack of progress, his mom was now willing to explore the possibility of enrolling him at Faith Academy. She came for a tour with her son and older daughter. You could tell the siblings were tight and it appeared that his sister wanted to check out the school for herself. I connected easily with Jeremiah's mom – she was a teacher at a public school and was pleasant to work with. She knew her son very well and when we were back in my office after the tour, she started sharing some of his struggles with school. The older daughter felt a sense of uneasiness with this discussion and asked if it would be okay if they went to play in the gym. I immediately agreed.

Why hadn't I suggested that?! What an intuitive girl.

I didn't know what Jeremiah's mom was going to say at our meeting, but I tried my best for kids not to hear adults talk negatively about them in their presence. I had a feeling that the boy was angry and suspicious of adults he didn't know. As we talked, I discovered that was all true, according to his mom.

From the things his mother was telling me, we had every reason to not accept his enrollment. Jeremiah already had an Individual Education Plan (IEP) in place at the public school he had been attending, had behavioral issues, and only had one grade of elementary school left. Allowing a high-needs kid to join our class at that late juncture could be very problematic.

His mother finally agreed to his enrollment at Faith Academy, and his dad was elated when he found out it was going to work for Jeremiah to come to school with us. Jeremiah settled in at Faith Academy, but I could still feel he was suspicious of us. He definitely kept his guard up. It soon became apparent he was willing to retreat into standoff mode to protect himself. He wouldn't even eat lunch. This was not the first time I'd experienced this – medications can cause kids to not have an appetite.

Elder Bernie was his van driver and intentionally picked Jeremiah up first so that he wouldn't be home alone after his mom left for work. She played praise and worship music on the route and remembered which songs he liked best and wanted to listen to on the way to school. Making sure his day started off on a good note was part of her strategy as a social worker. Some days that required her to have one-on-one conversations with him and some days it just meant listening to uplifting music.

One day early in the school year, I was called outside from our handheld radio to help Jeremiah at recess. He had become very angry at what he saw as an injustice when he was reminded of the rules of the game he was playing. The staff member present was concerned about his and the other scholars' safety as she could not give Jeremiah the individual counsel that was needed and supervise the other children as well. His reaction was not fitting to what happened – it was clear he was behaving as if he felt personally threatened.

As I talked with him, I could see his anger escalating more and his disrespectful language amping up. I just calmly stayed present to assist in de-escalating the situation. It was tense, as I didn't know which direction this was going to take. Jeremiah paced back and forth, keeping me in sight out of the corner of his eye. Eventually he decided he would comply with what had initially been asked of him regarding the game. Staying calm and present with Jeremiah that day was key. Thankfully, his behavior changed gradually as the school year progressed. I never saw that level of anger from him again. I know his classroom teacher still saw his anger now and then, as she was the one who spent more time with him. But his protective shell was beginning to melt away.

Jeremiah started asking questions – thoughtful questions after Chapel and Bible time in his classroom. He was leaning in when Doug taught during Chapel. Jeremiah soon would state, even without being asked, that Chapel was his favorite part of the day. His mom was reporting that he was a different kid. He was helping around the house. She hadn't seen this side of him in years. Most important, he was actually happy. He felt successful and like he belonged at our school. This is among the most rewarding and dramatic changes of any scholar during my time at Faith Academy. As I think back on my experience, I'm pleased that all of us at school played an important role in helping him along.

I'd like to say that it was smooth sailing from then on, but I know Jeremiah had challenges after he left. Our hope is that he will remember that feeling of peace and contentment he had the year he attended Faith Academy and know that it was the presence of God in his life that made the difference.

Children are often forced to deal with big changes in their lives, and it is our job as educators to help them however we can. Right before another scholar, Noah, came to Faith Academy, he had recently moved in with his dad for the first time. His mom was no longer able to be his primary caregiver because she had to serve time in prison. I could tell his dad was new to the role of being a parent. It also was obvious to us that he was trying to do the right thing for Noah, and he cared about him. They discovered the school because the dad's younger brother lived in our neighborhood and had some friends whose siblings came to Faith Academy.

The newly assigned caregiver brought his son to visit our school to see what they thought of it and if there was an opening for Noah. They were tentative around each other and were both polite. We realized this probably wasn't unusual because they were pretty much strangers. It didn't appear the boy had much enthusiasm for school. When we told them there was room for him and that we would be happy to have him join us, Dad was elated. He even hugged every one of us as we were leaving that meeting. That was the day our relationship with their family began.

We had our ups and downs with Noah over the next four years. It became evident in the last semester of his final year with us that things were falling apart. When a child knows a big change is coming up, such as being done with our school and moving to someplace new, that can be stressful for them. In those situations, they often will unconsciously deal with it in an unhealthy way. We were concerned that was the case with Noah. We wanted him to be able to graduate with his sixth-grade classmates. Graduation was a big deal at Faith Academy.

For Noah to complete his schoolwork and graduate with his class, it came down to an ultimatum. We felt we needed to be clear that if he complied with several requirements that we laid out, such as following his teacher's directions without disrupting the class and turning in specific assignments, he would be able to graduate with his class. Otherwise, he wouldn't complete the requirements to move on to middle school. We hated to put it in these terms, but this was after all of us went the extra mile to make things work for him. He had to be willing to take some ownership.

Annnnnnd... he didn't do it.

As a result, he missed the last week of school and did not graduate with his class or take part in the ceremony and festivities surrounding graduation. We were heartbroken. It wasn't the first time something like this had happened, nor was it to be the last. As a staff, we were getting better at "letting go of the ski rope," rather than being dragged around and allowing a mouthful of lake water to be taken in. We had a problem with continuing to allow ourselves to be pulled around by the ski boat – letting students and sometimes parents manipulate us for longer than we should – long after we had fallen down. We were learning to admit when we were not having success with a situation and moving on.

This was a time when we felt like laying out reasonable expectations and holding the scholar accountable was an appropriate balance. He had to hold up his end of the bargain. However, we didn't want him to think that we gave up on him, either. When kids have challenging behavior, they often get too many negative messages in our society, and we wanted him to know he was important to us.

Noah still needed to complete the requirements of sixth grade to move on to the public junior high school that was within the boundaries of where he lived. During the summer when kindergarten through fifth grade were attending summer school, Noah's teacher Shay drove to his house to drop off and pick up assignments every couple of days. After several weeks, Noah finally completed all his schoolwork. On a Tuesday after the school year was over, Elder Bernie contacted Noah's dad to see if it was okay if we went over to his house and presented his son with his diploma.

"You bet!"

His father was excited, but he wouldn't be able to leave work and come home. So, the three of us — Elder Bernie, Shay, and I – left school together and drove to Noah's apartment. We knocked on the door and he came out. Noah had the most awkward look on his face, even though he had been told we were coming. Seeing his teacher outside of school is weird enough, but to have all three of us show up at his door was well out of the ordinary.

We did some catching up small talk and then got right to it. I hummed "Pomp and Circumstance" for the occasion and we each said something positive and encouraging specifically about him. This was similar to what we would do the following year for our "Graduation on the Go" during the pandemic. He grinned and his beautiful eyes sparkled. One of us handed him his diploma with a grandiose gesture and we all shook his hand. Before we left, Elder Bernie asked us to focus for a moment.

"Noah, we're going to pray for you before we leave."

I remember right about then a couple of guys walked by. This was kind of humorous because I'm sure they were thinking "What in the world have we here?!"

We were standing under the stairs outside his apartment, beside the grassy area which had grown bare from the kids playing on it. We stood in a circle as we each took turns praying for Noah and his life moving forward. We also thanked God that we had the privilege of having Noah at our school. He gave each of us a hug, told us thank you and went back inside his apartment. The three of us walked to the car in silence. When we got in the car, I know at least a couple of us let the tears flow.

Just as we took it upon ourselves to hold a graduation ceremony outside a scholar's home, we also provided transportation when needed to carry out an educational plan for our scholars.

In the early stages of our school, we didn't have a system worked out with the public school system to transport kids where they received special-education services. After getting permission from the parents, this required me to take two scholars over to Alexander Elementary four days a week for their sessions. I would stay at the school and find a quiet spot where I could work from my laptop.

It was then that a new family across the street from Faith Academy started attending our school with a kindergartener and a second grader. The older boy joined the carpool over to Alexander to fulfill the requirements of his Individual Education Plan already in place. I loved the chance to chat with the boys, even though I had to plan my schedule around it every day. We were able to work out a time that was most efficient for their Faith Academy class schedule. We were also fortunate to be working with Chris Gibson and her Special Education teachers at Alexander. They made our scholars feel welcome, and their secretary called them by name when they entered each day.

One day Xavier noticed a new bracelet I was wearing and complimented it. I had just returned from a trip to Florida where my good friend had given it to me, so I was telling him about it. Xavier lit up.

"Ah... a best friend. Nothing like a best friend – I got me one of those!"

Like the other boy I transported, Xavier had a heart of gold. By the time he was in fifth grade, other staff members and eventually ICCSD took care of the transportation piece. While I missed the special connection with the boys, it made more sense for me not to be tied down to that schedule.

It was early in the school year when his sixth-grade teacher let me know that Xavier was having a particularly difficult time in class. The way he was interrupting and distracting others had escalated to an unacceptable point. I pulled him into the library when I saw him in the hall lined up for PE class. I asked him what was up. I told him I had been hearing things about his negative behavior and I said that wasn't the Xavier I knew. He was all tough and did not admit to doing anything wrong at first. Then he melted and spilled the beans.

"What *is* wrong?! Why can't I be that good Xavier like I used to be in second grade?! I know – it's that new kid. He has interrupted our mojo."

I laughed out loud. This new kid that he was talking about was quiet and highly intelligent. But Xavier was serious. There was something about the new kid that just rubbed Xavier the wrong way, and he was letting it show by displaying disruptive behavior.

It reminded me of when my son was at his first daycare with only two other kids. They played so nicely together and were just comfortable with each other. Then the sitter accepted Eric, a new boy. It wasn't long before we started hearing about Dylan not being nice to Eric. Dylan was almost two and little Eric was younger than him. One Friday after school I went to pick up Dylan. I sat down to chat with Lois, our day-care provider, when it happened. Eric had gone to the front door and pulled himself up to look outside. Dylan tottered over there and proceeded to pull him down and moved him out of the way. *What the heck?!* I guess Eric had messed with their mojo!

I realized that when a group of people – even kids – have been together for a while they often reach a place of contentment, and their personalities click. Adding a new person to that comfortable mix can be upsetting. Xavier's feelings of displacement were legitimate, and it was evident that he needed help navigating them.

Xavier and I talked about how to deal with his new feelings. Together we came up with ways to adjust his actions. He also had support from others on staff that helped him learn to work with his emotions.

Another advantage we had at Faith Academy was that even if families moved to a different place in town, the kids were still able to continue at our school. Typically, a move for the parents would mean a change of schools from one elementary school to a new one within the boundaries of their new residence. There was a time, after Xavier had been attending Faith Academy for a couple of years, when his family moved across town. There was a fear that he would have to give up the consistency and adult relationships that had been critical to his success by moving to another school, as he could no longer walk to ours. Thankfully we had room for him on one of our van routes that picked up scholars from all over town. To remain in a setting that is consistent and nurturing is beneficial to the lives of children. We were thrilled to be able to sustain that consistency for him and many others.

These boys I had the privilege of knowing all had different personalities and different stories, and they – along with so many others at Faith Academy – hold a special place in my heart.

These were not the first minority children I had grown to love in my years as an educator. However, when I was working in Des Moines, the occurrence of hate crimes, where a victim is targeted because of their membership in a certain group, wasn't on my radar. Once I arrived at Faith Academy, I realized those crimes had been happening all along. They were just not being recorded and publicized like they are now.

The events that played out on television and were a constant presence in our news media seemed much closer to home as the intensity rose in 2020.

CHAPTER 23

MAKING OUR WORLD
A BIT SMALLER

I watched the images on my iPhone screen as I took in the horror of what had just happened in Minneapolis. I saw George Floyd, a young Black man, being slowly asphyxiated by the hard-faced police officer with his knee on Floyd's neck. Floyd was crying out – even asking for his mom as he lay immobilized face-down on the ground. This cruel murder hit me particularly hard since one of our boys at Faith Academy had similar physical features and I realized he could look just like George when he grows up.

As time went on during my years at Faith Academy, I had a new fear, especially as the boys at my school grew older. I was afraid that someone would not know them, not know their open and loving hearts, and just react to them when they saw the color of their skin. In their innocence, they could be shot like Trayvon Martin, or beaten to death like George Floyd. Just looking at their exterior without knowing their soft boyish hearts, they might appear to be tough. Someone might assume they fit *their* stereotype of a young Black thug. The term "adultification" has been created to specifically describe the racial bias in which some people perceive Black children as older and less innocent than white children,

As I was making gains in cultural competency, I learned about "The Talk" that Black parents feel compelled to have with their sons. It refers to the conversation where parents inform their Black children, particularly boys, that they face a danger that white children typically do not. The Talk addresses the danger that Black children might be treated in an unjust or possibly violent way by authority figures, law enforcement, or other people who see themselves as self-righteous vigilantes. More specifically, The Talk describes what Black children should do to keep themselves safe. They are taught critical survival do's and don'ts.

"If you are pulled over, keep your hands where they can be seen at all times, and never make movements without stating what you are going to do first."

It saddens me that this needs to be communicated to males of color, especially now that I think of our boys who are well on their way to becoming young men. I also know it is hard to hate once we've been up close to someone. I am grateful beyond measure that my life has been expanded to include people who are Black, Asian, Muslim, poor, disabled, or immigrants who only speak English as their second language. I am grateful for knowing these individuals because I have learned to love people from these groups who are different from me and what I grew up with. I know they are worthy of love and am aware of the importance of not placing a blanket judgment on people because of their race, ethnicity, or other appearance.

After 9/11, it was tempting to group all Middle Easterners as potentially being extremist members of al-Qaeda. I never imagined I would become good friends with an Iraqi immigrant woman in our small southeastern Iowa town of about 2,500. Here was another opportunity for me to learn. The situation was so unusual, there was an article about us in the *New York Times* on January 2, 2008.

When I was a teacher at Kalona Elementary, I was part of a federal grant that involved teaching Arabic to our students. It was life-changing for me as I met and became great friends with Zahra from Iraq. I learned about life from her perspective. Our goal was to hire a native Arabic speaker as our teacher, and we were able to accomplish that because of our proximity to the University of Iowa. Zahra's husband was a doctor at the University Hospitals.

From left: Me, Zahra Al-Alattar our Arabic Teacher,
Susie Swartzendruber - teacher at Kalona Elementary and
Program Administrator

Unfortunately, my son had already moved on to junior high by the time the Arabic program came to fruition; otherwise, he would have benefited from it as well. I had some of my materials in the back seat of our SUV when I picked up Dylan and a friend of his after football practice one day. His friend took a look at the brochure on the car seat as he moved it out of the way. He glanced at it and matter-of-factly stated, "Glad I didn't have to learn any of that dang 'A-ray-bic'...."

"And that, my friend, is exactly why we are bringing this dang 'A-ray-bic' to Kalona!" I responded to him.

Dylan knew how serious I was. We needed this kind of cultural exposure to help expand the minds of our kids at Kalona Elementary.

Our staff benefited from this program in immeasurable ways. Zahra was a fun and outgoing woman who became a valuable part of our staff. She was in her early 40's, had two young children, and her mother lived with her family in Iowa City. In addition to teaching our students to speak and even write the language, she shared personal stories from growing up in Iraq. She came to the United States at the age of 24 as a refugee from Iraq as she and her family escaped Saddam Hussein's brutal dictatorship.

Hearing her tell the students how one of our most basic rights – freedom of speech — was not granted in her home country, it was clear she was willing to risk everything to come live in the United States. Her gregarious personality made it easy for us to become friends. I particularly remember one evening when she invited us all into her home for a gathering. Her mother made some delicious Middle Eastern food for us. She cooked for us more than once, with stuffed grape leaves being among my favorite dishes.

The attack on the World Trade Center on September 11th was only five years behind us when our Arabic program started. I am thankful we had the opportunity to meet this fascinating and gracious Muslim woman, as we realized that she was much more similar to us than she was different.

Zahra and I in 2015 after she had moved to Kansas City

She explained this to us in simple terms "Just like most groups of people — there are good ones and there are bad ones."

I also realized she had just as much disdain for the group of terrorists who crashed into the Twin Towers as we did.

Part of the grant to provide for an Arabic program included symposiums our school staff could take part in. These took place during the summer months for three consecutive years in New York City, New Orleans, and San Francisco, with all expenses paid. This type of expenses-paid trip hardly *ever* happens in the field of education. In addition to the knowledge gained through the various workshops and travel experiences arranged through the symposiums, there were other benefits as well. Many teachers gained the courage to travel on their own, which enriched their lives and the lives of their students due to sharing their experiences. I again think of the quote by Oliver Wendell Holmes, "Man's mind, stretched to a new idea will never go back to its original dimension."

Expanding the minds of educators through travel and other experiences, as what evolved through our Arabic Grant, will always benefit the students who participate in them. I felt fortunate to be a teacher at the time this expansive project was happening at Kalona Elementary.

This political cartoon appeared in the Iowa City Press Citizen in 2007 when the editorial staff became aware of our foreign language program taking place amid Amish country.

I am grateful I have had the opportunity to expand my limited view, something I didn't even realize I needed before I participated. I have also embraced watching movies and reading books that gave me the chance to experience life through the lens of a person different from me. It is from looking through that lens that helps us all to develop empathy.

In this lifelong learning experience, I have come to realize having empathy would help solve many of our most intractable problems, from the smallest issues to our biggest challenges. Empathy enables us to appreciate others and develop positive relationships with them, whether we interact in our personal lives or in the workplace. It even helps us understand those we're just meeting. We develop a much better understanding and appreciation for others when we see things from their point of view and put ourselves in their situation.

CHAPTER 24

A TIME TO WEEP, A TIME TO HEAL

O ne of the joys I treasured in my role as an educator was the opportunity to become close to my students, especially when that meant supporting them and their families through painful and sometimes tragic times. Some of our scholars stayed with us for all their elementary school years and some were only with us for a time. I was always sad when scholars would leave. The year after I taught second grade there was a mom who was going to pull her kids from our school because of some inaccurate information she received. I remember Doug texting me when I was attending a math conference out of town.

When I received Doug's text telling me about the family potentially pulling out, I couldn't focus for the rest of that session. As soon as the session was finished, I made a beeline for an out-of-the-way place in the conference center to talk in private. I remember feeling nearly sick to my stomach about the fact that one of our families would choose to go to another school after the progress their children had made with us. We had worked so hard to build a strong relationship with them that year.

This just can't be – they have to stay. I can't imagine them leaving.

This family did end up staying – Doug was able to clarify the misinformation the mother had received. But I will never forget that feeling of desperation I had, not wanting them to go elsewhere. I realized later that I was a bit over the top about it.

I never liked it when a family left Faith Academy, but I later came to terms with the fact there are going to be times when scholars do not continue with us, no matter what the reason. I acknowledged to myself that we need to do the absolute best we can with them during the time they are under our watch and in our care. It doesn't matter whether they have been with us for one year or seven.

One year we had a family move to North Liberty – a suburb outside of the transportation route that we reached. They would have to bring her to school if they wanted her to keep coming and that was not possible for their family. So, their daughter Grace was no longer able to attend Faith Academy. I was disappointed to hear that she wasn't going to be with us the next year, as I felt she had been making gains in both academic and behavioral areas. She was gone for a couple of years, but then fortunately moved back to Iowa City. When she returned to Faith Academy, she brought her younger brother and sister with her, as they were now old enough to attend school.

Grace had matured and was much more responsible, having two younger siblings along with her at our school. The younger sister, Katy, loved to sing and was enjoying our daily Chapel immensely.

We were all so glad to have another chance with Grace and were enjoying getting to know her sister and brother. Katy had a raspy voice and big brown eyes and always took a special interest in people. She noticed everything. One day she was being tended to in the office by Doreen, our secretary/nurse. She had an injury requiring an ice pack when she saw me come in. Even though she was just recovering from her injury, Katy looked up at me and lovingly said, "You're a good singer, don't ever forget that!"

She was referring to me singing in Chapel. I had noticed she participated enthusiastically while singing in Chapel, so it was obvious she loved it. Katy willingly spread praise on others – it was part of her nature. She would often compliment me on my accessories or on my hair or physical things she would notice. I would do the same to her, but I would follow up with "but it is what is in your heart that matters." It's important to me to let girls know they are valued for more important things than their outward appearance and beauty. Their little brother was also making new friends and finding his place at Faith Academy among his classmates.

When we got the news that their new baby sister had died from Sudden Infant Death syndrome at the age of four months, we were crushed for them.

The funeral was held in October, 2019 at our school, which also served as the East Campus of Parkview Church.

Grace and Katy showed up in beautiful matching outfits of cream and gold, and there was an open little casket up front with baby Gia. The family was milling about, which was unusual from what I had experienced. The funerals I was used to, had the families hidden away in another room in the back, but that was not the case this time. Grace looked like the preteen she was, but with an unfortunate new maturity level. I realized that happens when a child experiences a premature death in her life that causes her to grow up faster than she needs to.

The service was touching. A friend of the mother's flew in from Arizona to sing. She was beautiful and had a powerful voice as she sang touching songs at the funeral. There wasn't a dry eye in the place.

At the end of the service Pastor Doug announced there would be one last time to walk by and view the casket for those who wanted to. To view a small child who has died suddenly is emotional under any circumstances, and some of our staff opted out and just remained at their seats, choosing to leave the service from there. I wanted to participate. I walked by the body of this beautiful four-month-old in her frilly cream dress in the miniature casket and then I found myself face-to-face with the family. I hugged the kids of course and the parents, as I walked slowly along with the line of mourners. This funeral was one of the saddest occasions I had experienced.

When the kids came back to school it was a challenge to keep them engaged and allow them to be comfortable so that they could try to just be kids. Our dear Katy spent a lot of time crying and we loved her as best we could. The one downside to having had the funeral at East Campus was that it was the same space we used every day for Chapel at Faith Academy. It seemed to hit Katy especially hard when we were singing in that space during Chapel. For many of our young staff, it was a first-time experience and so we talked it through every step of the way. Thankfully we had a pastor, social worker, and counselor among us.

On one occasion, a scholar came up to Grace and asked something about her baby sister. A staff member saw this and reprimanded her for making Grace feel uncomfortable. I approached the girl later that day and just asked what her questions were. It was apparent she didn't know how to approach a peer who had lost a baby sister, and she had questions. The staff member who let me know about it was pretty upset with the girl – and I get it. It was painful and awkward for Grace.

I have learned that kids want to do the right thing when they know what that is. If our young scholar knew how to ask her question in a socially acceptable way she would have. It is our job to help the kids in the best way we can. And giving them the training or information that they need to do that is a must.

218

I feel it was God's divine intervention that brought this family back to Faith Academy that year. With the tragedy they endured, I was grateful that we were able to help lighten their burden. Being there for the kids and providing a church for the services had to help make a terrible situation a bit more bearable. Our staff provided meals for their family for a couple of weeks, and I know church people supported them in other ways as well. We walked alongside them for the following year.

Much later, at the end of the next year, I ran into Katy when she was coming out of the girls' restroom. It was just me and her in the hall.

"You sure seem happy," I said to her.

She looked up at me with her big brown eyes. "I'm feeling so proud," were her exact words.

"Let me guess," I responded, matching her tone of enthusiasm. "Your award?"

"Yes!" she blurted out.

And we both said it at the same time — "The sweet soul award!"

I put my hands square on her shoulders and looked right at her.

"That is so appropriate for you. Mrs. Shawver sure picked the perfect way to describe you and your best trait."

Starting in 2016, we liked to acknowledge our scholars individually at the end of the year school-wide assembly – rather than honoring more routine things like perfect attendance. Teachers came up with awards that included one word of vision or encouragement to honor that scholar.

Two other examples were:

Damiyah won the resilience award – she has grown and now recovers quickly from setbacks and is ready to move on even after facing something hard.

Atarion won the integrity award – he has displayed the ability to do the right thing even when no one is there to check on him.

219

Because this became a yearly ritual, we started to keep a record so that scholars wouldn't be getting an award focused on the same word year after year. It was evident that this tradition was something scholars found meaningful as I heard conversations about it beyond the one I had with Katy. Pointing out positive traits that we observe in children is a great practice. Building people up with words is something I always strive to do.

Once in a while, a scholar would build me up with words. That is the way I knew I had made a special connection with Jasmine, another one of our wonderful scholars at Faith Academy.

"Mrs. H – you make me feel like I can do anything! Love, Sweet Jasmine"

She always signed things that way — Sweet Jasmine.

Receiving this note from Jasmine was the first time it was made clear that the two of us had a special connection. Her whole class was writing notes as assigned by Mrs. Stoltzfus, their teacher. As a combination of a writing activity and showing appreciation, they could choose whoever they wanted to write to.

I had worked with Jasmine on memorizing her lines for the first Christmas musical that we put on in 2016. DeDe and I picked mostly third graders for the speaking roles, as they were the oldest class at the time. Noticing Jasmine's exuberance during Music class, Miss DeDe thought that she would feel comfortable in front of an audience and could handle having a part.

Jasmine would come to my office at times and I would set aside what I was doing and we would get out the script with her parts highlighted. Seldom did she sit on the cushioned bench that I had, as sitting required her to be too still. I would sit and she would pace back and forth as she worked on memorizing her lines. This was common among future actors who graced my office for musical practice over the years.

Her mom made a special request of me one summer.

"Hey, Mrs. H – Jasmine doesn't want to miss summer school next week and we are going to be staying in Chicago past the weekend. Would it be okay if she spent a few days with you?"

If there's any kid I wouldn't mind having around it would be her.

I did have one caveat, though.

"Well – we're going to move our son into his apartment in Des Moines on Saturday, so we won't really be around. She would need to come with us."

"Oh – she's up for going along wherever!"

Something I gained from our families was how willing many of them were to take care of other people's kids.

This phone call took place while I sat in my car outside Faith Academy.

"Sure. We'd love to have Jasmine hang with us."

So there we were – all five of us moving Dylan into his downtown apartment in Des Moines: Dave, Dylan, Jenna, Jasmine, and me. Jasmine's presence helped keep it light and none of us got grouchy with each other – moving typically has a way of bringing out stressful responses. Dylan was moving from Ankeny, a smaller town north of Des Moines, to more of an urban professional setting in a downtown loft. Jasmine's favorite part was pushing the cart supplied for people who were moving their belongings in. The original Terrazzo floors didn't slow her down any, but the narrow hallways maybe should have. Dylan tried to keep his cool in front of us.

After we were back home, Jasmine went to church the next day with us at East Campus, which wasn't new as we sometimes picked her up to go with us anyway. Jasmine and I had built a special bond. We still keep in touch today.

While she was attending Faith Academy an ongoing occurrence of physical abuse came to light in Jasmine's family that had lasting effects on all of them. Doug and I had the privilege of being able to help as we walked through it carefully and compassionately with them. God guided us every step and we became closer as a result. As in many times before, I could see God's hand in the timing of it all. We were grateful that this precious family had close relationships with all of us and we could be there to support them when this tragedy emerged.

Each of these stories include times where we were able to minister to families going through deeply painful experiences. I am grateful for God's timing that it was a season where they could benefit from our Faith Academy family walking alongside them, and that we could play a role in their healing.

CHAPTER 25

A TIME TO LAUGH

Doug could not stop laughing as he came into my office to tell me about the inspector's report. I can still see him attempting to talk and then leaning over with laughter again and again. I couldn't help but laugh as well … but I was really curious what was going on and what he had to tell me.

Earlier that week I was helping with serving lunch. We didn't have the number of people needed to do the job so I jumped in. I don't remember if we were short on volunteers or if it was our actual staff who were missing that day. Ultimately, I was needed all the way through cleaning up. After wiping down all the tables where the scholars eat, I was taught that we are to spray a fine mist of Clorox water on them and allow the tables to air dry. This clean-up procedure is part of the regulations required by the state.

As I was finishing up that task, I noticed that the spray bottle was close to empty. A feeling of guilt gnawed on me to fill it up. It was the same guilt I felt when Dave and I were living in an apartment in our first years of marriage and were sharing washers and dryers with the whole complex. In that situation, my guilt required me to empty the lint trap when I was done. I wanted to leave it clean for the next person even though I found that most other tenants did not do the same.

So rather than go back to my office, I had paused to help out in the cafeteria, and decided I would fill the bottle. I looked around for the bleach. Searched all over and finally found it in the closet next to the chapel that houses the janitor bucket and mop. I took the bleach to the kitchen to complete the task of filling up the water/bleach solution.

I am being so helpful! And no one would have known that I was the last person to use it, but this is the right thing to do.

I mixed part water and part bleach, screwed back on the sprayer, wiped off the bottle, placed it under the sink in the kitchen, and put the bleach back where I found it. Mission accomplished.

On with my day.

I don't remember doing it, but I must have shared my good deed of the day with Doug. He knew I had been the one to refill the bottle.

The Health Inspectors dropped by for a surprise inspection of our kitchen a few days later. This was an unannounced visit and as luck would have it the person normally in charge of the kitchen was absent from school that day. It was very nerve-racking as the inspector moved from place to place with her clipboard taking note of different details in our kitchen. One of our staff hung around in case she had any questions. It was reported to me that she was very stoic during the process, as inspectors often are. At the end of her inspection, she relayed her final report verbally to Doug and let him know that the official written report would be sent to us later via email.

"So how did we do? Did she threaten to shut us down?" I asked Doug jokingly. Yet, I was anxious to hear the report.

I knew that we have had people go through the "ServeSafe" training and we were conscientious about following the codes. But still, it concerned me that our kitchen manager wasn't there that day. What if something was misplaced or left in a way she wouldn't have done?

This is when the laughter started. I was sitting at my desk and stayed there when Doug came into my office.

He managed to get out the words indicating that we passed. After that, every time he tried to speak he couldn't stop laughing.

"We only got dinged in one area…"

More uncontrollable laughter.

"… The bleach water."

"WHAT?! You're joking," I blurted out. Doug is timely with his delivery, and I figured this was one of those times when he was pulling my leg.

"No … I'm not. She had one of those test strips with her and dunked it into the bottle under the sink."

"No way!"

Doug went on to explain that there is a certain proportion that the bleach water is supposed to be. And ours had too much bleach in it.

"… And I didn't measure it – I just dumped it in! So much for *me* being a helper."

Pretty soon Doreen came over to see what the ongoing laughter was about. She enjoyed the story just as much as we did. The laughter continued.

And the lesson all of us learned on that day was that Mrs. H should stay out of the kitchen.

Reactions to a game we played at our staff Christmas party in 2017 –
spouses and significant others enjoyed the evening as well.
From left: Natalie Fern, Dave Hochstetler, me, Ariel Perez, and
Blaine Thompson - husband of first-grade teacher.

We shared many heavy and serious moments at Faith Academy, so it was important to keep it light when we could. This is why I wanted to tell just a few of the moments of laughter that we shared which kept us enjoying ourselves day to day. Laughing increases the brain's release of endorphins and lowers a person's stress.

Another humorous event took place in that same kitchen a year later. Dave and I were in our car on our way home from Iowa City on a Saturday evening when I received a call from Ronnie on my cell phone. Ronnie was a 30-year-old man in charge of programming for the Spot — one of the programs that shares our space at Faith Academy. He had arrived with a group of guys to set up for a retreat they were having the next day.

While they were there Keontae, one of his kids, ran into the kitchen to get something. Pretty soon he turned around and was running out of the kitchen screaming, "There's something alive in there! Something is coming out of that box."

Ronnie ran to see what he was talking about. He put his hand on the lid of the box he was yelling about and felt it being nudged up – something was definitely moving around inside of the box. Of course, this freaked him out as it wasn't anything he would expect in our kitchen.

His first reaction? Call Mrs. H.

"Mrs. H!!," Ronnie screeched into the phone, "There is something in the kitchen. I don't know what it is. I think you guys have rats!!"

Then he yelled at someone who was with him.

"Don't let 'em get out!"

I tried to remain calm and asked him where he was and what was happening. It was rather hard to understand what he was saying with all the pandemonium in the background. I actually got a kick out of the fact that whatever was happening, he thought I could do something about it.

I must not have satisfied him because he called Elder Bernie next.

Ronnie finally took matters into his own hand. He and Keontae grabbed the container and threw the "rats" outside —- and ran.

Turns out they had walked in on a portion of the third grade science kit. The crawfish had arrived that afternoon from the FedEx driver. Rather than interrupt during class and have the scholars go crazy with their reactions to the crustaceans, the office staff decided to store them temporarily in the kitchen.

The teacher's plan was to tell the scholars all about the crawfish and the part they were going to play in the Science unit. Then, she would bring the crawfish into class the next day. However, on

227

Monday there was only one that remained alive after all the trauma and cold temperatures they endured following the "rat emergency." The remaining survivor was saved by Zach Fern, Doug's son. He was always up for rescuing or at least investigating animals of any kind. I learned that about him during our trip to Belize, where there were many opportunities for animal exploration. Someone told Zach about it when he came around after school. He went straight to the crime scene where the crawfish were last seen and was able to rescue the one remaining crawfish. New ones had already been ordered, so he got to take that one home with him. At least there was one happy person at the end of the whole debacle!

Kids innocently say funny things all the time. When we had funnies like that we would share at our Circle Up time in the morning.

One scholar asked our third grade teacher why Mr. Fern has been talking about the Dollar Tree for several days now in Chapel. She was perplexed — and then it hit her.

"Idolatry! Oh no, he wasn't talking about the Dollar Tree ... I can see how they sound alike but that is something much different."

She proceeded to clearly explain what idolatry is and took the time to break it down to its root word: idol.

That was a good reminder for all of us to slow down and be super explicit when using new vocabulary – and give us a lighthearted laugh as well.

Another funny comment came after a field trip to the Pumpkin Patch the year I was teaching second grade. We were writing an experience story together and I was taking ideas from the scholars as they sat on the carpet in front of me. One particular scholar named Simone spoke up.

Simone: "Oh yah, and the dog Bingo!"

Mrs. H: "Did you hear one of the owners call him that or how did you know that was his name?"

Simone (in an insistent tone): "There was a farmer had a dog and Bingo was his name-O."

Made perfect sense to her! That was one of those times when I wished another adult had been in the room so they could enjoy the moment with me.

Our Christmas party held in February of 2020 —
a face-off question during a round of Family Feud
From left: Doug Fern, Jenna Hochstetler, and
Matt DeLange, husband of our third-grade teacher

While we were serious about our mission at Faith Academy, I also wanted to tell just a few of the moments of laughter we shared that kept us enjoying ourselves day to day. Our ability and willingness to laugh together as a staff reinforced our connections with each other and brought a greater sense of unity. I believe we were more resilient during the hard times because of our positive environment. A critical part of keeping things positive was supporting each other, which included frequent laughter together.

CHAPTER 26

SINGING ON THE INSIDE

"How was Prison Choir last night, Mrs. H?"
It was Wednesday, and Joni, our second-grade teacher, was asking about an activity I enjoyed that was totally different from my day job. "Prison Choir" was also where I learned far more than I expected. For a couple of years, from 2015-2017, I carpooled with several people to drive almost an hour each way every Tuesday evening during the school year to Mt. Pleasant Correctional Facility, a large men's prison located in the town of Mt. Pleasant.

Because of this experience, I saw how I had been categorizing a group of people based on stereotypes. I also realized I was not looking at prisoners as individuals with the understanding they deserved. This experience inspired me to do all I could to help my scholars become aware of how important it is for them to control their own impulses. They needed to avoid making abrupt or emotional decisions that had negative consequences that might impact them in a life-altering way. We talked about self-control a lot with our scholars.

I became involved in the prison choir through my good friend, Heather (Blosser) Herschberger. She had been directing a choir in the prison for several years. Heather is a childhood church friend, and I ended up teaching next door to her at Kalona Elementary. She was the music teacher there when I taught fifth grade. It was amazing to cross paths like that again, as she spent five years in Rosslyn Academy, a private Christian school in Nairobi, Kenya, early in her teaching career.

Our Bible School class at Sugar Creek - 1971
Front row: Heather Blosser, Pam Wyse, me, Maria Freyenberger
Back row: Shawn Cheney, Ronnie Conrad, Ted Roth, Kevin Wenger

A group of eight to ten of us volunteered every week to spend our evening interacting with inmates who sang in the prison choir. This experience opened my eyes to a hidden segment of our population with which I was completely unfamiliar. Like many of us, I subconsciously grouped all incarcerated people into a category based on negative stereotypes. To that point in my life, I hadn't had a reason to put much thought into this, other than those few times I knew of a student who had a parent in prison.

There was one incident long ago where Mt. Pleasant prison and my students crossed paths. One weekend when Dave and I were visiting my parents in Wayland, I got in their car to find a wrapped gift in the back seat. I was teaching in Des Moines at the time. When I asked Mom what it was for, she explained that she had it in the car so she would remember to drop it off next time they were at church. It was a present for "Project Angel Tree." This was a mission where members of the church could buy a gift for a prisoner to send to their child, so the child knows they are loved and not forgotten about during the Christmas season. This program continues to this day, although I doubt they still have names attached. At that time, though, the label Mom had picked off the tree at church had the name and age of the gift recipient. It was a name I recognized.

Are you kidding me? This kid goes to my school in Des Moines!

When I questioned her further, all Mom knew was that this child's dad was incarcerated in Mt. Pleasant. She had a list of suggestions for gifts, and she had purchased one, wrapped it and was taking it back to church for the organization to pick up and deliver in time for Christmas.

This child was a fifth grader in my school where I taught fourth grade. I had met him when I was supervising the lunch line early in the school year. It was memorable because after chatting with him, I asked him his name, and he answered, "George!"

I thought he was messing with me because of the tone of voice he used and the unlikelihood of a kid that age having a name that was more fit for someone 20 years older than him.

"Yeah, right... What's your real name?"

He promised me that it really was his name. Wanting me to believe him, he added that he was named after his dad.

"So really I'm George Junior."

After finding out that it was indeed his name, I felt bad for doubting him. Afterward, we would joke around when I would run into him in the hallway, and I would call him George the second or King George. Finding out his dad was in prison was eye-opening for me. He was a gregarious kid and since I wasn't his teacher, I had no idea what his story was. It hit home how important missions like Project Angel Tree were. Because of this program, George would get to open a Christmas present from his dad, even though his dad had no ability to shop for and deliver a gift to his son while he was three hours away, in prison.

From that point on, whenever I would see Project Angel Tree set up in our church, I would happily select a tag and go shopping for a person who didn't have the freedom to buy a gift for their child for Christmas.

To participate in Prison Choir, we were required to attend an orientation before we started every year. At the orientation, we learned the "do's and don'ts" of the prison and the reasons for their rules. For example, we were not allowed to wear blue jeans or gray sweatpants, because that is what the inmates wore. Large pieces of jewelry were discouraged, as they would likely set off the metal detector. And we had to insert a quarter in a locker to put our valuables in before going inside. We weren't allowed to take a purse, phone, or a jacket with us, either.

We were also briefed about the expectations surrounding our interactions with the inmates. As this was going on, I remember thinking about the new concept we were learning at school regarding Trauma Informed Care (TIC). TIC is a framework we use for working with people who continue to have negative reactions after exposure to traumatic experiences. I described some specifics in a previous chapter.

As I went through the orientation, I wondered if any of these concepts had made their way into the prison and whether they were being used in interactions with inmates. As the orientation ended,

I still had questions. I asked some questions at that time, and there were a few I thought I might be able to figure out as time went on.

We had a carload from Kalona go to the prison every week and several people from the Wayland area simply met us there. The people from Wayland were mostly from my home church, Sugar Creek. Reconnecting with people I had known forever was an added bonus. I also enjoyed getting to know some new people from both places.

My cousin, Lynette, also participated in this choir, so it was a chance to get to spend time with her as well. A big reason I started on this journey was because I knew some people who participated in Prison Choir and I thought it sounded intriguing. Prior to the fall of 2015, when I began with the Prison Choir, our schedule had been dominated by our kids' high-school activities. Since we were empty nesters, I thought it would be a good time to become engaged in something new and worthwhile.

When my friend Heather, the choir director, saw that everyone coming for the evening was there, we "outsiders" would gather up and go to the prison together. For our first session that fall, I was the only newbie. The others had all been there before and felt comfortable with the routine. I took my cues from others getting checked in, as I put my purse in a locker, showed my ID to the prison guard, and walked through the metal detector. I was very nervous and was anxious to see how this would go. The guard who let us in seemed as if he were trying to find any error possible to slow down our entry. I'm sure he just wanted to be thorough. Sadly, the guard that night seemed to be a bitter person. I usually like to lighten the mood with humor almost anywhere I go, but not in this case. Joking seemed very out of place and I was laying low.

We proceeded through the double-locked doors known as the sally port and I noted them loudly closing behind us as we were escorted down the hall to our designated room. We met the prisoners in a dim, institutional, cold, gray classroom used for Bible studies, church services, and other classes. We could tell these other uses by the posters on the wall. Looking very out of place in this austere, institutional setting was a huge mahogany grand piano.

Interesting – I've always thought it would be fun to have one of those in my home. Wonder how that ended up here?

The "insiders" (inmates) started shuffling in at the same time we were arriving. Lynette was happy to see the men and was calling some of them by name. We were not allowed to have any physical contact – no handshakes. This was something stressed to us in the orientation.

Of course – Why the heck would anyone ever do that?

I felt tense and very ill at ease. I was self-conscious of all my actions. Everyone else seemed super comfortable.

Would I ever feel comfortable here?

The men were mostly wearing denim jeans and gray t-shirts. I noticed some of their glasses were not normal glasses — they were prison issued and looked more like the safety glasses that we had to wear in junior high shop class, where we learned how to work with industrial equipment. The shoes — some slides with tube socks — looked like something my son would wear to and from basketball practice. They were not like the Nikes he wore, though. Others wore plain black sneakers.

The men who were part of our group sat among the prisoners and we women sat together on the other side of the room. We were all connected in a circle.

I never want to be the one who sits by an insider, just let me be comfortable between two people I know.

Heather started the evening with a welcome. I realized she was just as comfortable as I always see her, and I admired her for that.

Man, she's good at this!

It was routine to start each session with a question for everyone in attendance. We would go around and say our names. We gave first names only, and then we answered the question. We gradually got to know these men through their sharing and just casual conversations between songs. Some topics were used to just get us talking. It could be something as simple as asking "hamburgers or hot dogs?" meaning which one do they prefer.

Other questions allowed us to learn things about each other. One I remember in particular was "Have you ever broken a bone?" That led to one insider revealing the reason for him being in prison. He told us he had fallen off a ladder, broken some bones and ended up getting addicted to prescription painkillers. We don't know the details that connected the dots to him serving time, but it started with something that innocent. I remember this experience in particular slowed down my rush to judgment.

Attendance varied among the insiders, but there was a group of them that was pretty consistent. It was voluntary of course, and some were trying choir for the first time in their lives. On the other end of the spectrum, there was one inmate who had been a member of a college choir. As we got to know them better, we wanted them to know they were missed when they didn't join us. This wasn't a requirement or even an expectation. It was just a way we all showed we cared about them. One evening when someone noticed that Kyle (not his real name) was not there, and we asked about him, one of the men said "Oh, Kyle is in the hole."

Solitary confinement? How could that be? He seems so easy-going and positive when he is here with us! What could he have done?

At that point, I realized I no longer saw these guys as I did on that first night. I no longer saw them just as prisoners. I finally saw them as individuals. The man I sang beside once told me how much he misses his daughter, and that he knows her momma is telling her only bad things about him. One guy with long, thinning gray hair told us about his most recent favorite song, "My Church" by Maren Morris. I looked it up later and listened to it that week so I could talk to him about it the following Tuesday evening. He lit up when I told him I listened to it and we were able to talk about the lyrics.

At the end of each semester, there was a concert where each insider could invite a guest from the outside. Other insiders were invited to attend as well. It was very small and casual. The week before the program I heard the funniest conversation between two guys standing next to me.

"Aren't you going to feel kinda funny singing in front of people – like even embarrassed?"

The other man's response was classic. "Dude … We're in prison!"

They both looked at me and laughed. I joined in and we laughed for quite a while.

During the last practice of the year, several of the men took the opportunity to thank us, as we were taking turns sharing, during roll call. I will never forget a comment from one man.

"Thank you for doing this for us. It is the only time all week that I feel normal — like a normal human again."

Wow.

That next year, as I rushed to get down there every week, if there was ever a doubt about the validity of me going, I just thought back to that comment.

One of the men asked why we came — why would we give up our own time every week to come to a prison. No one really jumped out with a response. We weren't really supposed to talk about God, but I found there wasn't really another answer for me.

To answer his question, I casually threw out, "It's God — He wants us to show others love. And singing is fun!"

I've often wondered what happened in the lives of these men who ended up there. Is it that they didn't learn to control their impulses? Is it because the significant adult in their life only spoke negative, harmful things to them and they developed a destructive self-image? Have they been hurt, let down, or abandoned by someone important to them and, as a result, they end up acting out? Is it because the friends they chose helped lead them to make poor choices, because of their negative influence? Did they refuse to back down in a confrontation and do something they regretted?

Of course, I really can't answer those questions without knowing each of them far better than I did. As a result of my experiences, I felt more compelled than ever to continue the important work being done at Faith Academy. We need to help the boys and girls cope with the many challenges they face so that they do not end up making decisions they regret for the rest of their lives. Introducing them to God played a major part in that.

In the end, I also learned and grew from this experience of singing with the inmates in the prison. I learned about how they each have value and deserve to be seen as individuals, not simply be labeled as "them."

In the words of Bryan Stevenson, the founder and Executive Director of the Equal Justice Initiative, a human-rights organization in Montgomery, Alabama, it's so very important for us to realize that "Each of us is more than the worst thing we've ever done."

CHAPTER 27

THE WORLD TURNED UPSIDE DOWN

On the Thursday before Spring Break of 2020, our Title One reading teacher, Char, asked if she could talk to me.

"So, when this pandemic hits here, are we going to follow the same protocol as Iowa City schools? If they close, will we close?"

I honestly thought this was kind of silly when she posed the question. I couldn't really imagine the situation being so dire that we would close our schools. Still, she was asking an important question — and so I responded, thinking at the time that I was speculating about something that was never going to happen.

"Unless we see valid reasons to do something different, it is likely that we will follow their protocol."

Inside, my thoughts were going a mile a minute in the other direction.

There's no way. Does she really think schools are going to close because of this? There's just no way. But I can tell she is seriously stressed so I'll go along with it.

Wow – Char was justified in her concern. Out of an abundance of caution, a phrase that became commonly used during Covid times, the following week we made the decision to cancel our first event. It had been planned for the Friday night leading into Spring Break. We were going to hold a School Fun Night sponsored by our newly organized Parent Boosters. The word "postpone" was used because we thought we would be able to have it in a couple of weeks.

We already held several planning meetings to organize our first ever Parent Booster-sponsored event. A couple of moms were interested in starting a group similar to a Parent Teacher Organization (PTO), and we referred to it as "Parent Boosters." Elder Bernie and I had been meeting with the boosters and a few additional parents and had a "Fun Night" planned for the school, which was to be our first event. The part that was most exciting to me was that some of our alumni who had graduated to junior high school agreed to come to the event to be helpers. Unfortunately, Fun Night and many other school events never came to fruition. Because of our lockdown, we didn't return to classrooms after Spring Break and, as it turned out, not for the rest of that school year.

Of course, I'm referring to the Covid-19 pandemic that became omnipresent in March 2020. The "19" is added to the name as an identifier because the virus was first identified in an outbreak in the city of Wuhan in China in December of 2019. Covid rapidly became a global pandemic caused by a highly contagious coronavirus. There were millions of deaths from the severe respiratory disease, there was no cure, and even in those cases that weren't fatal, the symptoms alone were very unpleasant. I experienced it firsthand – twice. It was no joke. Once before the vaccine and once after. There was also uncertainty about what the long-term effects could be. We had no idea what was about to hit, how long it was going to last, and the way it would turn our world upside down.

Jenna was temporarily living with us while she was studying for her graduate college entrance exams and applying for graduate programs in Industrial Organizational Psychology. She moved out of her apartment in Lakeland, Florida, where she had been working in her field since graduating from Southeastern University in December of 2018.

Her wanting to work part-time during the six months leading up to starting graduate school ended up being a win-win situation. Doug inquired if she would be our physical education (P.E.) teacher at Faith Academy, since ours resigned right before Christmas that year. Jenna is usually up for an adventure, so she accepted the challenge to be our part-time P.E. teacher for the second semester. She is athletic, good with kids, and loves Faith Academy. Knowing it would only be temporary was good for everyone, as I wouldn't want her hiring to be seen as nepotism. After all, I was her supervisor. Having her there every afternoon to really see the inner workings of our school was exciting.

Dave and I returned home right before travel was being discouraged at the beginning of March, 2020. We felt fortunate we had enjoyed a week away in sunny California, visiting his sister, Barb, prior to travel coming to a standstill. Toward the end of Spring Break, Doug and I started communicating on a regular basis about how to handle this pandemic that had become a reality. We did not return to school that following Monday. None of the schools in our area were in session. While it was a scary time, I also was at peace about it knowing that God was in control. I remember having the same feeling when 9/11 happened. As terrible as it was, I was able to remain calm, knowing that ultimately God knew the plan.

We had a Zoom staff meeting on Monday at 1:00 p.m., the day we had all planned on returning from our week-long break. Doug and I touched base in the morning before our staff meeting to pull our thoughts together for a united front. At that point we thought we might miss another week or two and then be back. We felt it was a good chance for us to practice living day to day – at least that is what we told ourselves.

Faith Academy teachers meet on Zoom for the first of many times during the pandemic

Food availability was an issue. I remember the eerie feeling when I went to the Hy-Vee Supermarket close to school and saw shelves that were almost empty. Never in my life had I seen it like this. It seemed like we were in a movie about end times or something. I remember locking eyes with another shopper. "This is weird," I said reluctantly, not knowing if this was a person who would want to chat.

"I know, I can't believe it's like this," he responded through his blue medical-grade face mask that most people were now wearing. Some people thought it was foolish to wear a mask. I would soon see this as just one of the controversial issues that would unnecessarily divide us when we really needed to pull together in the upcoming months.

I had trouble sleeping during this time with so much on my mind. I got into a bad habit of looking at my phone when I woke up in the middle of the night, usually around three in the morning. Everything was happening so fast – I would anxiously flip through different news apps seeking out any new developments regarding Covid, locally or globally. There had also been many funny memes created about Covid, which gave us some comic relief. My favorite one was, "Wait ... has anyone let the Amish know what is going on yet?" This one struck me as so funny that I laughed out loud – and kept laughing. I laughed so much I woke up Dave. He didn't think it was all that funny.

For some people the pandemic meant a break from rushing around to activities and a refreshing chance to hang out at home. This was the case for Doug, as he was always burning the candle at both ends trying to keep up with the demands at Parkview Church, Faith Academy, and as a husband and father to five kids. For others it meant being confined to a small living space with many family members. While some people had the luxury of working from home, others had to physically go to work and run the risk of being exposed to the virus. It seemed like those who suddenly had school-age kids at home 24/7 had the most stress, especially if their job was in an industry where they needed to continue working from home.

Once it became apparent that this was going to last for a while, our biggest concern was for our scholars' well-being. Knowing that many of them rely on us for breakfast and lunch Monday through Friday we wanted to get some needed nutrition to them and, often, to their other family members too.

Our immediate focus at school was to provide food for our scholars. There were a few families who did not participate in the program, but for most it was a lifesaver. As a team we developed an efficient program. We had drop-off hours when people from churches and our community of supporters would bring food to

Faith Academy where a couple of staff members would be there to accept it. Thanks to Collin Bockelman ("Mr. B"), we had developed a partnership with Table to Table – an Iowa City-based nonprofit food distribution organization — prior to Covid striking. Mr. B was "all in" as an employee who took on projects outside of his designated role as Behavior Coach. Being Behavior Coach meant, in addition to supervising lunch and recess, he coached scholars through situations where behaviors had escalated.

He was a jack of all trades, which was a huge asset to our small organization. In addition to helping with fixing things around the school, Mr. B. was a certified chef. Being interested in the food-service industry, he managed to connect us with their services. Table to Table had been in existence since 1996. They collected perfectly good, wholesome food on the verge of going to waste from grocery stores and distributed it through appropriate agencies. Weekly deliveries helped our kitchen coordinator, Juleissa, determine her menu for upcoming lunches. The service had been a blessing to us and, as usual, God's timing was perfect as we were able to utilize it for our families at the onset of Covid.

While everyone was affected by Covid in some way, thankfully there were people on the lookout for how they could help others during this stressful time. Certain items became scarce, such as toilet paper and wet wipes. When we received any of those as donations, we rationed them out like gold in our deliveries to our families. Products were also donated from people who worked at Procter and Gamble in Iowa City. They gave us shampoo, toothpaste, mouthwash, and shaving cream, among other things.

We collected food from our generous community donors on Mondays and Wednesdays. All staff would then come in on Tuesday and Thursdays to sort food and supplies into bags and boxes to be delivered to 35 families. Our problem-solving skills were put to good use in creating this system and working out the kinks as they arose or as a situation changed.

I was also grateful to Trader Joe's, a national grocery store chain that had recently opened a store in Coralville, when they responded positively to a request I made. The manager willingly gave us a large number of their grocery sacks with handles to use as delivery bags when I explained what we were trying to do for our families. The plastic bags that people dropped off were frequently too small and the handles sometimes broke. Trader Joe's bags were the perfect solution.

The willing response from the Trader Joe's manager and his praise for what we were doing for our families made me take pause. The manager was clearly impressed with the way we looked out for our families. Once the idea of providing food to them was brought up, none of us thought twice – we just set out to make it happen. It was nice to be reminded that what we were doing was of such immense help to people we cared about. It was a chance for me to shine the light back on God.

We created labels with the family's names and number of adults and kids per household. The bags needed to be separated by delivery areas around the city by the non-teaching staff. Teachers then added individualized schoolwork and supplies to each scholar's bag.

It was fun working together as a staff to accomplish this – all while "social distancing." Social distancing was a new term that meant staying a minimum of five feet away from each other. We did have a scare when a staff member was exposed to Covid and had to stay isolated at home for 14 days. It raised our concern and tightened our levels of sanitation, as we went through lots of masks and plastic gloves. Some people chose to wear fabric masks, and I had a cool zebra one I wore for a while, until it proved to be uncomfortably warmer than the blue disposable ones. We had some seamstresses in our circle who sewed masks in kid and adult sizes and donated them to the school.

Each session started with a Circle Up time where we gathered in a big, spread-apart circle. We shared updates about our Faith families and sometimes talked about individuals we knew who had become sick. We took time to pray for all of them before we got started with the packing. We loaded the teachers' cars with the deliveries, and they went out to drop off the much-appreciated commodities. The day ended with cleaning-up and saying goodbye.

After they learned what we were doing, Boys and Girls Club staff members came and helped. They wanted to be part of the delivery crew so they could maybe see some of their kids who were also Faith Academy scholars. Since we shared kids, our overlapping made it feel as if Sam, the director of the program, was one of our staff. These wonderful helpers included Sam, his sister, and a variety of other employees who loved our kids.

That was one of the many things that made this Faith Academy effort so very special. People from many entities – Boys and Girls Club included – came through our doors and became embraced as part of our team, whether they meant to or not.

Our relationship with the Boys and Girls Clubs began a couple of years before the pandemic. Doug had established a partnership with the Cedar Rapids branch of Boys and Girls Club to use our facilities to start an afterschool program in Iowa City in 2018. To get the program up and running, they began by inviting children from Faith Academy as part of the program.

The original mission of Boys and Girls Club in the 1800s was simply to give boys who roamed the streets a positive place to spend their time. The Cedar Rapids branch was established in 1993. After getting its start in our building in Iowa City, it is now known as Boys and Girls Club of the Corridor. The Corridor is the nickname for Iowa City, Cedar Rapids, and the smaller towns in between. Their mission is to provide a safe harbor for kids and an opportunity to make positive changes in their lives and the communities in which they live. This enabled us to offer after-school programming to our families until 6:00 p.m. daily at no cost to our families. It was a huge win.

After the decision was made and announced to shut down in-person school, I phoned all the teachers individually. We followed up with a Zoom meeting where we helped each other come up with ways to continue making academic progress with our scholars. I didn't want to mandate one particular platform for the teachers to conduct class, but instead listened to their ideas and supported them as the professionals they are. Some teachers already had platforms where they were communicating with parents. For example, the first-grade teacher used an app called Seesaw and families were already using it efficiently on smartphones and tablets. Other classes had Facebook Groups set up as a way to communicate with parents. Everyone offered help in the areas in which they had expertise.

We created a schedule for the classes to hold their Zoom or Google Meet meetings. To help make it workable for families, we did our best to ensure the classes didn't overlap if there were siblings in them, as many had only one device in the house to use.

Our "special teachers," instructing classes such as Art, Music, and P.E., participated as well – to the extent that was possible. Laura Ankrum, our music teacher, created her own YouTube channel with interactive videos of songs our scholars learned in class. It was quite impressive.

My daughter Jenna, in her role as the Phys Ed teacher, created some videos teaching the scholars some dances, such as the Cha Cha Slide, that they could learn and practice at home to get some exercise. She also recorded a tutorial on "The Cup Song" they had learned in their Cup Stacking unit in P.E. class. The song was made popular from a scene in the recent hit movie *Pitch Perfect*. Separately, Jenna used her information-management skills to create a template for an onboarding slide deck for me to use with new employees. It proved to be an amazing way to have all the information that a new teacher or staff member would need to know housed in one place.

Not everything worked perfectly, though. DeDe, our art teacher, sent home projects a time or two with the materials needed to complete an activity, and while some were enthusiastic about it, overall there wasn't a lot of participation. We discovered that we walked a fine line between providing an expected service and being sensitive to everything on the plate of parents during this turbulent time. We became aware we didn't want to assign students too much.

This segment of a newsletter I sent home in March of 2020 articulates the fine line:

*We **miss** being at school with your children every day. This situation gives us all a chance to practice trusting in God and living one day at a time... While we hope you are able to take advantage of the learning opportunities our teachers have provided, we don't want the things we send out to you to cause undue stress, as we are all dealing with our world being turned upside down. Routine is valuable to all kids, so hopefully you can keep that in mind as you help give structure to their day. Our main concern is that we give you the **support** you need and that we **stay connected** with our scholars.*

Our Title One Reading teachers conducted small-group lessons to keep scholars moving forward in the skills they needed to gain competency in reading skills. Our therapist from Tanager Place, Miss Dawn, continued to meet with scholars for sessions over the phone or via video conference. Consent forms needed to be signed by the parents to switch to teletherapy.

Internet service and devices were additional issues to be dealt with. It would have been best if each of our students would have had a laptop with access to reliable internet. It soon became clear that we needed to concentrate efforts on making sure each family had access to the tools needed for the necessary switch to online learning. We learned that parents' phones were the only devices some scholars had access to that could connect to the internet. The screens were too small and handing them over to their children to use for an hour was not ideal for the parents, either. Again, we pulled together to problem-solve.

Elder Bernie, in her role as Family Liaison, took the lead in investigating which families needed help with reliable internet. Of course, continuing schoolwork was not the primary focus of many families. This was at a time when parents were mainly concerned with keeping their families safe and away from exposure to Covid. Some parents were struggling with maintaining jobs and having safe childcare for their children who were now at home 24/7.

Additionally, we had previously spent time preaching cautionary tales of kids having unsupervised access to the internet. We did this by sending articles home as part of a newsletter or as the topic of our keynote presentation on our Parent Connection Day. Now we were telling them that their children must have access to it and were even delivering devices to their homes that we wanted their kids to use!

Using the many resources she knew about as a licensed Social Worker, Elder Bernie went to work and found ways to get all families set up with the internet. At first, that meant finding common spaces that provided internet service, such as the library. She transported some scholars herself.

When it came to devices, we did not have the resources to start handing out the prized laptops that we shared among the classes. We had painstakingly fundraised to get the limited number that we had at that point.

As we were working through getting our families set up for virtual learning, Sam, the director of the Boys and Girls Club, was happy to help out with some MobyMax devices. The MobyMax was a type of tablet used for accessing the internet. He gave them to us and trusted us to loan them out as needed.

The club had these devices on hand, but they had not set them up for kids to use yet. The MobyMax tablets were not a typical tablet or Chromebook that people were familiar with, so we created step-by-step setup and operating instructions and printed those to go along with the tablets. While we were thrilled to be able to offer these to our scholars, the setup of these devices was a huge learning process. I spent time fielding calls on simply how to sign in.

I found our families to be patient and appreciative as we worked through all these steps together. Thankfully, parents, teachers, staff, and scholars worked together well. Still, everyone on our staff commented about missing our scholars. We deeply cared about them and their well-being. One day as we were going around the circle with prayer concerns prior to our work session starting, our first-grade teacher opened up and shared a very emotional experience.

"You know you guys, this is really getting to me. There I am bringing the bags up to the family's front door, and I see Wendy's little red shoes outside the door on the step. I just started bawling. And I just had to turn around and leave. I miss her and all my scholars so much!" Wendy was one of her sweet first-graders.

Turns out that she was not the only one feeling that way. While we were taking the necessary steps to meet our families' needs met by delivering food and continuing to engage the students academically, we were missing a critical piece of what school is all about for us – the emotional connection between our staff and our scholars. We felt there must be something we can do. Fortunately, a unique idea for connection was right around the corner.

CHAPTER 28

WE MISS OUR PEOPLE

Doug was very concerned. Among all the issues surrounding Faith Academy's response to the Covid emergency, our financial health loomed large. He knew that without our spring banquet, there would be no way we'd be able to meet our yearly budget.

"We can't just skip the banquet. That's our major fundraiser. We're doing everything else over Zoom. Do you think we could pull off having a virtual banquet?"

Coming back after Spring Break the previous five years had always been "go time" to get everything ready for our annual fundraising banquet. It was on the calendar for April 4, 2020, the same day as Parent Connection Day. We needed to work around Spring Break and Easter and didn't want it to get any later in the spring as we needed to know what we were working with financially to make decisions for the following school year. It had been a little problematic in past years to have it that weekend because it was almost always the same evening as the semi-finals of the NCAA Final Four Men's Basketball Tournament. I saw several people who kept checking their phones on the sly to either watch the game or at least check the scores. My husband was one of them. I was pleased that he was willing to come to the banquet and, as long as he wasn't too obvious about it, I didn't mind him checking the scores.

Because of Covid, the NCAA Basketball tournament was actually canceled in 2020. When the cancellation was announced, it was a sad day at our house. Not having March Madness college basketball games to watch was another gut punch to Dave and Dylan. Dylan loves the tournament and takes in as many games as possible. When he was in high school, he would round up every screen in the house that was capable of playing a TV channel and would have them all displayed around the main TV in our living room with the variety of games that were being played at the same time.

There was no concern of a conflict in 2020 — neither the basketball games nor the banquet was held the evening of April 4 due to Covid-19. We decided to go with Doug's suggestion of having the banquet virtually.

With the help of the Parkview Church Tech Team, we held our annual banquet by doing a Live Facebook event at 7:30 p.m. on Thursday, April 23. Churches weren't meeting in person at that point and the idea of gathering for a nice, catered meal like we had the previous five years was out of the question. Instead, the evening only consisted of Doug, Elder Bernie, and me giving presentations, and then showing various videos we recorded. There was always lots of laughter when the three of us were together and that evening was no exception. We hadn't had much occasion to laugh in recent weeks, so it felt good – even refreshing.

There also hadn't been any occasion to get dressed up. When we were up front with Elder Bernie we knew there was no contest about who was going to be the best dressed — it was going to be her. We sat on stools up on stage five feet apart from each other, looking fine, as the crew streamed us on camera in various combinations. On the positive side, the event was easier to coordinate, as it was just the three of us who had to prepare. This was different from having to coordinate the many staff and additional volunteers pulling the evening together and executing it.

My favorite video of the evening was a "Plan B" video. Right before Spring Break I had gathered illustrations from our teachers that our scholars had drawn of the song "Who Am I?" When watching the movie *Overcomer*, the lyrics stood out to me as being meaningful to our scholars.

Who am I that the highest King would welcome me?
I was lost but He brought me in, Oh His love for me
Who the Son sets free, Oh is free indeed
I'm a child of God, Yes I am
Free at last, He has ransomed me
His grace runs deep
While I was a slave to sin
Jesus died for me
Yes, He died for me
I am chosen, not forsaken, I am who You say I am
You are for me not against me, I am who You say I am
In my Father's house
There's a place for me
I'm a child of God
Yes I am

This song soon became one of our scholars' most requested songs to sing in Chapel. My idea was to record the scholars singing and have their drawings on slides that coincided with the lyrics. I provided sheets of paper with one line from the song and we asked the scholars to draw an illustration related to that line. Our teachers, in turn, gave their scholars time to work on this project. I gave the more complicated lyrics to the fourth through sixth grade classes for them to interpret in pictures. The stacks of pictures I collected were on my desk when everyone left for Spring Break, and I was looking forward to seeing what they came up with.

As it turned out there was no time to redo any of the student drawings or ask for those who didn't make the deadline, as we didn't see the scholars again until well after the banquet. We hadn't even taken our all-school picture yet. To my disappointment, that is something permanently missing from our display in the front hallway, and it was one of those things I just had to get over. *It is what it is.*

We decided a modified version of this project was something we could pull together and share at the banquet. After scanning all the pictures digitally, I set out to arrange the slides in an iMovie like I used to make for fifth-grade graduation at Kalona Elementary.

Umm, it's been a while since I've done this. It takes a lot of time. I know there are other people who are good at tech on our team and could finish this in no time.

I got to a certain point in the project and turned it over to Shay, our sixth-grade teacher. She was good at putting together digital movies and I had other things to work on. Shay made it known, early on in her time at Faith Academy, that she was happy to help out with projects outside of her own classroom. I knew that about her and felt a big sense of relief when I was able to turn the video project over to her. Having complete confidence that it would be done on time and that it would be a quality product enabled me to focus on preparing my talk for the banquet and other projects at school related to the Covid situation.

As I watched the finished video for the first time, tears streamed down my cheeks, thinking of the scholars who had drawn each picture. Even though I had seen all the drawings previously, having the music playing in the background sparked strong emotion. There is a link to the video on my author page, www.JansInk.org

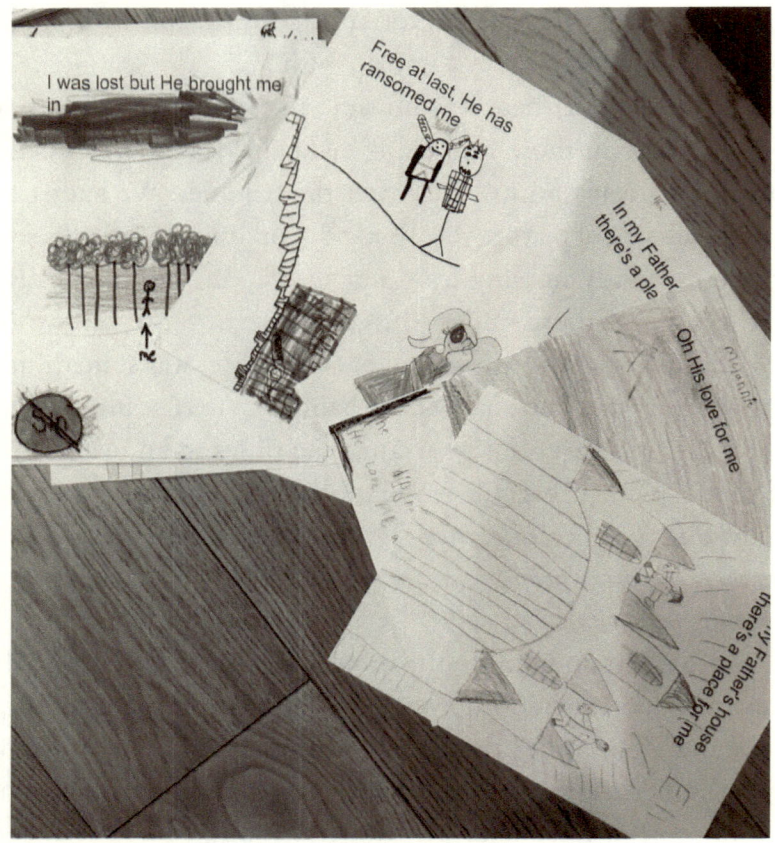

Our scholar's illustrations that were used in the video.

Illustrations included the words "I want Him to save me, I'm sorry." It was followed by a picture of Jesus saying, "Join me!"

Another beautiful drawing went with the lyrics, "In my Father's house, There's a place for me ..." One of our scholars had drawn a picture of a castle that included herself beaming with a smile between two spires of the castle. She was presenting herself as belonging in Jesus' mansion in Heaven.

The slide that was the most striking of all to me was another representation of having a place in our Father's House in Heaven. Again, it was a drawing of an ornate mansion-type castle. This time the words, "Welcome Home" were scrawled on a banner just above the Heavenly Palace.

They do get it!

At a time when everything was so uncertain in our lives, this awareness gave me renewed confidence. This earth is only our temporary home. We should live every day with an eternal perspective. This is the peace we are offering these kids when we share Jesus with them. It is the most important thing we can ever, ever do.

Part of the annual banquet I enjoyed and really missed that night, is being in the same space with a large group of people who care about the ongoing success of Faith Academy. The night has always been a time of celebration and feels so upbeat. I got a bit of that feeling after I got into my car to drive home when we finished. It warmed my heart to see 11 text messages afterwards of encouragement from friends and family who had been watching the banquet live on Facebook. They stretched from family in Wayland and Frytown to friends around Iowa City, Kalona, and Florida! Beth Noeller, my Christmas Musical partner, made me chuckle when she commented that I was "effervescent."

Overall, our Faith Academy community felt fractured by Covid. By March, teachers would have established a close bond with their students and have overcome many obstacles together. When we sent the scholars out the door on Friday, March 13, saying, "Have a great Spring Break!" we had no idea we wouldn't be seeing them again in person for the rest of the school year. School is far more than just an academic environment. This pandemic was a major world event and we wanted to be able to walk alongside our scholars in making sense of it, and talking through how they were feeling about it. As challenging as the circumstances were, we were thankful for the technology that allowed us to see our students on screen several times a week. Even so, we really missed being with them in school. We were scattered all across the city.

The idea of a "Reverse Parade" for Faith Academy was suggested by a teacher as a way to get to see our kids and for them to see us and know that we cared. Our staff would sit outside the school in lawn chairs from 4:30-6:30 p.m. and wave and talk at a safe distance to scholars and their families. The first one of three parades, held on April 9, required coats and blankets – it felt like we were tailgating at an Iowa Hawkeye football game. We used the same procedure as we did for the end of a school day pick up. The scholars' families entered on the street, which was more like an alley, going one way only. As they got closer to us, they rolled down their windows. The joy and the love we shared was amazing. This was the best idea ever. Almost all our families participated.

Once the first car came through, we were energized beyond belief, seeing our scholars and families in person! Several of them made posters and signs.

Getting to share the experience of working at Faith Academy with my daughter Jenna was a bonus that God gifted us. This photo was taken during the first Reverse Parade.

We witnessed one mom start crying. Another family brought ALL their kids with them to the parade – even the older ones who had never attended Faith Academy. A couple of our families decorated their vans. One mom sat along a side street in their vehicle with her kids after they had gone through the parade just to watch everyone else come through. We had treats at the end of the parade for them – just like when people on the firetrucks throw out candy at a parade. The treats changed each time. Ice cream treats, sidewalk chalk and other goodies were among them.

On the final parade of the year, as a good-bye there was a poster addressed to one of our third-grade teachers that read, "Thank you for helping me every day, Miss Delange, I will miss you, (signed) *Messi*"

Mrs. Thompson holds up a sign a family from Faith Academy for our second Reverse Parade. "We stand together – we miss our school, we miss our teachers, we miss our principal, never give up – we miss our school bus driver."

While we didn't get to have any in-depth conversations with our scholars, at least we did get to see them in person. That was heartwarming for both sides. There were some scholars who busted out of their cars and ran to their teachers for hugs. Going home after those parade days, it was safe to say that everyone's buckets were full!

We had one more occasion that we didn't want to overlook. We wanted to properly acknowledge the class of 2020, who would move on to seventh grade and not return to Faith Academy. The previous year, graduation for the sixth graders had been a momentous occasion, as it was our first graduating class ever. Knowing we couldn't gather at the school this year, Doug suggested taking the graduation to them. Elder Bernie reached out to all the families and got the schedule arranged. Juleissa decorated our minibus with a celebratory Ice Cream Truck vibe. Elder Bernie drove it to each of the scholar's homes and had an individual ceremony to honor their time at Faith Academy. We had a procession of vehicles as we needed to, again, distance ourselves from each other when inside the vehicles.

Graduation on the go in June 2020!
From left: Shay Rauch, Jenna Hochstetler, Elder Bernie, Dawn Neff,
Doug, Angel, me, Collin Bockelman (Mr. B), Crystal Johnson. Doreen
Schlabaugh is kneeling (photo by Ariel Perez)

It made it all that more festive to see a line of cars coming up the street honking horns on a Saturday morning. We played Pomp and Circumstance from a speaker as we approached the house. The scholars lit up when they saw everyone that had come to celebrate with them. Many of them had additional family members waiting at their house to witness our Graduation on the Go. Special memories were shared by Doug, their sixth grade teacher Shay, and me. Their diplomas were presented, pictures taken, and Doug prayed over them — all in their front yards or sidewalks. We also left treats for the family. There may have even been some quick hugs that were given. Once more, Mr. B came through with the dry ice to keep the ice cream treats frozen throughout the morning delivery schedule. Again, we accomplished our goal of taking care of our scholars and letting them know they were not forgotten during this time of Covid.

While this makeshift ceremony didn't have the grandeur associated with being held at school amid fancy clothes and helium balloons, they knew they were loved and cared for. It was heartwarming to see we were accomplishing one of our most important missions: that our scholars at Faith Academy feel seen, known, and loved.

We were familiar with what it took for us to operate a school. We just needed to put one foot in front of the other and do what it takes. When it all came to a screeching halt and we were challenged to come up with an entirely different way to meet our mission, there were times when the challenges seemed insurmountable. The Faith Academy team that God had orchestrated into place didn't give up. We benefited from everyone's ideas and all of us showed up to do the work.

I always knew how much I relied on our team, but it soon became even more evident as I had to shift my focus to my family at home and life happening there.

CHAPTER 29

COVID ON THE
HOME FRONT

On Mother's Day of 2020, Dave's phone woke us up at 5:00 in the morning. I could hear Jenna telling her dad that his mom had just passed away. She was the one with her when she took her last breath.

"Are you okay?" Dave caringly asked Jenna.

I sensed it was his way of acknowledging that we would have not expected our daughter to be the one who would be alone with Grandma Marvel when she died — that we knew this was a lot for her. Jenna has never been one to shy away from significant responsibilities, though, even when they were more than someone her age would be expected to take on. Dave told her he would be right there. He woke up his sister Barb and arrived at his mom's place within minutes.

As empty-nesters, Dave and I had moved to a different house in 2018 with a beautiful open view in a rural subdivision where we would enjoy watching the sunsets. It actually had more space than the house the kids had grown up in when we lived in town. I remember saying before Covid happened that I was sorry the kids had never gotten to live there with us. I learned to be careful what I wish for. For six months the four of us once again lived as a family unit in our new house. Even though we dealt with some communication issues during our months of confinement, I loved it.

Dylan had been living in a loft in downtown Des Moines for several years. He worked as a Certified Public Accountant for an accounting firm where he could walk to work through their skywalk system. Due to the pandemic, he was now working from home. As a result of Covid restrictions, his activities in Des Moines were significantly curtailed — no basketball or volleyball leagues or trivia nights at the local establishments. He was feeling penned-in. The final straw was when they closed the fitness center in his building.

"Would it be okay with you if I came and worked from home at your place for a while?" Dylan proposed.

"Of course! We would love that," I immediately answered.

Despite the scary circumstances surrounding our enforced isolation, we were pleased to have both our adult children under our roof. I even took advantage of the situation to apply some parenting advice I heard in recent years – thinking that I had missed the boat. Every night at dinner I made each of us go around and say the high and low points of their day. It was quite insightful, and I was pleased to get the chance to implement this simple routine in my own home. Everyone was held captive and was willing to participate – even Dylan, our minimal talker. We watched Netflix series' together and played family games such as Settlers of Catan and Code Names. Our dog, Mick, who was in his golden years, also got lots of attention, which he loved.

While Dylan, Jenna, and I were all working from home, Dave went into the bank except for the few weeks when it was closed. His work ramped up even more than usual with the Paycheck Protection Program (PPP) loans. Many banks agreed to facilitate these loans as part of the Covid relief funding from the government, and his bank was one of them. This meant gathering all the loan application information needed, and then approving and administering the loans. Making things even more challenging, the rules and procedures associated with these specific loans changed frequently, causing additional stress on Dave and the team he led. This work was in addition to his routine workload. As usual he bent over backwards to help his customers, which often meant working again after dinner until the system shut down and kicked him off at 10:00 p.m.

Once the school's fundraising banquet was over, I felt we could turn to taking care of operating the school and set aside the focus on connecting with our donors. Unfortunately though, things happening in my own home quickly took a front seat. While Dylan and Dave watched the banquet together at home, Jenna watched it with her Grandma Marvel, Dave's mom, from her room in the hospital. Marvel had happily attended every banquet and was always so interested and supportive of everything going on at Faith Academy. It meant a lot to me that my mother-in-law saw the relevance of the work being done at my school.

The day following the banquet, Dave's family, along with Marvel's medical team, made the decision that it was time for Grandma to go into Hospice care. There was nothing left to do for her medically, due to congestive heart failure, so she was dismissed from the hospital. Covid really complicated things in healthcare. We saw for ourselves how our wonderful healthcare workers willingly risked their own health to continue to care for the sick during that stressful period.

If we decided to have Marvel cared for at the local nursing home, we knew the family would not be allowed to spend any time with her – which was hard to imagine for her final days. At the time, nursing home facilities were closed to visitors. Dave knew about that controversial policy firsthand, since he had served on the Board of Directors at the Pleasantview Home nursing facility in Kalona starting in 2015. He continued in that role through the pandemic.

Fortunately, with the addition of a hospital bed, Marvel was able to return home to her duplex, which was part of that nursing home complex. We contracted with Home Instead Senior Care to have a caregiver on site, even though a family member was almost always there as well. All the family was grateful that this was an option.

Dave's sister, Becky, had been the primary person taking responsibility for monitoring Marvel's care. Since Becky had retired, we were all so thankful that she was willing to take Marvel to all her doctor appointments and spend time coordinating all that it involved. Jenna had always been close to her grandma, growing up just down the block from her in Kalona. Becky was happy to have Jenna at home the last several months to spend time with and care for Marvel. She even helped to monitor her medicine, which included giving her insulin for her diabetes. Not many 23-year-olds would be as willing to take on that role as Jenna did. She is close to her Aunt Becky, and they were in regular communication with Dave about Marvel's medical care.

Dave's sister Barb came from California and stayed with us so she could be with her mom during her final days. I was happy to have her there and thankful the weight of the banquet was behind me – again God's timing. Each of us had our workstations set up around the house. Due to all of us being at home, I was even conducting Zoom calls from our bedroom. Those three weeks before Marvel passed were a bit of a blur.

Looking back, I can see the incredible amount of stress placed on Dave during that time. His job alone was overwhelming. He and the rest of the bank management team were working through new policies for Covid, dealing with issues such as in-person versus remote work, and when to open the bank back up. They were also keeping up with the changes associated with the PPP loans, as they worked on implementing those. Additionally, in his board position at the local nursing home, Dave was often pulled into consultations regarding Covid procedures for patients and staff.

On top of all this, he had his adult children and his sister living at our house and his mom in her last days. Regretfully, none of us stopped to think of all *he* had going on. He was the one to calm us down when things were tense. He always played the role of peacemaker in our family. He had no down time. When he got home after his five-minute commute from the bank, we updated him with the details of the day and pulled him right into our pressure cooker. All of this happened with the overhanging fear of someone we love coming down with Covid. It wasn't until a month after Marvel passed that the impact of his overwhelming stress showed up physically for him in an unexpected trip to the doctor that resulted in ongoing treatment for his heart arrhythmia.

When Dave's mother declined and then passed on Mother's Day, we already knew traditional funerals and visitations were not happening during Covid. Marvel was a private person, so a small funeral seemed appropriate for her. The intimate graveside service we held included almost all the elements that she would have wanted, including a recording of the Hallelujah Chorus. The pastor who conducted the service was a close friend of Marvel's, so it was very personal and meaningful.

Both Dylan and Jenna were able to take part in the service, as were two other grandchildren who lived in the Kalona area. Sadly, her five grandchildren who lived out of state were not able to attend. Funerals are a meaningful part of the grieving process and a special time to be together as a family, so their absence was felt. My close friends brought meals to our home during this time. We felt so loved and cared for by Emily, Ruth, Shari, and Maria.

The obituary stated that a public memorial service would be held later. But like a lot of families who intended to hold those services after Covid, it didn't happen. At least it was approaching summer at the time she passed, and we could be outside comfortably. That expanded our living space and enabled some exercise opportunities, which improved everyone's wellbeing.

But summer was when things really heated up for me at school. Up to that point people were being troopers just doing what we needed to do to assist our scholars and their families in getting through this unprecedented time. Once we had to start working on our "Return to Learn Plan," things got intense.

Fortunately, there were exciting things in our family that showed signs of hope for the future as well. Both kids were making arrangements to start their coursework for their master's degrees in the fall.

Jenna was accepted to the school that was her number one choice for her master's program. Dave and I helped her move to Boone, North Carolina in early August to attend Appalachian State. Her graduate program in Industrial Organizational Psychology allowed in-person learning that fall due to the small size of her cohort going through the program together. The 13 of them would attend class together, as long as they masked and agreed to stay away from large gatherings to protect their health and decrease the likelihood of exposure to the Covid virus.

During our time getting Jenna settled in, Dave helped her sell her Camry and buy an SUV that would serve her better in the mountainous terrain of her new home. The used-car dealership would only accept cash for her vehicle. Since we weren't at home with access to our bank, Dave and Jenna made it an adventure going around to different ATMs and withdrawing the maximum limit of cash at each one until they had the amount they needed. Not the usual way of doing business but it was pretty entertaining to see them come up with the stack of cash needed to make the deal.

Dave and Jenna outside Boone, North Carolina - August 2020

She was fortunate to be able to secure an apartment in the lower level of a home owned by a professor and her partner living upstairs. Having a roommate in a smaller apartment was not something she was interested in at this point, so she was happy to find these accommodations. We felt secure about the arrangements as well. It was not easy leaving a daughter in a new town where she knew no one, but seeing her place in a nice wooded residential area was reassuring.

We noticed that everywhere we went in Boone, masks were required, and it appeared that Covid safety precautions were being enforced. People didn't object, either. I appreciated these restrictions as there were places in Iowa where we were looked at unfavorably when wearing masks.

On the other side of the country, Dylan was starting his master's in business administration (MBA) program that September at UCLA's

Anderson School of Management. He had already connected with a group of four other guys in his program to live with. They were able to rent a home in the upscale Bel Air neighborhood of Los Angeles, complete with a pool. The owner conducted interviews first to make sure it was a wise decision to allow them to rent from her. After that, and a substantial deposit, they were set to move in. Unfortunately, I was not able to make the trip to check out his new home due to my school starting. Dave and Dylan took off across the country with Dylan's Jeep Cherokee pulling a U-Haul. Dave flew back after Dylan moved in and explored the area a bit.

Dylan and me at home - 2021

UCLA did not allow any in-person classes even at the master's level. All classes were online. This enabled Dylan and his new group of friends to do some traveling, as they could tune in to classes from anywhere. It evidently was a tradition for students in that particular program to take some trips together – but not to the degree that this group was able to travel. They started by going to Hawaii that September and traveled to 12 different destinations throughout their two years together. Five of them were international trips.

All of this was on Dylan's dime. He had been in the working world and had lived fairly modestly to save up money during the previous five years. He was also awarded a merit-based fellowship to attend UCLA, so his hard work had paid off. He had to take Covid tests before and after travel with each trip. Fortunately, they were provided free of charge on campus.

Of the four of us, even with all that traveling, he was the only one to never contract Covid. It was crazy! We were happy for him, but concerned every time he went on an international trip that he might get stuck somewhere having to stay and quarantine if he tested positive for Covid.

All of this taking place during just a few months that summer seemed hard to take in. With the pandemic shutting everything down, our adult kids living with us, Marvel's death, and decisions about how to proceed at Faith Academy, it seemed like we faced endless changes and adjustments. Then we moved Dylan and Jenna to opposite sides of the country. The highs and lows would continue for the next couple of years. The roller coaster ride had just begun.

CHAPTER 30

RETURN TO LEARN (R2L)

"This has just been so stressful to me," one teacher shared through her face mask. "I have even more concerns about exposure to Covid – I have a compromised immune system and I'm older. I don't know if I should even continue teaching!"

"The thought of being here with kids and having to all be masked up … and if we can't hug them? That's just hard to comprehend." The first-grade teacher's frustrations were clearly showing.

"Thank you for asking how we feel – thinking about how we are going to make this work has been keeping me up at night. Honestly," answered another staff member as she was near tears.

Our Faith Academy teachers and staff shared these comments as we went around the group at our first of several meetings as a Return to Learn (R2L) Committee in the summer of 2020. I started the meeting by going around the circle – where all the desks were at least five feet apart – and asked each person to share how they felt about everything that was going on with Covid.

The Department of Education for the state of Iowa was requiring all schools to submit a plan for Fall 2020 describing how we would proceed teaching students in the midst of a worldwide pandemic.

To create our plan, I felt it was important to hear from each staff member, no matter what position they held, on how this was directly affecting everyone. Fortunately, we were a tight-knit group and respected one another. There had been plenty of stressful situations at Faith Academy over the years, but I realized if ever there was going to be a time of division among us, this was it.

The R2L Committee was one of several that met during the time we didn't have scholars at school due to Covid closure. It was evident that the staff members who chose to serve on this committee were the ones with the strongest feelings surrounding Covid. I thought it would be best to get those feelings out in the open right away, to know what we were dealing with. It proved to be a fruitful exercise. Feeling heard, especially during a traumatic event unlike any we had experienced, meant a lot to people.

Despite the many difficulties we faced, there were also some "silver linings" we took advantage of during Covid. To make positive use of our time away from school I connected with math consultant Amy Keller. Amy was one of our experts – there were several that we built strong relationships with -- from the Grantwood Area Education Agency (AEA), and she led us in professional development throughout the year. I was thrilled to find out she was willing to create a math concepts class catered to our staff and had already gotten approval to teach us under the auspices of professional development.

The focus of her course was an enhanced book study on *Choral Counting & Counting Collections: Transforming the PreK-5 Math Classroom* written by three researchers from UCLA and the University of Washington. The book explored ways in which two routines — Choral Counting and Counting Collections — can transform the elementary math classroom, enhance students' math understanding, and create partnerships with families.

We were excited to take advantage of this opportunity, because the approval for this course meant it would count toward one hour of continuing education for our teachers. In the state of Iowa, five of these continuing education credits are needed for teacher re-licensure every five years. We met via Zoom three days a week to discuss these principles and how we could implement them. That month was an extended time of learning; a bonus for our staff. Ultimately our scholars were the ones who would benefit from the boost in math instruction.

During my teaching career I always found it stimulating to take classes with educators from other districts, whether it be at my local AEA or area colleges or universities. After those sessions I was always fired up to implement new ideas and strategies just learned.

In our case, it was challenging for Faith Academy teachers to take these classes as our summers were shorter than they were for other teachers because we had a summer school program for all scholars, lasting four additional weeks. After summer school was over, we knew teachers needed the remaining time for recharging. Teaching is an admirable and rewarding profession – and it is extremely draining. I've always said that if you are a teacher, or married to a teacher, you get it.

Before Covid, I had been contemplating a plan to enable teachers to take a summer off on a rotating basis, but with everything else going on, I hadn't fleshed that out yet. Once we made the decision to not have summer school in 2020 due to Covid, we formed some committees to work on items that were best served with input from all staff members. The timing was ideal to accomplish those things. I wanted teachers to be able to work in the areas they were most interested in, so they let me know which committee(s) they preferred serving on.

There was a Report Card Committee, focused on modernizing the grading process. Since our school was in the beginning stages, we were still doing attendance, parent communication and report cards in a variety of ways. We hadn't yet invested in a program that would manage all those tasks and the reams of data associated with them. The timing to do this intensive work was perfect, as we were getting ready to implement our first-ever electronic student reporting system. The system was created by an education company named JMC.

To begin with, we took a step back and read the book, *A Repair Kit for Grading: Fifteen Fixes for Broken Grades*. I was familiar with this program, as I read this book as part of my coursework while becoming certified to be a principal. I had wanted our staff to read it and discuss the implications — but when? The summer of 2020 was the perfect opportunity to have a small group dive into it. Rather than having a report card full of educational jargon that benefits only the teachers, we were able to pull together a parent-friendly document sharing the scholar's progress.

We also had a Curriculum Committee that explored the new Social Studies standards for the state of Iowa. Because we were going through the initial process to become an accredited school, it was crucial for us to create a thorough "scope and sequence" that met all state requirements. A scope and sequence spells out what concepts and topics students are going to be learning in each grade. In addition to complying with the state standards, Faith Academy had been using *Story of the World*, a book that enabled us to present a timeline that coincides with Christ's time on earth.

In the Curriculum Committee, we curated the most important topics for our scholars and came up with ways to address Iowa's standards in cross-curricular ways. This allowed us to meet these requirements within the parameters of a school year. Having too much material to cover is typically a problem in elementary schools, so we worked on ways to streamline it. We also wanted to go deeper into what we covered, rather than trying to cover too much and not do it well.

In the end, I was quite pleased with the amount of great work being accomplished by our staff. Including the work that Jenna was doing on the Onboarding Slide Presentation, which contained all of the information that a new employee needed when starting at Faith Academy, there were three projects that took a great deal of thought and preparation to implement successfully: developing the Social Studies scope and sequence document, implementing the structure of our grading process, and creating an organized way to present all the necessary data a new employee at Faith Academy needed to know as part of the onboarding procedure. I was thrilled not to have to rush through them. Having the time to do these things in an organized and thorough way was another silver lining to Covid. We were in the middle of gaining our accreditation and all three of these requirements needed to be met. There would be even more work outside of school hours to complete the arduous process. Having this time to focus on these important tasks was a huge bonus for our already thinly stretched staff.

The last committee – the R2L Committee — was the one that took the highest emotional toll on the people involved. Nationwide, educators had coined the phrase "R2L" when referring to how they were going to proceed with school in the fall of 2020. Our plan was required to be submitted to the state department of education by July 1. As part of the R2L plan, we needed to determine whether we would return fully in person, create an online platform where students learned remotely from home, or teach using a hybrid model combining the two.

Even though our local public school made the decision to start the school year teaching remotely, we decided to hold in-person classes. We felt that our small class sizes and having fewer than 100 students enabled us to more easily work within the limits of Covid regulations than larger schools. While we felt good about deciding to open in the fall, the model we chose required a lot of detailed planning and creating new procedures.

As we focused on the safety of students and faculty alike, we soon realized the number of items shared by the scholars in our school was endless. With concerns about social distancing and limiting the spread of germs, we had to create individual bags of art supplies and math manipulatives, such as counting cubes or place-value sticks. We recognized the playground equipment, such as jump ropes, balls, and hula hoops, were all shared at recess and used in P.E. as well. The list of things we had to address to ensure the physical safety of our scholars was extensive and, at times, almost overwhelming.

The mere act of allowing children to enter school became far more complicated, too. We had to create a new drop-off routine in the morning, as we needed to take every child's temperature to make sure no one was coming to school with a fever. And we had to do all of this without an official school nurse. This meant that Doreen, our experienced school secretary, was going to be leaned on heavily.

Sanitizing rose to the top of our list. We only had a part-time custodian who came in to clean when school was over and was not in the building during the day. During Covid, we needed to add a cleaning routine to the responsibilities of our para-educator, an employee who was usually dedicated to student support and supervision and was not involved in cleaning.

We recognized it was best to have children interact with as few people as possible. This meant instead of having two or three classes in the lunchroom at once, every class had to eat separately. This required additional supervision and caused teachers to have to eat with students in their classrooms. This also required scheduling additional lunch periods and recess sessions. To help manage the situation, we created cohorts for group activities. This meant kindergarteners and first graders went to lunch and recess together, and the same with second and third graders, etc. This structure made it possible for just two classes to be on the playground at once. That way, if we needed to quarantine a class due to Covid exposure, it would be just two classes at most.

Of course, buses are a prime breeding ground for germs, so we decreased the number of students we allowed on each bus by half. They would need to spread out to reduce germ exposure. The bus drivers were provided with electronic thermometers as well, so they could take the temperature of each child. If the child was running a temperature, they could just turn around, get off the bus, and go back into their house. This was not a popular policy for working parents, yet it was necessary. Additionally, our buses needed to be disinfected daily.

Despite the restrictions we needed to impose to keep scholars and faculty safe, the vast majority of parents understood and supported us completely. I appreciated that support immensely. I didn't take it for granted, either, as I observed other local schools where parents fought administrators over tough decisions when it came to things like mask requirements. One unfortunate consequence of their combative behavior was that in many cases the children saw their parents display disrespect toward school leaders. That is impossible for a child to "un-see" and we know it plays a part in the level of respect shown to authority figures moving forward.

I only recall one controversy when a parent actually drove off as I was telling her it had been reported that her daughter was running a fever. I was disgusted. More than that, I couldn't believe this parent had acted so irresponsibly. Fortunately, we were able to keep the child in the office until her father was able to pick her up. Elder Bernie recognized I was angry when she said "Woah – I don't think I've ever seen you this upset!"

The most sacred time of day for us was Chapel and we knew that would need major adjustments to make it work. We always opened Chapel by singing together. That luxury came under reconsideration as articles on the ways the virus spread were continually written by anxious reporters and broadcast by news anchors trying to keep readers and viewers informed on the developing information about Covid. We learned singing indoors was one of the quicker ways to pass the virus due to the substantially larger number of respiratory droplets expelled during singing. It was even reported that a big church choir in the state of Washington had gone against the Covid recommendation and held a practice anyway prior to large gatherings being banned. Three weeks later two of the members who had been at choir practice lost their lives to Covid and three others were hospitalized. As much as we loved singing in Chapel, we knew we had to change things dramatically.

Fortunately, we had recently moved into the worship center built for Parkview East, the church that meets in our school. The result was we went from meeting in a small space where everyone sat together on the floor during Chapel, to a spacious area where each person had their own chair.

Our accommodation for group gatherings was having only half of the classes present for Chapel – and having each class sit separately from each other. We alternated which classes came to the worship center in person with the other classes watching via Zoom from their classrooms. Once school started that Fall, not being present for Chapel was the biggest complaint we received from teachers about our new procedures. We realized starting the day together by singing uplifting songs, focusing on God, and praying together was such a crucial part of our day. Because we wanted to incorporate Chapel activities as part of everyone's school day, we went back to the drawing board to see if additional adjustments could be made.

So that scholars in different classes would not be passing in our narrow hallways at the same time to get to Chapel, we designated separate entry and exit points for incoming and outgoing classes to use. Another adjustment gave us more room — we pulled a dividing curtain back to spread out into the overflow area and allow everyone to be in the Worship Center together. We made it work! Masks were required at this time, so while our singing was not nearly as robust as usual, at least we could all be together in the same general area. We also discovered it was crucial for the speaker at the front to use a microphone, which hadn't been the case before Covid.

It was affirming to find out how meaningful our daily Chapel was to our teachers. We didn't realize how important this was to us until it was gone. We were comforted by starting the days with a common time of learning and worship all together again.

Brian Scott, fourth grade teacher, ready for teaching during Covid with his microphone and shield

We set up hand sanitizer at all entry points of the building. Once Covid relief funds became available from the government we were able to purchase stands to put the big jugs of hand sanitizer on for easy access. I will forevermore refer to hand sanitizer as "hanzitizer" because that is the way one of our second graders consistently pronounced it and I found it adorable. Some staff members even spent their own money and stocked up on it, as we were limited to purchasing no more than one or two jugs weekly at our local Costco. We also learned that not all hand sanitizers were the same. There was one brand that had a nasty smell to it — and I think some of that still remains on the shelf because no one could stand its repulsive odor.

Before Covid, at the end of the day the scholars who were picked up by parents gathered in the front hallway and waited to be called. During the pandemic, a group gathering like that was no longer allowed due to classes not being able to mix with each other. Everyone needed to wait in their rooms until their names were called over the handheld radios.

As difficult as it was for students, classroom teachers were most impacted by all the changes that we implemented. Teachers no longer got to gather with each other for lunch while their students were supervised by others in the lunchroom. At the end of the day when they used to chat with each other as they supervised their scholars in the pickup line, they were instead secluded in their classrooms with their students. The teachers missed the camaraderie. I took over their duties now and then so they could eat lunch with another teacher and I wished I could have done that more often.

Sadly, five of our scholars couldn't return for in-person learning due to their own health concerns – such as asthma – or in one case it was due to their parent's compromised health concerns during cancer treatment. Those students participated in online learning through our public school district. Conversely, we added three families who were looking for in-person learning.

We decided not to tackle online learning as an option at Faith Academy. I felt that would be too much to ask of our teachers in addition to all their other responsibilities with in-person learning adjustments.

We were very fortunate that all staff found themselves able to return in the fall. Initially when we started our R2L conversations, there was at least one teacher who questioned whether it would be wise for her to come to school during the pandemic. She felt more comfortable in the fall due to the safety measures we put into place.

Under any circumstances, a school is not a great place for anyone with a compromised immune system because of the enormous amount of interpersonal interaction going on. This was even more true during the pandemic. We were all very concerned about Andre, our young para-educator, who had been undergoing treatments for Hodgkin's Lymphoma, a type of cancer that attacks the lymphatic system.

Andre Walker – lower right – on Easter Sunday at
PV East Campus in 2019.
Wisdom Nwafor, Zach and Emory Fern,
Ronnie Smith in back row, Doug Fern lower left

It was a blessing that he had even gone to a doctor to discover the cancer. In 2019, as an otherwise healthy 24-year-old, he was complaining about back pain. Several of us had encouraged him to get it checked out by a doctor, but it was one of our faithful volunteers who made it happen.

Joanne Shelman, with whom I grew up at Sugar Creek Church, volunteered regularly at our school by helping with lunch. She became acquainted with Andre as she was working in the kitchen with him. He was easy to connect with as Joanne had twins the exact same age. She overheard him talking about his pain. Her husband is a doctor and she insisted that Andre see him. Since Andre was reluctant, she just took things into her own hands, calling her husband who agreed with Joanne's recommendation. Because of her insistence, Andre went to see him that afternoon. Without Joanne's personal call, it was highly unlikely this would have happened, given his very busy schedule.

That one appointment started the ball rolling, and we were shocked to later discover that the pain was caused by cancer in his system. But thanks to Joanne, Andre was diagnosed and started treatment. He is healthy and active today, and worked at Faith Academy for several more years. I shudder to think what may have happened had Joanne and Andre not crossed paths. Another God moment. He cares as much about the people who are doing the mission as He does about the mission itself.

Another effect of Covid restrictions was that our morning "Circle Up" could no longer be held in the rotunda, the space in the front hallway. We needed to move it to a bigger space so we could socially distance. That meant Doreen was no longer able to watch the office and participate in prayer time at the same time. This is one more example of how it was challenging for all of us to stay connected at a time when we needed support from each other the most. It took constant communication with each other to successfully accomplish the stressful job of running a school during a worldwide pandemic.

Our small pool of substitute teachers got even smaller when a couple of them were not comfortable coming in to work during Covid. I couldn't blame them, but the amount of extra stress this caused for our teachers and staff alike was enormous. The need for substitute teachers increased due to teachers having to quarantine any time they were exposed to the virus. For the teachers who had young children, the need was multiplied, as daycare facilities often had exposures that would require their children to quarantine. This caused the teacher, who was completely healthy, to have to stay home with their child, requiring a substitute to teach their class.

I struggled with this. When I was in my teaching years and there were not sufficient subs to cover classrooms, I remember thinking the principal should just be the substitute. That seemed to be an easy enough solution to me.

What I didn't know then was the extent of the role a principal plays. During Covid, it was particularly difficult for me to settle in and exhibit the patience it took to work with a group of young kids when I had an extensive "to do" list dancing around in my head. As much as I loved our scholars, I had long since lost the desire to be a classroom teacher. Regardless, I stepped into the teacher role quite a bit during that time.

There were days when I would wake up to multiple texts indicating someone wasn't able to be at school that day. Thankfully, DeDe would often come in if she was needed on her day off. In later years our new Title One teacher, Annemarie, often helped us out by filling in when needed. While her primary job as a Title One teacher was to give small groups of students extra support in Reading, her willingness to step in as a substitute with little notice was a lifesaver for me. Even though I expressed my appreciation to her many times, I still don't know that she realized what a Godsend she was to me and to our school. But it was a rare day in 2020-2021 when I wasn't scrambling and reworking people's schedules, including my own, to get everything covered when a substitute was needed on short notice.

Summer planning for the upcoming school year in the fall of 2020 weighed very heavily on all of us. The detailed issues that needed to be addressed, resolved, and then carried out by our already overworked staff seemed insurmountable at times. We continued to get glimpses of God moments knowing that He was there for us and wanted Faith Academy to be able to continue operating. It truly was a time of God carrying us. Our staff at Faith Academy just took things one day at a time and worked together to solve the enormous obstacles that were placed in front of us. Before Covid, none of us ever imagined that working through a pandemic would be part of our story at Faith Academy. Thankfully, God did, and He guided us day to day.

On the toughest of days, I had a song that I played on Spotify over and over prior to arriving at school.

Turn your eyes upon Jesus
Look full in His wonderful face
And the things of earth will grow strangely dim
In the light of His glory and grace

When the myriad of issues I faced began to weigh on me, I desperately needed the things of our current earth to grow dim! I knew God was greater than everything we were facing. I realized this was a time when we had to keep our eyes on Jesus – every single day.

CHAPTER 31

"NOT ME, LORD"

I'll be long gone by the time Faith Academy gets around to getting officially accredited.

Going back to its very beginning, I had always been a part of the school board. I served on the initial school board prior to working at Faith Academy, I continued as the staff representative to the board, and then of course, as the school's principal. I loved the informality that was woven into the fabric of Faith Academy. That casualness and ease of getting things accomplished was a big part of what drew me to the school.

As we grew, we became more structured. Along with the board's increased structure and the school's growth, there came an awareness that official accreditation would be necessary for a host of good reasons. While we recognized that accreditation was desirable and probably inevitable, I wasn't pushing it.

Darice Keating, a former teacher working for Pearson Educational Services, had been part of the board in the early days. After we officially were recognized as a 501(c)(3) organization — a designation for nonprofit groups that allows tax-exempt status – our school board became more official as well. Unfortunately, the first time it came to our attention that we needed to seek out this status was when we were disqualified from receiving grant money because we did not have the status.

After finally receiving the 501(c)(3) status in 2017, Darice periodically brought up "accreditation" and how it would bring validity to what we were doing as a school. Pearson is an academic testing company based in Iowa City, so she had credibility in the world of education. Even as Darice raised this topic, I didn't make it a focus of mine.

One of the things that drove me out of public education was all the bureaucracy that went with it. For example, I was irritated when we had to spend valuable time creating things such as "Curriculum Maps," where we indexed and diagrammed the curriculum we taught. For elementary teachers who were responsible for covering all subject areas it was an overwhelming and seemingly insubstantial task.

Another frustration I experienced firsthand was the unrealistic expectation placed on me as a classroom teacher when I saw the need to have a student evaluated to see if they qualified for special-education help. To support my recommendation, I had to design and implement multiple instructional strategies for these students and document the resulting outcomes to prove they should even be evaluated prior to being placed in a special-education program. I came to learn that it was only the particular psychologist we were working with at my school who made the process so laborious for classroom teachers such as me. As with other things that drove me away from teaching in 2013, maybe God allowed this to be the case.

At Faith Academy we were able to informally provide our scholars with the additional help they needed as we had an academic support person and the flexibility that came with our small class sizes. As a result, creating hoops to jump through and establishing a bureaucracy within our school was not on my immediate list of ways to enhance Faith Academy. Despite my personal beliefs, I didn't want to show my cards to everyone and be the person who resisted accreditation. I knew we were already doing what we needed to provide a quality education to our scholars, so I felt it wasn't anything we needed to be concerned about. I didn't say much one way or the other.

We'll see what happens.

We had been kicking around the idea of hiring a Director of Development for some time, but providing the funding for an additional position was always an issue. We also knew we would need to hire someone who was fully qualified, was all-in on our mission, and was flexible enough for this to be a success. In the fall of 2017 things fell perfectly into place. Due to the merger of Darice's employer with another company, she had the opportunity for a professional reset. She came to work for us as our part-time Development Director. With her understanding of Faith Academy from serving on the board and with her professional connections to the education community, there was no learning curve and she jumped right into action. One of the first tasks Doug and I assigned her was to research the various agencies through which we could be accredited in the state of Iowa.

Let's go ahead and see what this is going to take.

Even though there was general agreement this was where we needed to go, we did have constituents who were concerned about us "selling our soul" by allowing the state to get their fingers in our business. My easy explanation was that most of the requirements for accreditation are things we would have been working on anyway. These activities included establishing protocols, creating procedures, and writing handbooks as we got our proverbial ducks in a row.

We knew that meeting the requirements to become officially accredited would result in us having an organized and purposeful way of doing these things moving forward. We also wanted to assure our parents that we had all our bases covered in their child's education. We decided to seek accreditation through Christian Schools International (CSI), one of the five institutions our state recognized as a valid accreditation agency. We had no intention of giving up Chapel or excluding Biblical teaching in our classes — state accreditation, of course, didn't require those faith-based activities. By going through CSI, they would be equipped to support us in achieving those goals.

There was a lot to learn about how accreditation worked, and we realized we needed to take things one step at a time. I never dreamed it would be me who would lead our school through this process. My situation reminded me of when I started my master's degree in 1988. Getting a postgraduate degree wasn't something I ever envisioned doing, nor did I realize all it entailed, but because of the end results – higher pay, more effectiveness as a teacher, and more credibility as an educator – I started the process and had faith in myself. Sometimes you have to just jump in.

Once the train left the station and it became obvious I was the one who would be driving, I found myself in disbelief that I was leading something so technical. I felt like my gifts were in other areas, and that I was an unlikely person to be leading this undertaking.

Not me, Lord....

I recalled a song we sang in high school choir about Moses — yes, in a public school. The lyrics came back to me. Moses was telling God that He surely must be thinking of someone else to lead His people out of slavery in Egypt. This is the way I felt. I was sure there must be someone else who was better suited to do this.

"Moses, I've chosen you to be my man,
Moses, 'way down in Egypt's land.
Moses, I've chosen you to work for me,
Moses, I've chosen you to set my people free!"
"Not me, Lord!
Don't you know I can't talk so good;
I stutter all the time.
Do you know my brother, Aaron?

He can sing like an angel,
Talk like a preacher.
Not me, Lord!"

I then realized that God doesn't call only the qualified – He qualifies the called.

We began by pulling together a very competent Accreditation Team. By the time we did this, Darice was no longer working as our Development Director, as she had recently taken a full-time job elsewhere in her field. Thankfully she remained on the accreditation team in a volunteer role.

Dr. Betsy Altmaier joined our team, too. She had recently retired from the University of Iowa as a professor of psychology, and her expertise in accreditation at the university level was a huge asset. Betsy was a detail-oriented person and in addition to proofreading all our work, she took charge of creating and compiling multiple surveys. Generating, conducting, and analyzing surveys were necessary tasks as we pursued accreditation.

Dollie Blackley served as our parent representative even as she maintained her busy schedule of working as a respiratory therapist and caring for four boys at home. Laurie Thompson – our most experienced teacher – started as our teacher representative, and later passed that off to Crystal Johnson. This dedicated group of people met monthly from 2018 through 2021. Dollie coined a phrase that we laughed at frequently as we strove to complete an unending series of tasks: "Deadlines are our friends!" We used it over and over during our time working together as we checked tasks off the list.

To begin this process, we completed the lengthy application for accreditation. Once we submitted our fee and were approved as a "Candidate for Accreditation," unexpected things started happening. I got a call from Diane Schumacher, the Executive Director of Teaching and Learning with Iowa City Community School District

(ICCSD), in September 2018. The district had been notified by the state department of education of our application, and Diane wanted to meet in person to talk about what this meant since Faith Academy was a non-public school within the boundaries of the ICCSD.

From my past experiences with private and public schools, I knew they didn't always "play nice" with each other, and I was anxious about that meeting. I made sure I dressed more professionally than usual that day and we cleaned up Doug's office for the occasion by removing the various sweet treats and sporting gear lying around. Doug let me lead the discussion as he had no clear idea what we were getting into. His degree in Anthropology and his recent focus on studying for the pastorate hadn't prepared him for such a conversation.

To my pleasant surprise, Diane was delightful. She was positive and seemed genuinely interested in what we were doing in the Broadway neighborhood. Doug gave her the background of The Spot starting as an after-school and evening program for neighborhood kids and how it led to the creation of Faith Academy.

By the time our meeting with Diane was over, we discovered there were more benefits from our accreditation application than we were aware of. Even though it would take three to five years to complete all the work for the initial accreditation, by completing the application process, we now had the ability to use the services of our local area education agency (AEA). This meant we could take advantage of professional development classes and get supplemental education materials on loan delivered to our school. Finally, we were able to utilize the AEA's consultants, who were experts in the areas of science, math, reading, technology, and English as a Second Language. We could also seek out advice from their occupational therapists and utilize their speech therapists.

It wasn't that we weren't offering speech services at that point. We had one kindergartener who came in with an IEP in place from preschool and was receiving speech services from the public school already. For other scholars we had made connections with Millennium Therapy and were being served by an energetic young woman who was a sister-in-law of one of our employees, Mr. B. The hassle of the insurance processing and other paperwork associated with speech therapy was a headache and it slowed down the process markedly. While we were sad to part ways with the wonderful therapist who we had been working with since 2015, it was better for us to be able to switch over to Grantwood AEA for all those services.

Prior to having access to all these resources, I would just gather information or assistance from various people I knew who specialized in those areas, just as I had sought out a speech therapist. Thankfully, I had friends like Beth Swantz and Frank Slabaugh who gave their own time to help set up our email system on Google Drive and help us with our technology equipment questions. They also led professional development sessions for us on various computer skills. They were both people I had worked with at Kalona Elementary and they wanted us to succeed at Faith Academy. I was continually amazed at how they each continued to say "yes" when I asked for their help.

We were also surprised to find out there would be a small amount of money that flowed through the Iowa City Community School District to Faith Academy in the form of "Title One funding." Later in the year when Diane got the report detailing the additional funding that each private school received in her district, she told me she had never seen a private school receive such a large amount before.

"You are not a typical private school, that's for sure!" Diane observed.

And that is why I'm here.

The money provided was based on the addresses of our families and the needs of our students. If the school they attended was determined to be in a low-income neighborhood, their school was considered a "Title One" school. The additional money provided to the school under this program could be used for certain things, and hiring staff for extra support was allowed.

At the time this funding became available, Elder Bernie was graduating from the University of Iowa with her bachelor's degree in social work in December 2018. Doug and I couldn't believe our luck when this unexpected money came in right at that time. From our understanding of the parameters associated with the funds, hiring her to support our children was a slam dunk. We talked to Elder Bernie about the possibility of her coming onboard as a social worker in the second semester by using this "Title One" money.

Elder Bernadine Franks graduating at Carver-Hawkeye Arena –
picture was shown on The Today Show on January 4, 2018.
(Photo courtesy of Bernadine Franks)

Her ceremony at Carver-Hawkeye Arena was a time of great celebration as her going back to college was the fulfillment of a promise she made to her mom many years before. Just as she had pledged, this came to fruition at the age of 67. Dave and I were out of town attending Jenna's college graduation ceremony in Lakeland, Florida or we would have been with some of our scholars in the arena cheering Elder Bernie on. This was such a momentous event that her success story caught national attention. She was flown to New York and featured on the Today Show with her granddaughter, who attended the university at the same time. There is a clip of her interview linked on my author website: www.jansInk.org

A group of girls from Faith Academy celebrate with Elder Bernie at her graduation party held December 2017 at Parkview Church.

Everything seemed to fall into place beautifully – until it didn't. The proposal that we thought made perfect sense within the parameters of the program was disapproved. It turned out ICCSD had never hired a social worker as part of the Title One program before and they wanted to just stick with what had been working. I'll never forget having to make that phone call to Elder Bernie one evening to let her know that our idea had been declined, and due to the budget already being set, she would not be able to work at Faith Academy as we wanted. The tone in her voice was so low – "Okay, Mrs. H (pause). Well, you tried. You tried your best and I thank you for that." I teared up by the time I got off the phone.

How could this be happening? It was looking so perfect – like it was God orchestrated. How else can we make this work?

After some more time reading through the Title One requirements, Doug and I came up with an alternative proposal that was easily approved. We saw that Char, our current academic support teacher, could be hired by ICCSD as our Title One Reading teacher, enabling us to have her salary freed up. To fill this position, Char had to go through a team interview process with ICCSD and me. She also had to have all the state required licensure, including a reading endorsement, and extra coursework specifically in supplemental reading instructions. She met all those requirements.

Because we could hire Char into our Title One position, we were able to use the money we had budgeted for Char's academic support position to fund Elder Bernie as our Family Liaison. She started in February of 2019 and has been doing amazing work for Faith Academy ever since. Looking back, we all realized it was especially important for us to have a Black woman like her in our liaison position. She has credibility with Black families and a way of relating to them that opens the door to effective communication with our scholars and their families.

There were also many times when she provided a cultural perspective that was much needed on our leadership team. Staff members continued to consult her when challenges arose – or to prevent a problem from arising – with family communication. Ultimately, in addition to knowledge of navigating the social services systems and their resources, her greatest contribution is her deep and invaluable wisdom.

Over the next three and a half years, we spent an exorbitant amount of time on the detailed and very involved process of creating targeted content to satisfy the requirements of accreditation. The unexpected extra time I had during Covid was a gift, as I was able to work on fine-tuning handbooks, guidelines, protocols, learning goals, and other documents as part of improving our school.

After three and a half years of working on this project, we submitted the official 43-page paper containing 104 links to additional pages of documents on Friday, February 12, 2021. By turning the proposal in this early, Arlyn, our contact person at Christian Schools International (CSI), could get back to me if anything needed to be changed or improved prior to presenting it to our Site Visit Team. This way, the team would have at least two full months to thoroughly read over our documents.

The last task ahead of us was to prepare for our site visit during the first week of May. Leading up to the visit, it was uncertain whether this was actually going to take place because of Covid. In the back of our minds, we were concerned that a Covid outbreak might postpone the visit. A delay like that would have been a major issue, as we did not want to have accreditation bumped into the next school year, since there would have been personnel changes and other complications. Because of this, I asked if we would be able to conduct this virtually, in case a Covid incident prevented the in-person site visit. Since it was our initial accreditation, CSI declined that request. They stood by their need for it to take place in person. They wanted to have the Site Visit Team physically present on our campus. I respected that and chose to turn my worry about it over to God.

With Covid still in our community, we held our breath, knowing that our site visit could be forced to be postponed with an outbreak of the virus at our school or among the members of the Site Visit Team. It wasn't really until the team had arrived safely in Iowa City and came to campus on Tuesday afternoon, May 4, that I exhaled.

What a huge relief. The visit took place as planned, and it did not have to be pushed into the following school year.

Whew — thank you, Jesus.

We were responsible for hosting the Site Visit Team. We provided hotel accommodations, travel, and meals for the five people who made up our team. The team consisted of two people from CSI and three teachers we needed to recruit from various Christian schools in the Midwest. Two teachers were from schools in Iowa, and we were able to secure one from Hope Academy in Minneapolis.

I was particularly thrilled when Rena Hall accepted the request on behalf of Hope Academy. Faith Academy is not a typical private school and I felt strongly about having someone on the Site Visit Team who understood our mission and how it differed from other schools in many areas. Rena served as Hope Academy's Academic Director for grades 3-5 as well as the Tech Integration Specialist. She was the perfect person to have as part of the team.

Site visit week was different from what I had anticipated. There were details to be tended to every day – and our committee had all the bases covered. Betsy generously was on site, delivering food and staying on top of hosting accommodations. By the time the week arrived I felt confident all our work was complete and I wasn't nervous about what would take place. I knew the hardest work was behind us.

Initially I expected the visitors to spend their time combing through our files and being very formal about processes and procedures. Instead, the interactions were far more personable than I anticipated, and it was exciting to have conversations with the visiting educators about Faith Academy and all the things we were doing. They spent much of their time observing the school and interviewing students, parents, board members, and staff. And yes, going through files.

In the end, we were thrilled to receive many compliments about how far we had come in such a short time. Many of the evaluators commented on how hard it was to believe that we had been open for only eight years.

On Thursday afternoon of that week, they delivered their preliminary findings to Doug, our accreditation team, and me. They told us that they were going to recommend full accreditation be granted by CSI for Faith Academy! At 3:30 a joint meeting of staff and school board gathered to hear the anticipated news. The official word wouldn't come until their board held a meeting in July to approve their recommendation — but we knew that was just a formality.

All smiles after the accreditation approval at Faith Academy, May 2021!
From left: Dave Asprey - board president, Elder Bernie, Doug Fern,
Rich Hoefer - board member, Darice Keating - board member
and Accreditation Team, Craig Welt – board member, me, Crystal
Johnson, Dr. Betsy Altmaier - Accreditation Team, Dollie Blackley -
Accreditation Team, and Julie Dancer in front - board member

We enjoyed a day of celebration on Friday complete with the delivery of $100 bills to each staff member from Rich, a board member, to commemorate everyone's hard work. Another board member kindly delivered succulent plants to all the staff. It was truly a day of rejoicing and relief! The project we had started looking into in 2017 was finished – and it was a big success.

The thank-you email I sent to the five members of the Site Visit Team who came from out of town that week summarizes my thoughts and feelings succinctly. I'd like to share an excerpt from it:

Friends,

… (You were) a group of professional, highly qualified educators coming in to our school, to assure that all of our standards are met, and met with fidelity. And THEN, coming alongside us, entering into a place of WORK, to help us make things better at Faith Academy. You rejoiced with us by pointing out things that are going well and things that are in place due to some sincerely hard work. That was so encouraging. You asked questions and required clarification in areas that need more and ongoing work. BUT it didn't stop there — you offered specific resources, documents, websites, organizations, etc. that will help us in moving forward with those tasks. That was also so encouraging.

I feel like I now have five more partners in this mission. My cup is FULL because of you (and GOD — and the divine intervention that YOU were the ones that ultimately were the ones that came to Faith Academy). I also need to give credit to our school board for celebrating with us on Friday. And as you know, that is a lot to say that my cup is full at the beginning of May, after the most challenging year, ever, in education.

God's blessings to you.

Jan Hochstetler | K-6 Principal |
Faith Academy - A Kingdom School

CHAPTER 32

AN OVERNIGHT DECISION

"How long are you going to live in fear?"

In the fall of 2021, a teacher hurried down the hall to quickly make a copy before she needed to be back with her students. One of our volunteers who the teacher knew outside of school passed by her and gave that snarky, unsolicited comment regarding her mask.

Being a Christian school didn't isolate us from the dynamics that rocked society as a whole during the pandemic. The controversies surrounding Covid were difficult, and the divisiveness associated with mask-wearing was something we had not experienced before at Faith Academy. I only learned about the volunteer's unkind comment regarding the mask when I was researching this book. I'm not sure if I wish I had known it at the time or not.

While I always felt strongly about it being crucial for me to support our staff, there were scores of challenging issues that needed addressing during that time. Steve Jobs once said, "If you want to make people happy, don't be a leader – sell ice cream!" As time went on, I understood the usual conflict resolution techniques I used wouldn't have worked with people on this topic. It was next to impossible to alter people's views on mask-wearing once it became a hardcore political identity issue.

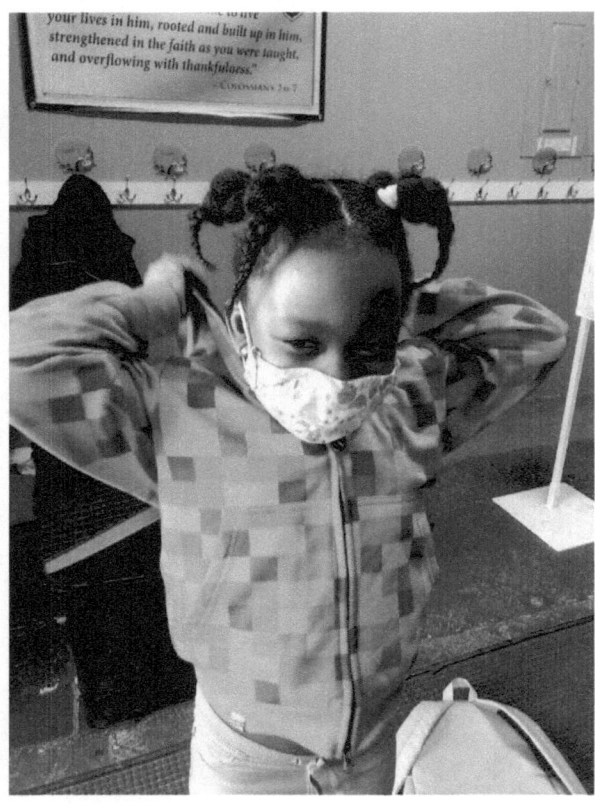

A scholar as she packs up for the day in 2021 – wearing a mask had become routine

Spending time as an elementary school principal on issues surrounding our scholars or their parents was something I anticipated, and I was willing to do whatever it took to work through them. Spending time on issues that were purely created by grown adults outside of the learning environment – issues that were hard to believe could carry such deep emotions in the first place – was exhausting.

In May 2021, less than two weeks after our exuberant celebration surrounding our accreditation, our staff and school found ourselves in turmoil because of a controversial action regarding Covid regulations in our state. Iowa's lawmakers threw a curve ball to educators and parents by introducing and passing a law immediately making it **illegal** to require masks in schools. Our governor signed the law after midnight and the entire legislative process from start to finish happened in less than 24 hours on a Wednesday in the middle of the school week.

Doug and I each learned of this new law just as we were getting ready to go to school that morning. We were gathering to have our morning Circle Up prayer time when Doug asked me a straightforward question, kind of off to the side.

"Did you see what the governor did overnight? We'll have to talk about that and decide how we want to present that."

But we never had the chance to process through it. After talking about a few other items, Doug casually brought it up to our group.

"I don't know if you had time to see what happened at the state house overnight, but we'll let you know how we're going to deal with that...."

It was then one of our teachers cut him off. She was clearly agitated as she spoke defiantly.

"You can't make me wear a mask – and I'm not going to make my kids wear masks anymore either!"

Woah - where did that come from?

Turns out our staff wasn't as united as it had appeared these past months.

I was stunned. The tension that cut through the air was something we had never, ever experienced previously. We dealt with differences of opinions on our staff and had personality conflicts before, just as in any workplace, but nothing this severe. I can't even remember

301

what anyone said for the rest of the Circle Up time, but it was clear we were in an unprecedented and very tense situation.

After the group dissipated, Doug and I talked in private about how to proceed. We knew everyone was going to be gathering as usual for Chapel in less than 30 minutes. We quickly found and read the report from the governor's office. Sure enough, the law had gone into effect immediately. We were given no choice but to address the issue **today** due to the teacher's bold comment.

We decided if all the classes walked into Chapel wearing masks as usual, we would not make any announcements regarding the change yet. If there was a visible change in mask wearing, we knew we would need to say something in Chapel right then.

We know it is important to be consistent with rules and expectations that have been set. For months we had been requiring the scholars to wear masks and we would gently remind them to put their mask on if it was not in place. Kids sniff out inconsistencies like bloodhounds, and we knew they would notice if things had changed without being told it was okay.

As the scholars filed in with the upbeat music playing in the background, it was evident that more than a few of them were aware they no longer had to wear masks. Doug handled it well, considering the tense situation.

"Scholars, I want you to know about a change that has been made by our lawmakers and state governor...."

He then told them that we would rather they talk to their parents first about whether they should continue to wear their masks or not. But at this point, we would no longer ask them to put on their masks.

After nine months of having a united front about mask-wearing at our school, this change was forced on us literally overnight. The state law conflicted with national policy, too. The Centers for Disease Control and Prevention (CDC) had released a statement just a week prior, advising face coverings to be worn in schools, medical settings, and public transit. The CDC did caveat that guidance by saying that people who were vaccinated against Covid no longer needed to wear a mask in most settings because the chance of them catching or transmitting the airborne virus was low. Children under 12 were still not cleared to receive any of the Covid vaccines at that time, so none of our scholars had been eligible to get the vaccine yet. Because of that, these CDC caveats didn't apply to our scholars.

I wondered if our governor had thought about the sudden and unnecessary upheaval this unanticipated law was going to create among educators statewide. If she had, I like to think she would have never passed the law on such short notice while school was in session. There were 10 other states that had banned mask mandates at some point during 2021, as well. The whole situation was frustrating and seemed so unnecessary. It felt like a real dig.

We are working our tails off for children in our state — this stressful school year is almost to an end, and you allow this divisive law to be passed overnight?!

The following day we had a couple of parents reach out to us. They wished they would have been able to talk to their children about the optional mask wearing *prior* to us making the announcement. I did too!

Once the parents' children saw some of their classmates not wearing masks, their kids stopped wearing their masks as well. Because I needed to remain professional by maintaining my objectivity, all I could state in response to those parents was that I totally get it, and I was sorry it had happened that way.

One parent came into my office to have this same conversation. She saw that I was continuing to wear a mask, so she likely knew I supported her concerns. I so badly wanted to tell her the whole story.

Again, I reminded myself I needed to remain objective and professional.

We let parents know that if they wanted their children to continue wearing masks, we would support it by saying "Your parents want you to keep your mask on." But peer pressure undermined the parents' wishes, as children naturally felt the need to do what others in class were doing – or in this case, not doing.

This controversy resurfaced in the fall when a federal judge blocked the state's mandatory mask ban in schools, stating that it created an unfair risk for students with serious health conditions to attend class in-person.

Because of this ruling, we were then able to require masks in our school building. This was on a Monday.

Whew! Consistency.

By the end of the week, it was reported that the judge failed to include accredited non-public schools in his declaration. Therefore, it didn't apply to us.

We suddenly returned to not being able to require masks.

I just want this issue to go away. I love our staff here at Faith Academy — how has this seemingly simple matter become so divisive?

It was becoming more difficult to remain thick-skinned. Doug and I – again – made the necessary policy adjustments. We let parents know that if they wanted their children to continue wearing masks, we would enforce it by saying "Your parents want you to keep your mask on."

In other areas, some of the things we did best at Faith Academy had been hampered by Covid and were slow to return. Many people enriched our school with their presence and by sharing their talents. Prior to Covid we had volunteers come in every day of the week. We were blessed with the number of people who helped by meeting with our scholars to read with them, to help with class activities, by using their skills to help with such things as maintenance or repair of our building, and by assisting with serving lunch.

A picture taken prior to Covid — one of our faithful volunteers has a "teachable moment" and looks at a map in the front hallway with a scholar. The map had labels on all 12 countries from where families at Faith Academy emigrated.

We had one woman who came in weekly to read to all our Kindergarten through third-grade classes from library books she picked out especially for our scholars. Since she didn't return after Covid, her very popular program could no longer be carried out. Occasionally we would have volunteers who came in when the students were no longer in the building to help with maintenance. We also had people who led special-interest programs in the classes such as chess, drumming, board games, and knitting. None of these could take place.

I already mentioned Joanne, who continued to faithfully help us in the lunchroom throughout the pandemic, along with a couple of others. But the one-on-one help scholars had been getting through our volunteer and mentoring programs came to a standstill. The retired couples who had served faithfully and enjoyed reading with our scholars couldn't risk being in the school sitting side by side with the scholars. We felt their absence and the kids missed the bonus adults to whom they had grown attached.

There was one special program started by my lifelong friend, Maria, that was really missed when Covid hit. When Faith Academy opened, the school contracted with a caterer who provided meals for some of the fraternities and sororities in our university town. He would drop off hot food every day around 11:00 a.m. There was a rotating menu, and the kids' favorite meal was when we would have egg rolls and fried rice.

With our already stretched budget, the dollar amount we were paying to have lunch brought in came on the chopping block. Since we were not equipped with a commercial grade kitchen, we didn't have the capabilities to create meals from scratch. Asking the parents to pay for lunch was also not a consideration. We knew at the public school most of our families would qualify for free or reduced cost lunches, and we wanted to provide that same benefit to them. Once we became accredited and researched our eligibility for Title One Funding, we discovered between 80-90% of our families qualified for free or reduced-price lunch.

About that time a generous donor who attended Parkview reached out to Doug to talk with him about ways he could help. As God would have it, this donor owned a sandwich-making business, where he sold to convenience stores, prisons and other facilities. He offered to give us sandwiches for free. The timing was perfect! We started a weekly trip to his facility to pick up a week's worth of sandwiches. With the addition of some fresh fruits, veggies, and occasional chips, we were able to serve our scholars a healthy lunch. Because of this donor's wonderful generosity, we provided our scholars with a variety of sandwiches, and the kids ate them pretty much every day for a couple of years. We would occasionally spring for Little Caesar's pizza on Fridays, but not often.

Then came the sandwich meltdown.

A typically quiet, well-behaved, fifth-grade boy sat down at a table one lunch period. I was in the lunchroom at the time, chatting with scholars as I sometimes did. When I sat down at his table, this boy became agitated and loudly commented, as he couldn't seem to control himself anymore.

"Sandwiches again?! Every day it is sandwiches, sandwiches! I want something else! I can't take it anymore!"

I felt like I was in the middle of a *Seinfeld* TV episode.

This seemed like a case of "displaced aggression" according to a psychology class I remember. At the time, I thought this surely had to be what this was – it had to be the straw that broke the camel's back for him, and it must have emanated from something else that was bothering him. In hindsight, I'm not certain it actually was displaced aggression. He may have just been really tired of sandwiches.

He actually found me later in the day and apologized for his outburst. I'm pretty sure the conversation he had with our associate, Andre, had something to do with that apology. They had a close relationship, and Andre witnessed the incident. It wasn't unusual for Andre to mentor a student when he observed an action that wasn't becoming of a young scholar.

Afterward, I told Maria about this incident because admittedly, a sandwich meltdown is a pretty funny story. I didn't use any names, of course. When she heard it, she immediately offered to help with the situation.

"I can fix them a meal once in a while."

"What? Really? There's 80 of them, you know," I responded hopefully.

But this friend of mine is a gifted cook with a kind and generous heart. As a result, a few weeks later we had our first lunch served by Maria. She even brought friends and her sister with her to help with serving the meal and cleaning up afterward. Her homemade food was amazing. And the kids did not let me down – they lavished her with praise and "thank yous."

My worlds intersected in an amazing way that day, and it made my heart full. Maria was my lifelong friend who lived across the road from me growing up. I have known her since birth. Except for the time when her family moved to Louisville, Kentucky from third to sixth grade because of her dad's job, we did almost everything together. We were with each other in church, school, youth group, softball, and even our first three years of college. To have her support me at our school by sharing her gift of cooking was so uplifting.

Maria and friends ready to serve lunch! From left: Barb Freyenberger (Maria's sister), Lisa Graber, Maria (Freyenberger) Roth

When I shared about the "Maria and friends" lunches at our banquet that year, I choked up unexpectedly. I was in a jovial mood, presenting with Doug, and this heartfelt emotion came out of nowhere. Her generous contribution obviously meant a lot to me. She served delicious homemade meals like walking tacos, applesauce she had canned herself with red hots dissolved in it to make it even more kid-friendly, and creamed turkey gravy on mashed potatoes. She had the electric roasters needed for this type of thing because fixing and serving food is how she blesses people.

There were rarely leftovers, as the kids kept coming back for seconds and even thirds. I'm pretty sure the teachers experienced some kids in "food comas" those days Maria served lunch. She brought enough for teachers too – so we all looked forward to the day once a month that "Maria and friends" would bring in lunch. This was an exciting monthly ritual until Covid severely curtailed volunteer activities.

Once Covid restrictions lessened, our volunteers slowly started to return. I still had money from Covid relief funding, and I had already spent a good deal of time learning how to navigate the various platforms and deciding how to best distribute the funds. The requirements associated with providing money varied with the different types of funding. I spent a good deal of time on the phone with helpful people from the Iowa state department that handled this. I even got to know a lovely woman named Susan on a first-name basis.

At the same time, we had to write our five-year Strategic Plan as a follow-up to our accreditation. Each of these projects could be a chapter of its own in this book and it exhausts me to even think about the time and effort they took. Because these were huge, daily tasks I needed to address when there was no end to the innumerable list of things I had to do, I was constantly exhausted.

Doug was around even less than before as he was the full-time interim lead pastor for Parkview. As time went on, we gradually saw things move back toward normal as Covid receded. Still, things were definitely not the same. After the stresses associated with running a school during the pandemic, I felt like I had aged 10 years in the last year and a half. I'm pretty sure I looked like it, too.

The accreditation site visit team even told me they saw problems with my role being sustainable at the pace I was operating. However, with their desire to "tread lightly," their comment about it was so camouflaged in their final report that the point they were making wasn't clear to anyone who read it. In the end, I was even beginning to wonder how much longer I could operate at this breakneck pace.

CHAPTER 33

END OF A SEASON

It's not unusual for people to wake up at night to go to the bathroom. When I got up one night in the fall of 2021, I must have briefly passed out because I fell to the floor in the narrow space between our bed and the wall, barely missing the footboard of our bed that sticks out with a sharp corner. Dave heard me hit the floor and sat straight up in bed.

"Dear, are you okay?!"

Even though the experience startled me, I minimized it by telling Dave I was okay, and was soon back in bed. My heart was pounding fast.

I spotted a minor scrape on my forehead the next morning. I thought this was unusual as I didn't remember hitting anything – or so I thought. That weekend when I pulled back the curtains from our bedroom window to raise the shades and enjoy our beautiful view, I noticed something strange. I saw an indentation on the wall beneath the windowsill in a round shape about three inches in diameter.

What the heck? Did that happen when I fell? Woah!

When I showed it to Dave, we both knew it could have only happened when I passed out earlier that week. While I acted unconcerned at first, it worried me more than I let on. I made a doctor's appointment for later that week to talk about it. After having bloodwork done, thankfully there was nothing medically significant discovered. But every time I pulled back the curtains in our bedroom that circular dent on our wall reminded me of my fall that night. I realized my body was trying to tell me something. It began to hit home that I simply had too much on my plate.

The Body Keeps the Score

That is the name of a book I read recently by Bessel Van der Kolk. The book is about how the brain, mind, and body work together in healing. My intent in reading it was to have a deeper understanding of our scholars who have experienced trauma. Our bodies carry our overwhelming experiences in physical ways that can play out in a variety of physical and emotional manifestations.

*Hmmmm – is **my** body telling me something?*

I believe God speaks to us in whispers. When we don't answer, He speaks a little louder to us until we respond.

Starting back to school in the fall of 2021, things had changed. We had weathered the worst of Covid, and it seemed a sense of normalcy was starting to return. Despite things opening up and recognizing we were moving in the right direction, it felt different. I wasn't the only one who realized things were not nearly as "back to normal" after Covid as we had anticipated. This feeling made the situation even more stressful because we were expecting things to return to the way they were – but they were not.

Along with this uneasiness, there were many different challenges that confronted us. Two of our seven classroom teachers were expecting babies in the spring, and we needed to find long-term substitutes for them, at a time when our sub pool was very limited. Complicating things even more, we were still dealing with periodic quarantines from Covid, but never more than one class at a time.

On the positive side, we now had a contract with Christian Schools Management for a pair of consultants to work with us to create a five-year strategic plan. This was great, although it included another weeklong site visit in November, which would mean even more preparation and focus would be required.

We were also in the midst of an exciting "build out" at Faith Academy that would add five classrooms and new restrooms to our school. We looked forward to this wonderful new phase that would make a big difference in our ability to serve our scholars. Everything in that part of our building was going to be new, as we had acquired the adjoining space in our building, and we were constructing walls within that shell. Again, as welcome as this was, it was another stressor, as I had become the school's contact person for that major project. This added to an already lengthy list of challenges to be overcome.

Previously, the sixth-grade class had been held in the north end of the strip mall we owned. We referred to this area as the Extended Learning Center (ELC). We referred to the ELC in this euphemistic way to soften what was seen as an uncomfortable topic. Calling it the ELC was much preferred to saying, "the classrooms away from all the others at the north end of our strip mall." The art room was temporarily there, as well. Their home had been bounced around, as had the music teacher's. With this new construction and an expanded facility, we were grateful that those teachers were committed and flexible enough to hang in there until they were assigned to their permanent classrooms.

It was a good thing we were all so thrilled about the construction project because the noise and inconvenience could easily have become an item of contention. As it turned out, there were a few setbacks due to Covid-related shipping delays regarding things such as hardware for the new doors. In the end, we were excited to finally move into the new space at the beginning of February 2022.

A couple of rooms in our new space – completed in February 2022

It was a domino effect during the moving process as once a classroom was emptied for scholars to move into their new space, another class typically moved right into their emptied-out classroom. Our teachers rose to the occasion as usual and came in on the weekend with additional volunteers to make the move. It was amazing to see our expansion project come to fruition step by step. One teacher had even planned on remaining in his classroom for the rest of the year and then moving everything into his new classroom after summer school was over. That seemed sensible to him, with his structured type of personality. But as everyone's anticipation of moving into their new classrooms grew, even *he* jumped on the bandwagon and made the move the first weekend after the project was finished.

When Shane, the project manager from Hodge Construction, handed me the master key that would open all the rooms, I felt on top of the world! But in a matter of months, I would be handing that key over to someone else.

Doug Fern and Trystin Luneckas, third grade teacher, praying in the new space the morning the scholars would occupy it for the first time

Despite my excitement and satisfaction at seeing the physical changes taking place in the building and recognizing that Faith Academy was slowly but surely recovering from our Covid challenges, I was having a hard time looking forward to continuing in my role at the school. I felt exhausted, and it wasn't simply the myriad of different job-related challenges that constantly demanded my attention. Looking back, I can see I was spending less time on the energizing things I was skilled at and passionate about, and more time on the draining things I learned to do but were not in my natural area of competence.

As much as I loved the people I worked with and the scholars and families we supported, there were issues that took my energy that I was not in the position to control. I'm aware that virtually everyone, especially those who hold leadership positions like mine, must face these challenges as part of their job. Even so, dealing with personnel conflicts was one more stressor that added to my exhaustion. Along with that, the challenges that came with our building being used by multiple groups and organizations, and the discord that arose as a result of their conflicting demands had always been frustrating. It was becoming clear to me that my time at Faith Academy might be coming to an end.

It was during a phone call to my friend in Florida, Sara Thompson, that I confirmed my decision to retire at the end of the year. I had worked with her at Kalona Elementary, but we hadn't become close friends until later. In 2015, her son tragically died in an accident. I reached out to her, and we stayed connected from that point forward.

I trusted Sara's intuition and I had talked about many things with her over the seven years since her son's death, even after she had moved out of state. We have that kind of friendship – where we can call each other on the phone and just pick up right where we left off. What made our relationship special was that we were able to talk about deep stuff, too.

Sara Thompson with some of the books she donated to create "Lukie's Library" for us at Faith Academy in honor of her son. On what would have been his fifth birthday, she requested books on Facebook and this was the result!

After hearing me talk, she reassured me that my thinking was on point. And she encouraged me not to feel guilty about my decision to retire. She reminded me that guilt feelings do not come from God. She told me to "go out on top," like Jerry Seinfeld – one of our favorite comedians – had done when he left *Seinfeld* while it was still the number one TV comedy. She told me not to wait until I was completely burned out. She was right. Dave had already agreed that we could make it work if retiring at the end of the school year is what I decided to do.

There were still things I wanted to accomplish at Faith Academy, yet I could see the school was in a great place. Our accreditation was complete. We had a strong staff. Laura had taken over the Christmas musical and could take on leading the music in Chapel as well. The new classrooms were going to be completed soon. Even our sixth graders and music program had a permanent home. I felt good about the academic special services our students were receiving through Title One and special education when they were needed. All areas of our curriculum had been addressed fully, with writing and computer science being the last ones to be finalized that year. Our five-year strategic plan was well on its way. To cap it all off, we even had an official sign on the outside of our building for the first time.

I knew it was time for me to leave ... on top.

CHAPTER 34

PASSING THE MEGAPHONE

I wanted Doug to be the first person I told about my retirement plans and I wanted to do it in person. The next couple of days he was at the central campus of Parkview most of the time, leaving school right after Chapel in the morning. That weekend after I made my decision, I tested positive for Covid, as Dave had contracted it from work.

The first time we had it in our house was before the vaccine was available and it was rough. We were knocked out sick for two weeks, even a little longer for me. I got it from a teacher at school who knew she contracted it at Thanksgiving. So, I unknowingly passed it on to Dave just in time for the Christmas season.

We weren't even able to be together as a family that Christmas as Dylan's flight was scheduled to arrive when Dave was still in his quarantine period. Dylan just stayed in Los Angeles over Christmas in 2020, which broke my heart. The day the realization came to us was the same day I lost my ability to taste and smell, and the combination of the two things happening together pushed me over the edge.

We are always together at Christmas – this is just unacceptable.

I broke down and cried. That's all I could do – sit down at our island in the kitchen and have a good cry. At least Dylan could get his money back from his flight – airlines were required to refund people during Covid times. And Jenna didn't contract Covid from Dave or me – she was sequestered in the lower level of the house.

December 2020 – After I was feeling better, but we were still in Covid quarantine, Jenna and I colored together and chatted – me at the top of the stairs and her at the bottom as she was quarantined in the basement. Mick, our Cavachon, looks on.

The second time I had Covid, Dave passed it on to me just in time for my birthday in January 2022. That time wasn't nearly as bad since we both had been vaccinated – but I was out of school for a week.

I was still at home at the time, and I hadn't been able to communicate with Doug about my retirement. I wanted to be fair to

319

him by letting him know as soon as possible. I texted him while I was home sick.

"Give me a call when it works for you."

He wasn't shocked when I told him the news over the phone. Even knowing that my retirement was a possibility, he was still melancholy.

"I get it … congratulations. But, dang."

I tend to tell people things right when I know them – but as I've gotten older, I have become more aware that timing is also important. I knew I had to be careful with this news as it would bring about questions and concerns over future leadership at Faith Academy.

When we told our kids, Jenna wasn't surprised. We talk daily and she has processed so many work things with me, over the last couple of years in particular. She knew the stress I endured. She also knew how much Faith Academy meant to me.

Dylan's response was very practical. "So … what are you gonna do?"

I told him I didn't know yet, and I just needed to take one thing at a time. I knew the first thing for me was that I was just going to recover and rejuvenate.

I also knew the first person I needed to tell at work besides Doug was Elder Bernie.

This is going to be hard. I love being with her every day – we work so well together, we are a well-oiled machine. I have learned so much from her and have an extraordinary amount of respect for her.

I remember the feeling that hung in the air after telling Elder Bernie in my office that I was going to retire after the school year. Disappointment. Disbelief.

Elder Bernie, one of my treasured friends from my time at Faith Academy, and me watching some of our former scholars play football for City High at the University of Iowa's Kinnick Stadium in September 2022

"No one here can do what you do – you come early, stay late – it has to be someone who is really into this mission," she said.

She told me she always thought she would leave before I did and that she assumed she would never be at Faith Academy without me being there, too.

"I was going to stay until our first class graduates high school – I don't know if I can make it now," Elder Bernie added.

I reassured her that it was going to be fine – there are many people who love our mission just as much as I do. But I felt I had let her down.

As I've discovered from personality tests – I'm a type seven enneagram — I'll do anything to not be sad. But that evening I just put on some Netflix and allowed myself to accept my sadness.

The most nagging feeling I needed to address within myself was guilt. I knew I had been important to the success of Faith Academy and that the school's mission genuinely made a difference in so many people's lives. I also knew how demanding it was to work there and how much we all relied on each other – and now I was leaving them.

Guilt is a feeling that comes when a person believes they have done something wrong. I knew I hadn't done anything I should feel guilty about, but it was hard to shake the feeling. My friend in Florida, Sara, had even cautioned me about that feeling.

I believe that no one is irreplaceable, including me. We had a great team in place, and we were not nearly as short-staffed as we used to be. In my heart, I knew it would be okay. I also knew that the following year there would even be a substitute teacher hired who was dedicated to our school. This was an enormous relief, and it was thanks to arrangements made through the Covid relief funds. *That will take a huge amount of stress off the person who replaces me.*

When a life change such as retirement comes up, I recognize there are certain people who need to hear it straight from the horse's mouth, so to speak. I thought of a few people who I needed to tell directly and decided that I would wait until I had announced it to our school board. That had to be my first official step.

I wanted Dawn, our therapist, to know ahead of time, as she and I had become close. We worked together on helping our neediest scholars, and I valued her judgment when it came to important matters concerning both students and staff around school. Since she was employed by Tanager Place, I didn't supervise her directly. That made it easier for me to talk to her about things that I wasn't able to reveal to anyone else – she was a therapist after all! She was grateful when I texted her the night before the board meeting, yet initially responded with a singular "Noooooo" and a bunch of crying emojis.

Doug and I spent some time thinking about what the best timing would be. We decided that we would announce it at the last January board meeting. Doug suggested saying it at the end of the meeting rather than the beginning.

"They won't listen to anything else that is said if you tell them at the beginning. Save it for the end."

I remember doing just that. Gauging from their overall reaction, it caught them off-guard. After some initial comments of shock – since it seemed out of the blue for them – they were professional in their responses and appreciative of my service. By that point I had worked through my array of feelings and felt confident in telling them. I could tell by the time we were ready to disperse from the meeting, many of the board members' wheels were turning, as they wondered "what now?"

That same morning, I told our teachers during Circle Up time that I was retiring at the end of the school year. I just had to blurt it out and allow them time to process.

It all felt a bit surreal. I loved Faith Academy. The board, the staff, the teachers, and I had accomplished so much together. Still, I felt relief that my retirement was finally out in the open.

During Chapel that morning, after what had been an emotional morning starting with the 6:30 a.m. board meeting, for the first time I let tears flow down my cheeks. It was during a slow worship song. I realized at that moment singing together in praise with these young kids is what I will miss the most about Faith Academy.

Another important aspect of my decision was that I never wanted to be that person who rides it out and just comes to work without giving it my all. I felt this role I had at Faith Academy is too important to not give it 100 percent.

I specifically remember what Shay, our sixth-grade teacher, said to me that morning – "I get it – you don't want to wait until it's no fun anymore. I mean I don't want you to go, but I get it." She was 26 at the time but has always been mature beyond her years.

"You're too young to retire!" was a comment I got a lot.

I don't feel young....

An hour-long phone conversation in mid-January with Karen Fisher, my former fifth-grade teaching partner who had moved to the Chicago area, left me very encouraged. She reminded me that she retired at 57.

"You need to take care of your health."

Karen Fisher, Jenna, and me.
Karen was Jenna's Fifth Grade teacher in 2008.

I learned so much from Karen about teaching, parenting, and just being a generous human. When I was new at Kalona Elementary, she modeled her warmth by making the art teacher feel welcome by inviting him to join us at our table for the first Back to School in-service day.

"Join us at our table, John!"

John was one of the few males on our staff and as a teacher who split his time working at three elementary schools, he wasn't around as much to develop friendships. That was the first example of many times when Karen made people around her feel noticed and loved.

At what would be my final spring fundraising banquet, Brett — our development director and creator of "Jan's Jam," my monthly video feature on Faith Academy's Facebook page – put together a tribute for me. People shared from their hearts. Shay spoke on the video, and told me later that she just thought the video was for my viewing only. They hadn't told her it was going to be shown at the banquet.

Elder Bernie and Doug on stage during my last Celebrate Faith Fundraising Banquet 2022

She had just returned from a field trip to The School of the Wild and she thought she looked like it, too. That course was an all-day outdoor learning experience with her sixth graders, and that was when Brett approached her about needing the video. I found that story humorous and completely appropriate for the way we operated at Faith Academy. Not much was ever scripted or polished – we had too much important work to do!

My good friends Heather and Ruth joined Dave and me at my table that evening. It felt great to have them alongside me to witness the festivities. They had each heard plenty about Faith Academy over the last eight years. Ruth, in particular, would catch the immediate scoop as we often walked laps on the track at the YMCA or on the walking trail at Terry Trueblood Recreation Area in Iowa City. I recognize even now it is great to have a friend who I trusted with the uncensored version of what I felt, knowing it would never go anywhere else.

Ruth, me, Heather and Maria at my retirement party in June 2022

At that point, April 2, I hadn't yet announced to the scholars that I was leaving. Several of them were present at the banquet that evening. In addition to some of the scholars coming to sing, Mr. Scott and his fourth-grade class had a special role in the program that evening. The idea was to give the audience a glimpse into their math class. It was executed perfectly and was well received. As a result of their performance that night, there were more scholars at the banquet than usual.

Afterward as people were milling about, one of our scholars heard her parents talking to us about my leaving. Her mother was talking to Dave.

"Your wife – she always had so much energy. She is talking to us parents – and then she goes up and is the one playing the piano, too!"

The girl stood alongside them, seeming so small in comparison to the adult conversation happening above her head. It was always such a change in dynamics when my scholars were with their parents.

The ouch came when little Wendy – the very same sweet girl who brought her teacher to tears when she saw Wendy's shoes outside her house during Covid – looked up at me and asked, "But Mrs. H – why are you leaving?"

I started to answer her and then I just stopped.

Oh, man – I hadn't really processed what I was going to say to the scholars.

"I'll have a better answer when I see you at school on Monday."

In all the complimentary things that were being shared that evening, the unspoken truth was that I was going to miss our scholars like crazy. They are absolutely *the* best part of this job. The sincere love and enthusiasm they show along with the funny things they say – nothing can compare to that in life. Nothing.

The Monday after the banquet where everyone said how much they would miss me and stated their appreciation of my contributions to Faith Academy, I woke up to a text at 5:46 a.m. It was from a teacher stating she didn't feel well and needed a sub. And there I went – back to reality – and I was reminded of what I would not miss.

On Monday during Chapel, I had Andre put up a picture of me on screen from my first year of teaching – the same picture I included in chapter nine of this book. I then turned and spoke to the scholars.

"I've been doing this for 34 years – that is longer than most of your teachers have been alive! Mr. Scott was only two years old when I started my teaching career. It's time for me to be done."

Heck, most of our teachers weren't even alive when I started teaching!

I continued by telling them all the jobs I had, including the many different places and grade levels I had taught. I even told them I never thought I would be a principal, but God obviously had it planned all along. I mentioned how I got to know Mr. Fern and Miss DeDe on a mission trip to Belize. I was cruising along through all these fun facts and was doing just fine until I glanced down and saw tears welling up in Melannie's eyes, one of our third graders. She had been one of my spicy ones and I loved her so much. The amount she had grown in the four years I had known her was very rewarding. I choked up and needed to pause a bit.

I ended my little speech by telling them to always remember that God doesn't care as much about what you're going to be when you grow up, but He cares a great deal about **who** you are going to be.

I was at peace with my decision. It was very different from when I left other places of employment. It wasn't that I did not have second thoughts – I was still right in the middle of everything that was happening and felt a deep connection with Faith Academy. But God was making it clear in the way things played out. Whenever something came up that made me wish I was staying, something else came along that sent a clear message that leaving was the right thing to do.

For example, I was talking to Brett about the need to update our website and got all excited about things I wanted to create and include.

I cannot leave Faith Academy yet!

Then later that day Jenna randomly forwarded an article to me about something I am very interested in – the negative impact social media has on young girls and what their parents should know about it. I have always been focused on supporting parents with meaningful research and tips. I wondered if maybe I could write a book about that. I know it was challenging to recruit speakers to talk about important topics like this on our Parent Connection Days. I was excited that I could research and put together a presentation for parents of school age children.

As the ideas flowed, I reminded myself that I wanted to finish strong and to do that I needed to focus. I jotted some of these ideas down on a Google Doc, closed it up, and vowed to not become distracted by thoughts of the future until I successfully finished my job at Faith Academy and handed off my responsibilities to other people.

It seemed like every time doubts would come into my mind, reassurances that I was doing the right thing would show themselves.

I don't know what it is yet – but there are other things for me to do – God's got me. It is the right thing to retire.

I will always love the mission of Faith Academy -- but I knew it was okay to pass the baton, or in our case, my prized possession … my megaphone.

After the last day of Summer School 2022 this picture was captured of me handing off the megaphone to Crystal Johnson, our second-grade teacher who was selected to take my place.

CHAPTER 35

LIFE AFTER FAITH

"**M**an, I would have thought you would have slowed down if you knew you were leaving."

As I was talking through the necessary transition process with Crystal Johnson, our second-grade teacher who was going to take my place and serve as the Curriculum Director, she commented that I not only had accomplished so very much during my tenure as principal, I was also in the middle of many other activities.

I didn't hesitate as I responded.

"I never thought about leaving – I just kept doing what needed to be done."

We were fortunate that with Covid relief funding we were also able to bring on Leigh Ann Erickson to work with Crystal and take over a couple of areas I had been covering. Leigh Ann took over the role of helping with student services as well as being in charge of professional development for our staff. That fall, after school had been in session for about a week, I received this encouraging email on August 31.

It has just been on my heart the past week to email you and just express a large thank you. I am so thankful for all you have done to set

up SO many things for FA. The amount of work you have accomplished here is incredible. Just wanted to say THANKS and WOW to all you have done.
Much love and appreciation-
Crystal Johnson
Director of Curriculum and Instruction
Faith Academy

That was kind, and I appreciated that she had taken the time to send me an email.

After leaving Faith Academy I was approached by a few places asking about my interest in employment in a variety of roles – being an interim principal among them. I had been given some heartfelt advice by more than one person who stopped by my office – "say no to everything for a year after you retire" – and I planned on following it. My intent was to take the time to recuperate and see what really seemed right before I committed to something else.

I was surprised at the wide array of feelings I experienced once school started back up in the fall without me. My primary emotion was overwhelming relief, but I also experienced an empty feeling and anxiousness about what was going on at school without me.

During the summer, I felt at peace about not having to focus on the upcoming school year. I felt like I used to when I had summers off after a taxing school year of teaching, which hadn't been the case for nine years. Once I knew that everyone was back in school, though, I struggled as I asked myself questions about what was happening at Faith Academy and remembered things I wanted to follow up on.

What are they doing? What songs are they singing? Is Melannie getting along with her new teacher? What jokes am I missing out on? I need to remind someone to spray that spot on the playground set where the wasps always build a nest!

Dave and I spent time that summer and early fall planning a much-anticipated trip to Greece and Italy for the end of September. Since I was available to help with the vacation planning, I put my focus on that as a way to distract myself. This wasn't my normal role, as Dave is usually the one who made our travel arrangements. But I was the one with the time to do this now.

When I saw the invitation for the ribbon-cutting of our new playground on Facebook, I realized we were going to be leaving for our trip the day before the big event and I would miss it. I couldn't stand the thought of not seeing the scholars' reactions to the beautiful new playground that we started planning for them three years ago.

Prior to the ribbon-cutting, I found out when the installation was going to be complete and when they would be letting the scholars play on it for the first time. I contacted Doug to let him know that I wanted to stop by and see the new playground before our trip to Europe, but that I didn't want to interrupt. I have witnessed many times over the years the way our scholars greet people they haven't seen for a while, and it is never low-key. They usually stop whatever they're doing and run to the person and greet them with exuberant hugs. If I arrived during recess, this behavior should be fine.

I pulled into the parking lot and was walking toward the playground just as the first group came out for recess to use the new equipment for the very first time. I walked from my car onto the playground and one of the scholars glanced in my direction.

"Mrs. H!"

It wasn't long before a whole troop of kids were at my side in a big group hug. My heart was full.

"We miss you!"

"Did you know we got a new playground?"

Did I know?!

They had no idea how much work was done by so many generous people to complete this project.

"Yes – can you show it to me?" I responded enthusiastically.

Scholars playing with the outdoor musical instruments for the first time in September of 2022. I had picked out these instruments as part of the new playground equipment.

I stayed for all the recess shifts that morning and went inside to visit with a few staff members. I knew that everyone was in the middle of completing many tasks and I didn't want to disrupt them. My discomfort about being a nuisance diminished as I was greeted with overwhelming enthusiasm from my old friends. It felt great to be inside Faith Academy again.

Scholars on the new playground in September 2022
when I stopped by for my first visit back to Faith Academy
since retiring a few months earlier.

I stood in the kitchen and helped myself to some amazing home-made salsa that Juleissa was sharing with the staff as I chatted with Elder Bernie, Dawn, Andre, and others who came along.

Prior to my visit, I didn't know how it would feel to be back at school. Even though it went really well, I knew that I wouldn't do it often.

"I don't want to be like a high schooler that graduates but keeps coming back to hang around on campus," I told Doug when I stopped to catch up in October. "But we used to talk every single day and I miss that. What is going on?!"

He and I went to the new library that was finally at home in its own full-sized room. DeDe had it decorated beautifully – she has a gift for arranging spaces and making them aesthetically pleasing. I had texted Doug ahead of time to find out when he planned to be available at school rather than over at the main campus of Parkview or in a meeting. We hid out in the back of the library so we could chat between ourselves without being interrupted.

I told him a little about our recent trip to Italy and Greece. He needed to know the highlight of my trip was not seeing the Acropolis in Athens or the Vatican in Rome, but the moment when my heart was happiest was when I got a text that said, "Hey Mrs. H, this Kentrell (it was from his mom's phone). I miss you."

Kentrell was a seventh grader who had been at Faith Academy from K-6. When I saw him the next time, which was months later, I told him just that – that the highlight of my big trip was when I received an unexpected text from him.

I'll never know if some of these kids realize the amount of love many of us from Faith Academy have in our hearts for them.

Doug caught me up on how it was going at Faith Academy as well as at church, which had faced one quandary after another for the past five years. Covid only added to the unsettled atmosphere there. The unrest at the church filtered over into Doug's role at Faith Academy and affected me and some others as well. Because of all the uneasiness at Parkview, Dave and I had drifted away from attending services there.

Even though we were no longer attending Parkview Church, it certainly did not mean we had turned away from God. I grew in my relationship with God during my time at Faith Academy more than any other time in my life. Changing churches happens. Our experience reminded me of a humorous story my brother Joe told me once.

A man was finally rescued, after having been on a deserted island for 10 years. The first question he was asked was why there were three huts on the island if he was alone.

He replied, "The first one is my home and the second is my church."

"What's the third one?" his rescuer asked curiously.

*"Oh…" he replied in a knowing tone, "That's the church I **used to go to**."*

In the fall of 2020, while I was still fully employed at Faith Academy, Doug asked casually, "Hey, are you going to be coming up here to church?"

Since he opened the door on that subject, I took the opportunity to tell him what I was thinking.

"You know, I just can't do it anymore with the whole women thing."

He was aware I have a difficult time accepting that women like me and others are not allowed in any position of leadership. I wanted to be at Parkview's East Campus so if Faith Academy families come, they see someone else they know and feel more comfortable. Dave and I had been doing that for over four years and I just couldn't anymore.

"We aren't going to be coming back."

"I meant this Sunday – I just wanted to see if you would play piano," Doug stated wryly.

Oh, whoops --

"Okay… well now you know," I admitted.

Even though the exchange became a little awkward and I dreaded that moment, I was relieved it was out in the open. Doug was my friend, and it was hard to no longer support him at church, but I knew that finding another church to worship at was the healthy thing for Dave and me to do. Doug knew how I felt about the theological "complementarianism" philosophy that emphasizes men and women have different roles and responsibilities in marriage, family life, and religious leadership. It is pretty much a euphemism for patriarchy. If the group of people who were in the position to make decisions at Parkview Church had been more balanced, some of the issues they were facing may not have turned into problems. A balanced approach includes women as well as men.

I had no idea that was the governing philosophy when we started attending Parkview Church years before. With the contemporary music style centering around the whole praise and worship band, I thought that everything was more modern there. Because we were on the periphery of church leadership, it took me many years to see it was more conservative than we realized. I'm glad that I was oblivious to it for a time, as I wouldn't have become involved with Faith Academy had we never gone to Parkview. Once I saw this side of the church, however, I could only ignore it for so long.

After about a year of just watching a variety of churches online, Dave and I are back at a church again. I really feel encouraged about so many aspects of our new church, including the cultural diversity, as I know that is what Heaven is going to be like. I also like the emphasis on both its local and global mission, the desire to love people the way Christ does, and especially the presence of women pastors. Still, I know our new church is not going to be perfect, as no church ever is. A wise philosopher, my friend Doug Fern, once said, "Where there are people there is poop."

As a person who has attended church all my life, it causes me angst to know that churches have done a good deal of harm in some people's lives. The term "church trauma" describes having negative and long-lasting experiences in church. I have come to understand that just because a person believes in the Bible doesn't mean they understand it. It has been my experience that it is not God who lets us down, it is people who are supposedly representing God. When others are being judged by churchgoers, those people are **misrepresenting God**. What I do know is that God does not disappoint. He will never fail us and will never let us go.

Above all, our desire in the work we did with the scholars at Faith Academy was to be clear about that message.

With all the highs and lows during my eight years at Faith Academy, I often thought "Man, I could write a book about all of these crazy things that are happening around me!"

As time passed, I decided this was something I genuinely wanted to follow through on. I was excited and full of ideas and couldn't wait to get started. Once Dave and I returned from our trip in October 2022, I sat down to start my book.

After a couple of hours on my computer writing thoughts and ideas, I closed my laptop. I was discouraged and overwhelmed by the enormity of the task that lay in front of me, and I started to make excuses for myself.

This is HARD. I guess not everyone is meant to write a book. It's okay if I don't write it.

Two months later, an interaction with Cynthia Ukah changed my perspective.

One of the many wonderful things that came out of my association with Faith Academy is the valued friendships I made because of being at the school. A month after I had reluctantly closed my laptop on my book idea, Dave and I were invited to a party at Julie Dancer's. Julie became friends with me and Dave on the Belize trip in 2012 and she had also served on the Faith Academy School Board. She is a hostess extraordinaire, and I was looking forward to the event.

Monique Washington, me, Julie Dancer and Cynthia Ukah downtown Iowa City

Monique Washington and Cynthia Ukah joined the school board and became friends of ours. They were at Julie's party as well. It was that night I learned Cynthia had just published her book, *A Marriage Made in Heaven*. I learned of her story earlier when just the four of us had gotten together at Julie's. Cynthia's husband Ferdinand, a prominent transplant surgeon, was killed years before and she was left to raise four children at a young age. Her book is a deeply moving love story that centers around a tragic event. More than that, it's about her inspiring recovery based on her inner strength and faith in God.

Cynthia and I had a chance to talk off to the side that evening, and she told me all about how she wrote and published her book.

"The day after my husband died, I knew that I wanted to write a book about his life to honor him. This writing coach I was introduced to is the one who helped me make it happen. It's like he is a 'one-stop shop'! He helped me with all the steps – writing the draft, editing it, publishing it, and everything. It's going to be available in a couple of weeks – can you believe it?!"

A month later, just before Christmas break was over and Cynthia would have to go back to work – she taught Special Education in the Iowa City School District – I asked her if she wanted to meet for lunch. I wanted to hear more about her book-writing process, especially now that I had read her book. This would be the first time it was just the two of us getting together, as we had always been part of a group gathering prior to that. I was excited to get to know her better. Of the four of us who typically got together, she was the quietest one, but if you asked her something, she was always willing to talk.

"I'm an open book – you can ask me anything."

We met for lunch at The Tribute, a restaurant in the Iowa River Landing area of Coralville. There were many things Cynthia and I had in common – Faith Academy, teaching, Parkview, and we even had sons the same age who played on a basketball team together when they were in junior high school. And now we share this common interest in writing.

I asked her many questions about her experience. I was curious about how she met Bruce Hurd, her writing coach. I asked about the cost of everything, and I even asked about simple details, like who she told she was writing the book. She gave me all the insight I was asking for. As we were nearing the end of our lunch, I surprised her.

"So ... I've signed up for the Make Your Book a Reality writers retreat next weekend. I ran it all by Dave and he is fine with it. I'm going to write my book!" I revealed enthusiastically.

"What?!" she confirmed, "I am so proud of you, girl!"

And she got up from her side of the booth, stood up and threw her arms out for a hug. I got up and hugged her back. About then our server came back to check on us – it didn't bother us in the least.

I told him about my book idea too! Cynthia could not have been more excited.

"You have no idea how happy this makes me! I am going to be your biggest fan – your biggest supporter."

And she has been true to her word. She has been my biggest supporter.

Starting six months after leaving Faith Academy, I have been fully focused on my book project. It has been challenging and it has been therapeutic. To write in detail about my life and all that has happened in the past eight years gave me a clear vision of how God gently and wisely guided me as I played my role in the Faith Academy story.

In July 2019 I read American Philosopher John Dewey's wisdom that "... experience isn't what teaches us, but reflecting on our experiences is where we learn." Upon reading that, I started keeping a journal. I had done this off and on over the years, but never using a structured format. My new journaling system included four specific things:

1. Things I had done well
2. Things I could have done better
3. Praises
4. Prayer requests

I am grateful that I kept this journal from that time forward. My intention was to write in it daily. I started out entering daily, sometimes weekly – but I kept it going. Not only did it help me to improve on my interactions as a leader, but it served as a primary source when writing this book.

To close the loop regarding some of the many extraordinary people I've introduced in this book, I want to finish by providing an update on each of them. Of course, I will discuss my wonderful husband Dave, and my amazing children Dylan and Jenna. I will also talk about some of the very special people I worked closely with at Faith Academy.

Dave retired from Hills Bank in January of 2024. While neither of us has decided what our plans will be, there are many ideas we kick around as far as what our next stage holds.

Dylan accepted a job in Los Angeles after graduating from UCLA. He works in the music industry for Global Music Rights in Revenue Strategy. Fortunately, he lives within walking distance of his work in Westwood and doesn't have to fight the daily L.A. traffic. He is Mr. Recreation and now gets to play golf year-round as well as beach volleyball and basketball. There are many opportunities for him to see live music and attend concerts and sporting events. Travel also continues to be important to him. He loves it there and we have a beautiful place to visit.

Jenna, Dave, me, and Dylan in the Fall of 2023 at a wedding in Iowa

Jenna is living in a suburb of Atlanta and works in Talent Development for a real-estate investment firm. She loves the milder weather and the beautiful setting for outdoor activities such as hiking and kayaking in Atlanta. Cooking has become an interest of hers and she is very good at it. She is active in her church and is happy to be able to spend time with her best friend from her undergraduate years who lives in Atlanta with her husband, as well as other new friends.

Doug accepted a job as a lead pastor at a church in St. Cloud, Minnesota and moved from Iowa City in late August of 2023. It is a great opportunity for him and his family, as Doug is able to answer the call he feels to be a lead pastor. His son, Zach, had just graduated high school and left for college. His younger kids will have an opportunity to get settled in their new school, thereby allowing for three more years before the next son would graduate from high school.

Doug was asked to speak at the Back-to-School night at Faith Academy in August 2023, which doubled as his send-off party. He shared that he always wanted to be part of something where it was evident that the whole thing would be unexplainable — except for God.

And that is what he felt Faith Academy had been. There were plenty of reasons why it should have failed, yet here we are starting year number 11.

I wasn't surprised when he decided to relocate, as I had seen the struggles he faced over the years as he worked to please everyone at the church in addition to performing his leadership role at Faith Academy. So many of us were sad to see him go and to know that he was leaving behind all the wonderful connections he established with many people in the Black community of southeast Iowa City. But I'm happy to report that several of his "Spot kids" are becoming leaders in that neighborhood, have children who attend Faith Academy, and several are even working at Faith Academy.

I know Doug had a hard time leaving, as it was a tough decision. We all know that if it weren't for the strong connections that he established and nurtured over many years, there would be no Faith Academy.

Connections. Isn't that what life is all about?

The good news is that Elder Bernie is serving as the Head of School. What better person to have in that role than someone who is a trusted leader in the Black community and has been around since day one of Faith Academy? She is killing it!

The evening of my final banquet, Pastor Boyer — a vibrant 70 something woman who is Elder Bernie's sister — decided to share her thoughts with Dave in front of me.

"Don't worry… after about a year and a half of retirement she will be back looking for something to do again. That's the way it was for me."

I wasn't sure what to think of that statement at the time, but I know what my response was.

"Don't count on it, Dear!"

We have each read a couple of books on these transitional years leading into retirement, including Bob Buford's *Half Time* and *From Strength to Strength* by Arthur Brooks. The big idea of both of those was to use the wisdom gained from the years in our respective fields of work and put it to use in areas that would be helpful to others.

One mission possibility is already taking shape and it is an idea that was generated from a past parent at Faith Academy.

Lucie, a mother I met during my time at Faith Academy, and I met for lunch over the summer, as I had some questions for her in regard to my writing. She is an amazing woman who moved here from The Republic of Congo as a teen. Her children attended Faith Academy. I respected her for the relationship she had with her children and the advocate she was for them. I have been honored to attend an award banquet with her where she was recognized for her work in advocacy of women in the community. Despite English being her second language, she earned a degree in counseling. She understands mental-health issues and does not attach a negative stigma to it like others in her family and many in her culture do. I am grateful to have learned so much from her.

As a result of our conversation, we are currently working with others at my church, Life Church of Coralville, to start an after-school program on the afternoons when school is dismissed early. The program is aimed at helping immigrant students who, as my friend Lucie has brought to our attention, often have unmet needs of being seen, known, and made to feel accepted. This population of students have parents who are occupied with making a living for their families and have many hurdles adjusting to life themselves in a new country.

This is another area where I am interested in devoting my energy.

Just like God worked it out for me to be involved at Faith Academy, I know there are other ways He can use both Dave and me — and we look forward to the opportunities that lie ahead.

FINAL THOUGHTS

By this point in my book, you have gotten to know me, my family, and the wonderful people in my life very well. I hope you have enjoyed it, as well as learning from my insights and experiences. Much of what I described is common to all of us, regardless of what career field we have chosen.

As I close this book, my hope is that it's apparent God wrote my story better than I ever could have.

Yes, I studied, worked, and accepted challenges along the way. I also made mistakes and God has given me grace. Throughout it all, I found I can impress some people with my strengths, but where I really connect with others is through allowing them to see my weaknesses. The following Bible verse addresses how God meets us in our weaknesses:

"... My grace is sufficient for you, for my power is made perfect in weakness. Therefore, I will boast all the more gladly about my weaknesses, so that Christ's power may rest on me" 2 Corinthians 12:9.

I have read many times that our regrets, especially when we reflect at the end of our life, are more often for things that we didn't do in life or the risks we didn't take, rather than mistakes we made. I would like to encourage you to embrace interesting experiences offered to you and take the time to get to know people who are different from you. We are all God's children, no matter what the ethnicity, religious background, political views, color of our skin, or socioeconomic status we have. We never know how one of those experiences we've had or people we've met will change us or shape our future.

During my time at Faith Academy, over and over we have been blessed to see how God puts people and resources in our path right when we are ready for them, God knows when we are genuinely ready for them to enter our life. That concept of my being ready for what faces me was demonstrated throughout my life. While I never sought out difficulties, I realize if things hadn't been challenging or difficult at times, I would not have learned to trust God so completely. In my imperfection I continue to strive to be more patient in the way things play out in life. Patience – this was my word of the year that I picked as part of our "assignment" in my book club in January of this year. We all picked a word for the year and shared it with each other.

Through my experience of feeling defeated and leaving teaching at Kalona Elementary, I feel now like God was saying "I wish you could see what I see ... there's more to it than how it looks. It's going to work out in the end. Trust me."

I did not feel this complete faith at the time, especially when circumstances were challenging. It is only upon reflection that I am able to look back over the years and see the dots all becoming connected. I can now see God's hand in how it all played out.

Faith Academy came together as a result of many people being faithful to how God was leading or nudging them. There are scores of wonderful people who blessed us financially and were generous with their time, energy and resources. Had it not been for them, none of this would have become a reality.

Just like Doug said at his going-away party, "… this kind of school does not make sense, but God." An example of what he was describing is how the school was supported. Donors pay for other people's kids to attend this very special school, and we all understand that is not the way our world usually works. That is one huge reason why Faith Academy is so special. When the mission is in tune with what God desires, a way will be found for it to be completed in ways that are unexpected and more joyful than we could have imagined. He will help us thrive.

I am grateful for my decision to go into education. It has been a fulfilling life for me. I have connections with so many "kids" that I treasure. I learned innumerable things about child development that I would have otherwise not known, and this knowledge helped me be a better parent, too. I saw life through the eyes of so many amazing souls as I got to know a wide array of people that I might never have interacted with otherwise.

Being an educator opened me up to the world of reading, too. As a primary teacher, I had to get kids excited about it, so I had to become excited about it, as well. Reading has been my gateway to growth. It's the same with learning about history. I am grateful for the way that both have enriched my life. I discovered there is always more to learn, and I continue to expand my understanding of people, of God, and of our world.

As I look back over my career I do not wonder "what could have been." I look back with satisfaction over the way I have touched lives as a career educator. Just last summer I went up to a young man I recognized at a wedding and called him by name.

"Derek?"

"You remember me?" he asked.

"Of course, I do!" I said, and then started to tell him who I was.

"Oh, I know…."

Later, as we passed each other again at the reception, he was talking to another person I knew as he spoke about me.

"She was my favorite elementary teacher."

My heart melted. This kid was so quiet when he was in fifth grade, and I remember I took it as a challenge to get him to open up. It fills my heart that he remembered me this way.

I recently had a student who sent me a Facebook message because she was starting her second year as an elementary teacher.

"Hi Jan! I'm going through some of my memory boxes and found some special artifacts. Thank you for everything – I loved 5th grade." She sent pictures of things she had saved: a handwritten note from me, a box of affirming notes from her classmates, and a special memory project we did at the end of the school year.

The project this Facebook message was referring to was something my last teaching partner and I had them do at Kalona Elementary. Emily Pennington and I cut special colored paper and had each of the kids write every person in the class a note telling them what they appreciated or admired about them. They had a week to accomplish the task and each student made a container similar to a Valentine's box to collect them. We set aside some time on a Friday afternoon for everyone to open their container and read the notes that had been written to them.

Seeing the smiles on their faces as our students read over their affirming notes was remarkable – a memory etched on my heart forever. Since then we have heard from many students that they saved those notes. We even heard from a young man who is now a teacher and is carrying that project on with his own class. To hear that something we initiated so long ago meant that much to our students is purely heartwarming and rewarding for both Emily and me in a way that's hard to fully describe.

Being an educator can be hard. It can be exhausting. People often feel free to critique our work or the work of our profession openly and sometimes harshly.

I was fortunate that my work was so intricately linked to my beliefs and mission. Of course, hindsight is 20/20. But reflecting on my experiences has been meaningful in a profound way. By reflecting on events in our lives, we are able to become aware of our actions, see ourselves in new ways and even change our behaviors or way of thinking. I know I have.

I hope my story can benefit someone else as well – perhaps even you.

If that is the case, that would make my objective complete. God Bless you.

ABOUT THE AUTHOR

Jan Eichelberger Hochstetler grew up just outside of Wayland, a small town in southeast Iowa. The farming community was home to a large Mennonite population, along with a smattering of other Christian denominations. Jan was the only girl and the youngest of five children in her family. The WACO Community School District (encompassing Wayland, Crawfordsville, and Olds) where she attended school served as a source of pride for Jan and her brothers, as they grew up as active members in their community.

Becoming an aunt at the young age of eight allowed her the opportunity to fall in love with children. She had 10 nieces and nephews by the time she finished college, each one with a different personality and needs. She credits this, and her experience as a youth camp counselor at Laurelville Mennonite Camp in Pennsylvania during college, for lighting her desire to become a teacher.

The church Jan belonged to, Sugar Creek Mennonite, also played a primary role in her life. For the first two years of college, she attended Hesston College, a private Mennonite school in Hesston, Kansas. She took advantage of the opportunities available at a small college by playing women's basketball and singing in the Hesston College Chorale.

Jan continued her undergraduate studies at Iowa State University (ISU) in Ames, graduating in 1987 with a bachelor's degree in elementary education. The summer after graduating from college she married Dave, whom she had met at Iowa State. The couple then moved to Des Moines where Jan started her career as a public elementary school teacher.

In Des Moines she taught grades one, four, and five. It was during this time she completed her master's degree in education at ISU, attending classes at night and during the summers. After five years with the Des Moines Public School District, she took a job teaching fourth grade in the suburban setting of Ankeny, Iowa. It was when she worked as a teacher in Ankeny that their son Dylan was born in 1993.

Thinking it would benefit their children to grow up in a smaller town close to their grandparents, the family of three moved back to Dave's hometown of Kalona, Iowa in November 1996. Their daughter Jenna was born in 1997. That fall Jan started a part-time job with the University of Iowa, supervising college students who were completing their elementary student teaching experience.

In 2002 she moved back into the classroom. She started at Kalona Elementary as a fifth-grade teacher when Dylan was in fourth grade – the same year her daughter Jenna started kindergarten there.

Twelve years later, as Jan was about to turn fifty, her career as a teacher had left her disillusioned and exhausted. She loved the children she taught, but the oppressive administrative demands of a well-meaning system had just ground her down. She knew she had to make a change. Resigning from her job as a teacher in her home community was a scary step. She realized she wanted to take a little time off, but she knew she would soon need to find another full-time job. She felt like a trapeze artist who let go of the horizontal bar before the next bar was in sight. It was difficult for her to stay above the discouraging feelings that came with having no direction. She continued to get a sense, however, that she had a purpose that God hadn't revealed to her yet.

That next year, Jan found herself filling in as a substitute teacher to cover for a friend in an emergency. Becoming a substitute teacher was something Jan had never planned on doing. It was because of that role, though, she became involved with Faith Academy, a Christian elementary school whose mission was to reach out to an underserved minority population in Iowa City.

Faith Academy was started by Parkview Church, the church her family was attending at the time. From the connections she had made the previous year on a church-sponsored mission trip to Belize in Central America, God had a way of putting the pieces together to give order and purpose to her life again. Jan met two of the people who were the driving force behind creating Faith Academy on the trip to Belize. Starting with that connection, they became good friends because of that trip.

Because she loved the staff, the atmosphere, the students, and most importantly the mission of Faith Academy, she accepted the position of second-grade teacher for the following school year when it was offered to her. She could see God at work as He allowed His plan to unfold.

Moving into the role of Curriculum Director the year after that was a new and exciting experience for Jan. This was a completely new role, and Jan was the first person to fill the job as the school expanded. Soon thereafter, it became apparent the school would need to create the position of school principal to lead the ever-growing staff and student body.

To position herself for greater responsibilities, Jan completed the program for principal certification to be licensed as a K-12 school administrator. This certification program was yet another major undertaking that Jan never envisioned taking on. It was because of her completing the two-year certification process that Jan was able to serve as the first principal of Faith Academy School in Iowa City, Iowa.

As she grew in her role as principal, her love for Faith Academy, the staff she led, and the students at the school expanded. Along with that, her joy of being an educator returned. As in any leadership role, challenges were ever present, yet the greatest hurdles she encountered in a lifetime of education were when she and Faith Academy faced the world-stopping Covid pandemic in the spring of 2020. She counts being able to help shepherd her school successfully through those difficult times among her proudest achievements.

Recently retired from education, she is now at home with her husband Dave outside of Kalona, Iowa. Their two adult children, Dylan and Jenna, are living their own exciting and productive lives on opposite sides of the country in Los Angeles and Atlanta.

Jan is a member of two book clubs and enjoys getting together with her friends and family and traveling with her husband. She loves running into former students and their families, and she stays active practicing yoga, golfing, doing Jazzercise, listening to podcasts, reading, and playing piano.

She continues to love interacting with children and stays connected to the world of education.

Always More to Learn is her first book.

If you are interested in learning more about Jan and her latest projects, visit her author page at www.JansInk.org.

Discussion Questions

1. The author and her husband needed to weigh the differences between having their children grow up in a small town where you know everybody versus a bigger town. Which was your experience? Pros and cons.

2. What things from your childhood would you like replicated for your own kids?

3. Were there any things that you intentionally did differently from your parents?

4. The author mentions her place in birth order, being the youngest with four older brothers. What is your birth order and how does that effect your relationships with your siblings? What effect does it have on your relationships in life?

5. In this book, the author worked at a school that raised 90% of the necessary budget and families were only required to pay 10% of what it cost to educate their child. That is one way to look out for other people's kids. This is a major undertaking and commitment. What are other smaller ways to look out for "other people's kids?"

6. In chapter 11 the author was intentionally trying to keep Keshwan from attending, but it turned out better when he was able to attend at the last minute. Think of a time where you have tried to intervene in a situation but it turned out better because your plan was not carried out. Was that God?

7. College bubble. For those of you who attended college, What was the feeling you had being away for the first time? How did your perceptions of the world around you change once you had lived away from home?

8. The author shares about a special friendship that has lasted since childhood. Do you have a lifelong friend such as Maria? How has your relationship changed over the years?

9. The author had an experience where a teacher did not encourage/support her in her proposed college major. What have your experiences been with this? Were you supported or discouraged with your college choice/vocational choice? Have there been times when you have weighed in on high school students' desires/potential plans?

10. Covid is discussed in several chapters. What were the high and low points for you during the shutdown? Any favorite memes?

11. The author goes into detail about the day-to-day operations of a school during Covid. What information was new to you? Share your reactions with the group.

12. In chapter 21, Jan ran into her former professor and she had declined cognitively yet not physically. Do you have any examples to share with the group of loved ones who have suffered from cognitive decline, such as Alzheimer's, at the end of their life?

13. The topic of racism is brought up in *Always More to Learn*. Do you have any incidents, people, books, or movies that have enlightened you in this area?

14. This story is about the author's life as an educator. Tell about an educator who:

    1. challenged you to do better
    2. made you feel special
    3. seemed to really enjoy kids
    4. you learned the most in their class/subject area

15. Final thoughts on *Always More to Learn*.

www.ingramcontent.com/pod-product-compliance
Lightning Source LLC
Chambersburg PA
CBHW030353130626
46549CB00004B/1476